Studio Visual Steps

MacOS Sierra®
for Seniors

Learn step by step how to work with MacOS Sierra®

www.visualsteps.com

This book has been written using the Visual Steps™ method.
Cover design by Studio Willemien Haagsma bNO

© 2016 Visual Steps
Author: Studio Visual Steps

First printing: November 2016
ISBN 978 90 5905 443 1

Resources used: A number of definitions and explanations of computer terminology are taken over from the *Mac User Guides*.

Do you have questions or suggestions?
Email: info@visualsteps.com

Would you like more information?
www.visualsteps.com

Website for this book:
www.visualsteps.com/macossierra

Subscribe to the free Visual Steps Newsletter:
www.visualsteps.com/newsletter

Table of Contents

Bonus Chapters

On the website accompanying this book you will find the bonus chapters. In *Appendix B Opening Bonus Chapters* you will read how to open these bonus chapters.

Bonus Chapter Basic Text Editing Operations
Bonus Chapter Downloading Apps and Music

Foreword

For a number of years, the Mac notebooks and desktop computers have increased in popularity among a growing group of users. In this book, you will learn how to use the Mac with the operating system *MacOS Sierra*, step by step.

You will learn how to use the *TextEdit* application to handle your basic writing needs, such as creating letters, notes and memos. The *Finder* app allows you to work with the folders and files stored on your computer. You can delete, copy, move and rename your files with the *Finder* app.

You can use the *Safari* Internet browser to surf the web. This program comes with some very useful functions, such as *Top Sites*. This feature keeps track of the websites you visit most often, and allows you to open these websites with just a single mouse click. The email program that is included in the Mac software package is called *Mail*. You can use this program to quickly and easily send and receive email messages.

Did you know that the Mac also has built-in programs for working with photos, videos and music? You will learn how to edit a photo, transfer a music CD to your computer and play video files and DVDs with *QuickTime Player* and *DVD Player*.

Furthermore, you will learn how to adapt the settings according to your own preferences. For example, you can change and adjust the mouse or trackpad settings to suit your own working method. You can also change the size of the icons, as well as the sound settings.

We wish you lots of fun while working with your Mac!

Studio Visual Steps

PS We welcome your comments and suggestions.
Our email address is: mail@visualsteps.com

Introduction to Visual Steps™

The Visual Steps handbooks and manuals are the best instructional materials available for learning how to work with mobile devices, computers and software applications. Nowhere else will you find better support to help you get started with *MacOS*, *Windows*, an iPad, iPhone, Samsung Galaxy Tab, Kindle and various software applications.

Properties of the Visual Steps books:

- **Comprehensible contents**
  Addresses the needs of the beginner or intermediate user for a manual written in simple, straight-forward English.
- **Clear structure**
  Precise, easy to follow instructions. The material is broken down into small enough segments to allow for easy absorption.
- **Screenshots of every step**
  Quickly compare what you see on your screen with the screenshots in the book. Pointers and tips guide you when new windows, screens or alert boxes are opened so you always know what to do next.
- **Get started right away**
  All you have to do is have your computer and your book at hand. Sit some where's comfortable, begin reading and perform the operations as indicated on your own device.
- **Layout**
  The text is printed in a large size font and is clearly legible.

In short, I believe these manuals will be excellent guides for you.

Dr. H. van der Meij
Faculty of Applied Education, Department of Instructional Technology, University of Twente, the Netherlands

Visual Steps Newsletter

All Visual Steps books follow the same methodology: clear and concise step-by-step instructions with screenshots to demonstrate each task.
A complete list of all our books can be found on our website **www.visualsteps.com**
You can also sign up to receive our **free Visual Steps Newsletter**.
In this Newsletter you will receive periodic information by email regarding:
- the latest titles and previously released books;
- special offers, supplemental chapters, tips and free informative booklets.
Also, our Newsletter subscribers may download any of the documents listed on the web page **www.visualsteps.com/info_downloads**

When you subscribe to our Newsletter you can be assured that we will never use your email address for any purpose other than sending you the information as previously described. We will not share this address with any third-party. Each Newsletter also contains a one-click link to unsubscribe.

What You Will Need

In order to work through this book, you will need to have a number of things:

 The most important requirement is to have a Mac with *MacOS Sierra* installed. This can be a desktop version including the Mac Mini, iMac and Mac Pro or the portable or notebook type of Mac including the Macbook, Macbook Pro and Macbook Air.

 An active Internet connection.

Apple's Magic Mouse, or another type of computer mouse.

If you want, you can also use the trackpad on your notebook computer, or a mobile Magic Trackpad.

The following items can be very useful, but it is not absolutely necessary to own these items or devices. Just read through the sections that make use of these things.

 A USB stick (also called a USB memory stick or memory stick).

 A printer.

 A digital photo camera, an iPad, iPhone, or other portable device that is equipped with a built-in camera.

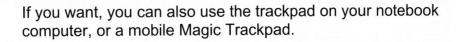

 A music CD and a DVD.

How to Use This Book

This book has been written using the Visual Steps™ method. The method is simple: just place the book next to your Mac and directly execute all the operations on your Mac, step by step. The clear instructions and the multitude of screenshots will tell you exactly what to do. The quickest way of learning how to use the Mac, is by working through the exercises.

In this Visual Steps™ book, you will see various icons. This is what they mean:

Techniques
These icons indicate an action to be carried out:

⊂▷ The mouse icon means you should do something on your Mac by using the mouse. Also, the mouse will regularly be used for operations where you can use a trackpad, as well as a mouse. In the first chapter you can read more about using the mouse.

⌨ The keyboard icon means you should type something on your Mac's keyboard.

☞ The index finger icon indicates you can do something on your notebook's trackpad, or on a mobile trackpad, for example, tapping something.

☞ The hand icon means you should do something else, for example insert a USB stick into the computer. It is also used to remind you of something you have learned before.

In some areas of this book additional icons indicate warnings or helpful hints. These will help you avoid mistakes and alert you when you need to make a decision about something.

Help
These icons indicate that extra help is available:

 The arrow icon warns you about something.

 The bandage icon will help you if something has gone wrong.

Have you forgotten how to do something? The number next to the footsteps tells you where to look it up at the end of the book in the appendix *How Do I Do That Again?*

The following icons indicate general information or tips concerning the Mac.

Extra information
Information boxes are denoted by these icons:

 The book icon gives you extra background information that you can read at your convenience. This extra information is not necessary for working through the book.

The light bulb icon indicates an extra tip for using the Mac.

Website

On the website that accompanies this book, **www.visualsteps.com/macossierra** Regularly check this website, to see if we have added any additional information or errata for this book. Also, you will find various bonus chapters on this website.

Test Your Knowledge

After you have worked through this book, you can test your knowledge online, at the **www.ccforseniors.com** website.

By answering a number of multiple choice questions you will be able to test your knowledge of the iPad. After you have finished the test, your *Computer Certificate* will be sent to the email address you have entered.
Participating in the test is **free of charge**. The computer certificate website is a free Visual Steps service.

For Teachers

The Visual Steps books have been written as self-study guides for individual use. They are also well suited for use in a group or a classroom setting. For this purpose, some of our books come with a free teacher's manual. You can download the available teacher's manuals and additional materials from the website:
www.visualsteps.com/instructor

The Screenshots

The screenshots in this book indicate which button, file or hyperlink you need to click on your computer or tablet screen. In the instruction text (in **bold** letters) you will see a small image of the item you need to tap or click. The line will point you to the right place on your screen.

The small screenshots that are printed in this book are not meant to be completely legible all the time. This is not necessary, as you will see these images on your own tablet screen, in real size and fully legible.

Here you see an example of such an instruction text and a screenshot of the item you need to click. The line indicates where to find this item on your own screen:

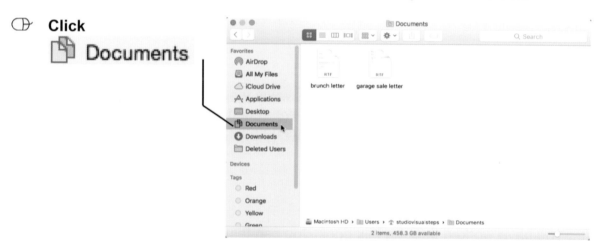

Sometimes the screenshot shows only a portion of a window. Here is an example:

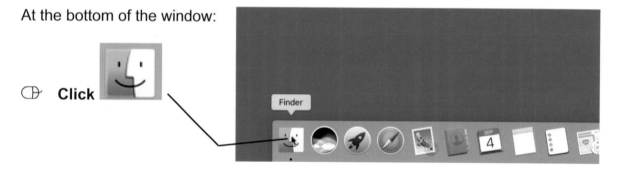

We would like to emphasize that we **do not intend you** to read the information in all of the screenshots in this book. Always use the screenshots in combination with the display on your computer screen.

1. Start Working With the Mac

Mac is the abbreviation for *Macintosh*, the name of a series of desktop and notebook computers manufactured and sold by the American company *Apple*. *Apple* also produces other devices, such as the iPad, iPhone and iPod.

The Mac uses the *MacOS* operating system. This is the counterpart of the well-known *Windows* operating system, produced by the American company *Microsoft*.

The *Apple* products are famous for their beautiful design and user-friendly, intuitive interface. When you start to use a computer for the very first time, you will need to learn some basic operations. This may take a while, but afterwards, you will see that working with the Mac is quite easy. And if you have previously used a *Windows* computer, you will be surprised by the simplicity of the Mac.

In this chapter we will start with an overview of the main types of *Apple* computers. Next, you will get acquainted with your own Mac. We will cover all of the basic operations for using your Mac.

In this chapter you will learn how to:

- distinguish among the different types of Macs;
- turn on the Mac;
- use the mouse and/or trackpad;
- open a program with *Launchpad*;
- use the *Dashboard*;
- view and move widgets;
- put the Mac into sleep mode;
- wake the Mac up from sleep mode;
- turn off the Mac.

1.1 The Different Types of Macs

Apple produces both desktop and notebook computers that use the *MacOS* operating system. A desktop computer has a fixed place and usually resides on a desk or a table. A notebook computer can be used anywhere. You can set it on a table or desk as well as on your lap while sitting on a couch or bench (hence the name *laptop*). Below you will find an overview of the main models:

The *iMac* is an all-in-one desktop computer, where the computer and monitor are integrated as a single unit. This means you do not have a separate hard case or tower. You can operate the iMac with a keyboard and a mouse.

The iMac is currently available in a 21.5 inch screen or a 27 inch screen with or without a Retina display for exclusive display quality.

The *Mac mini* is the compact, portable and very quiet desktop computer produced by *Apple*. The Mac mini comes without a screen, keyboard, mouse or trackpad. You will need to buy these devices separately. They can be purchased from *Apple* as well as other hardware manufacturers.

The Mac mini is also so small that a CD or DVD player or burner does not fit in this device. But you can connect an external player or burner to the mac mini.

The Mac Pro is another type of desktop computer manufactured by Apple. This computer comes without a monitor, keyboard, mouse, trackpad, and CD/DVD player or burner as well. This is the most powerful computer produced by Apple.

The *MacBook Pro* is an *Apple* notebook, specifically built for professional use. This notebook is available with a 13 or 15 inch screen.

The *MacBook Air* is a very slim and lightweight *Apple* notebook. The thickest part is a mere 0.68 inches and the 11 inch model weighs only 2.38 pounds. The 13 inch model weighs just less than 3 pounds.

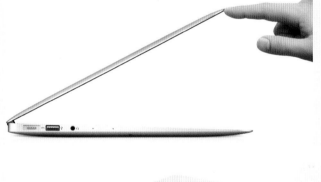

Apart from this, you can also purchase the MacBook. This notebook computer has a 12 inch screen and weighs only 2.03 pounds.

The MacBook Pro, MacBook Air, MacBook, Mac mini, Mac Pro and the latest models of the iMac are not equipped with a CD/DVD player or burner. If necessary, you can connect an external player or burner to your device.

It does not matter what type of Mac you have to use this book. You will be able to perform all the given exercises. But before you can use your Mac you need to turn it on. In the following section you can read how to do that.

1.2 Turn On the Mac

You turn on your Mac by using the power button. You will recognize this button by the ⏻ icon.

The power button of the MacBook, MacBook Air and MacBook Pro is located on the keyboard, in the upper right corner:

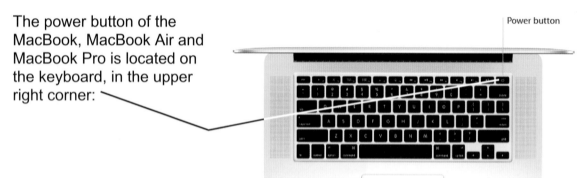

Source: MacBook Pro User Guide

The power button of older versions of the MacBook Pro is located next to the keyboard, in the upper right corner:

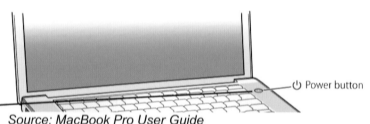

Source: MacBook Pro User Guide

The iMac has a power button on the back of the screen:

If you explore the back of the screen with your left hand, you will feel a round button at the bottom.

Source: iMac Quick Start Guide

The Mac mini has a power button on the back of the unit:

Source: Mac mini Quick Start Guide

The power switch of the Mac Pro is also located at the back.

Please note:

If you are using a Mac mini, the screen will need to be turned on separately. The power button of the screen is usually located on the front of the screen.

When you turn on your Mac and the sound of your computer is turned on as well, you will hear a startup tone. *MacOS Sierra* will start up automatically.

You will see a screen with one or more icons (small pictures). Below these icons, names will be displayed:

This is called the *login window*.

Somewhere on this screen

you will see a black arrow :

 HELP! I see a different screen.

Your Mac may be set up in such a way that you do not need to login with a password once you have turned it on. In this case, your desktop will display immediately:

On this screen you will also

see the black arrow :

☞ **Continue reading**

This arrow is called the pointer. You can move this arrow with a mouse or a trackpad. In the following section you can read how to do this.

1.3 Mouse and Trackpad

You can move the pointer  across the screen in any direction you want by using your mouse or trackpad. You can also use the trackpad (also called touchpad) as another means of moving the pointer. The trackpad has a special surface that is able to convert the movement of your fingers to an onscreen movement or command. Depending on the type of Mac you have, one or more of the following devices will be suitable:

The iMac always comes with a wireless *Magic Mouse*:

Put the mouse next to your keyboard on a clean, smooth surface.

This may be a smooth table top, or a special mousepad.

Loosely lay your hand on the mouse. Keep your fingers relaxed and not stiff.

Allow your wrist and lower arm to rest on the table.

💡 Tip
How do you hold your mouse?

Don't: **Do:**

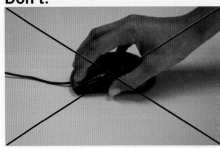   

- Do not grip the mouse with just a few fingers, while sticking the other fingers in the air.
- Do not dangle your wrist over the table.
- Do not pinch or press.
- Do not lift the mouse.

- Loosely hold on to the mouse.
- Let the palm of your hand rest on the mouse.
- Your hand follows the shape of the mouse.
- Loosely rest your index finger on the left mouse button, let the other fingers relax beside your index finger.
- Put your thumb on the table, next to the mouse.
- Rest your wrist and lower arm on the table.
- Make sure the mouse buttons point away from you.

It is important to teach yourself how to hold the mouse in the correct position.
By holding the mouse in the palm of your hand, in a relaxed and loose manner, you will be able to control the mouse.

This is how you move the pointer with a Magic Mouse:

☞ **Loosely place your hand on the mouse**

☞ **Move the mouse across the table**

You will see the pointer move: ———————

HELP! I see something on my screen.

If you see something appearing on your screen, move the pointer to a blank area on the screen and click this area.

The Mac mini and Mac Pro does not come with a mouse. But you can connect almost any type of mouse to one of the four USB ports located on the back:

Source: Mac mini Quick Start Guide

You can also buy a Magic Mouse separately and connect it to your Mac mini through *Bluetooth* (this is a feature that sets up a wireless connection between different devices). Ask your computer supplier about this option, or read the Magic Mouse's manual for more information.

After you have connected a mouse to the USB port on your Mac mini, you can move the pointer in the same way as with the Magic Mouse:

☞ **Loosely place your hand on the mouse**

☞ **Move the mouse across the table**

The MacBook, MacBook Air and Pro are equipped with a Multi-Touch trackpad. This is how you move the pointer with such a device:

☞ **Loosely drag the tip of your finger across the trackpad**

You will see the pointer move across the screen.

Tip

Use the mouse with a notebook
You can also connect a mouse to one of the USB ports on your MacBook, MacBook Pro or MacBook Air. If you are learning how to use a notebook computer for the first time, it is recommended that you use a mouse in the beginning. You will be able to be more precise with your movements right away.

Do you own an iMac, a Mac Pro or a Mac mini and do you prefer to use a trackpad anyway? Then you can use the *Magic Trackpad.* This can be purchased separately:

The Magic Trackpad contains the same functionalities as the trackpad on the Macbook, MacBook Pro and Air:

☞ **Practice moving the pointer across the screen for a while longer**

1.4 Clicking

You have just learned how to move the pointer across the screen. If you want to enter a command (an action that will do something), you need to click your mouse. In this section you can read how to do this on the various Mac devices. Then later, you can practice clicking with your own device. Here is how to click the Magic Mouse:

☞ **Position the pointer on a blank area of the screen**

☞ **Briefly press your index finger on the front side of the mouse**

You will hear a clicking sound.

If you have connected a different type of mouse to your Mac mini or MacBook, it will probably have two buttons.

 Position the pointer on a blank area of the screen

 Briefly press your index finger on the <u>left</u> mouse button

You will hear a clicking sound.

 Please note:

From this point on, if you come across the 'Click' command you will always need to click with the **left** mouse button, if you own a mouse with two buttons.

Clicking the trackpad of your MacBook Pro or Air works the same way as clicking a Magic Trackpad:

☞ **Position the pointer on an icon**

☞ **Briefly press the trackpad with one finger**

You will notice that there is not a lot of difference between working with the mouse and using the trackpad. While using a mouse you move the mouse, while using a trackpad you move your finger across the trackpad. You can click both devices with a single finger.

 Please note:

Whenever you see the ⊕ symbol in this book, it indicates that you need to do something with the mouse or the trackpad. If a certain action needs to be executed in a different way when using a trackpad, we will describe that action separately. In this case we will use the ☞ symbol.

Now you are going to try it yourself, by opening your user account:

☞ **Position the pointer on the icon with your name, for example**

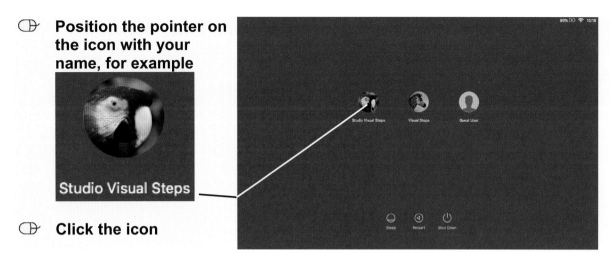

☞ **Click the icon**

HELP! I do not see an icon with my name on it.

If your screen does not display an icon with your name, you may already be viewing your desktop screen. If that is the case, you can practice clicking like this:

In the top left of the window:

☞ **Position the pointer on**

☞ **Click**

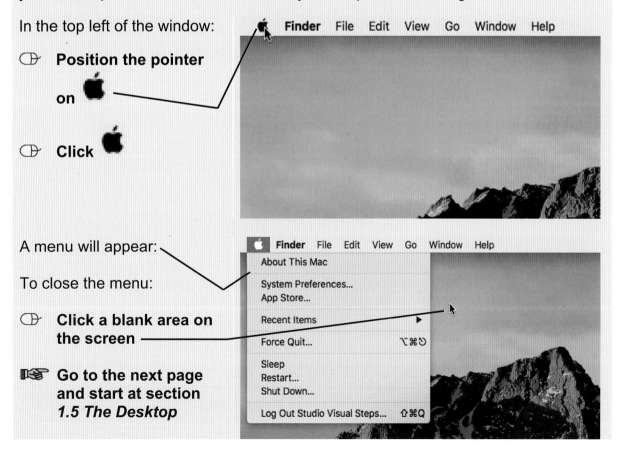

A menu will appear:

To close the menu:

☞ **Click a blank area on the screen**

☞ **Go to the next page and start at section *1.5 The Desktop***

In the next screen you will need a password in order to continue.

 HELP! I do not know the password.
If this is not your own computer, ask the owner to type the password for you.

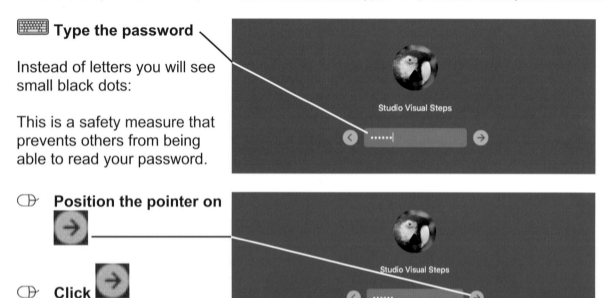

⌨ **Type the password**

Instead of letters you will see small black dots:

This is a safety measure that prevents others from being able to read your password.

☞ **Position the pointer on** →

☞ **Click** →

1.5 The Desktop

Once you have logged in, the desktop will appear. Every action you carry out on your Mac begins from the desktop:

The default desktop picture on a Mac is a photo of a rock:

You may see a different photo or a solid color on your desktop.

HELP! I see a window about creating an Apple ID.

You might see a window about creating an *Apple ID*. You will not be needing an *Apple ID* to work through this book. You can skip this option for now. Click *Continue* at the bottom of the window. A small window will appear and you will need to confirm the action by clicking *Skip*.

 HELP! I see a window about Siri.

You might see a window about *Siri*. In that case you click *Don't sign in* and *Continue* at the bottom of the window.

 Please note:

To display the screenshots in the rest of this book as clearly as possible, we use a simple, blue color for the desktop background. In the last chapter of this book you can read how to change the desktop picture to your own liking.

At the bottom of the screen you will see the *Dock*:

The *Dock* is one of the prominent features of the Mac. It is the horizontal bar at the bottom of your screen containing many icons. These icons are actually shortcuts for launching programs and opening folders.

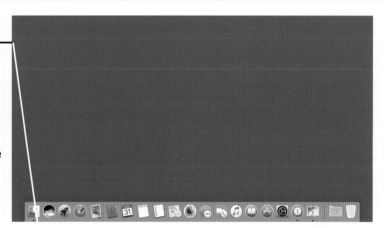

You may see more or different icons on your own Mac, or the icons may be in a different order.

At the top of the screen you see the menu bar:

Whenever you change to a different program, the text on the menu bar will also change.

At the top right you will see the current time, and the user's name:

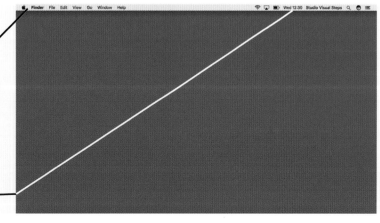

Your Mac contains many other programs. However, there is not enough space on the *Dock* to display an icon for each one of them. In the next section you will take a look at the default set of programs.

1.6 Launchpad and Dashboard

The *Dock* contains an 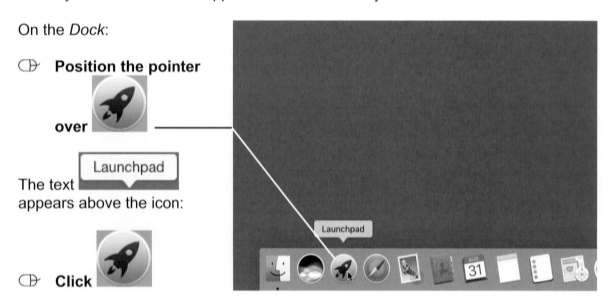 icon for the *Launchpad*. The *Launchpad* is the place where you can view all the applications installed on your Mac.

On the *Dock*:

☞ **Position the pointer**

over

The text [Launchpad] appears above the icon:

☞ **Click**

Now the *Launchpad* is opened:

You will see various icons for the programs installed on your Mac:

You may see more or different icons on your own Mac.

At the top of the *Launchpad*. you will see a search box: ─

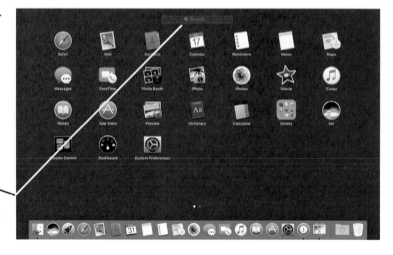

You can use the icons for opening the corresponding programs. Just try this for the *Dashboard* program:

 Point at `Dashboard`

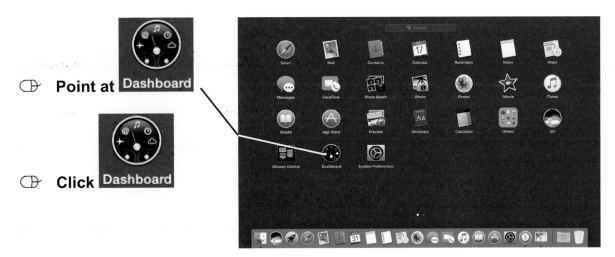

 Click `Dashboard`

Please note:

From this point on, the commands for ⊕ **Point at…, Point to… or** ⊕ **Position the pointer…** will be replaced by the shorter command ⊕ **Click…**

Dashboard is a program that provides access to all kinds of useful mini programs. These programs are called *widgets*.

Now you will see the *Dashboard* screen. It contains the *Weather, World Clock, Calendar* and *Calculator* widgets:

If someone else has previously used your Mac, you may see other widgets.

HELP! Dashboard has not opened and Launchpad has disappeared.

If you have not clicked the *Dashboard* icon accurately, but have clicked accidentally next to it, you may have caused the *Launchpad* application to close. You will then return to your desktop screen. Just give it a try once more:

Click

Click Dashboard

This is how you calculate a sum with the *Calculator* widget:

Click 7

Click ×

Click 5

Click =

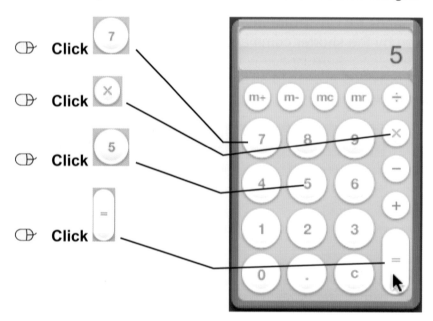

You will see the answer in the box at the top of the screen:

1.7 Dragging

The widgets do not have a fixed spot on the screen. You can move them across the screen by dragging them. This is how you drag an item with the Magic Mouse:

- **Position the pointer on the widget you want to move**
- **Press the mouse and hold it down**
- **Move the mouse until you have reached the desired place on the screen**
- **Release the mouse**

This is how you drag an item using a mouse with two buttons:

- **Position the pointer on the widget you want to move**
- **Press the left mouse button and hold it down**
- **Move the mouse until you have reached the desired place on the screen**
- **Release the mouse button**

This is how you drag an item using the trackpad:

- **Position the pointer on the widget you want to move**
- **Press the trackpad and hold it down**
- **Drag your finger across the trackpad to move the item to the desired spot**
- **Release the trackpad**

Now you can practice dragging one of the widgets yourself:

- **Position the pointer on the *World Clock* widget**

- **Press the mouse button/trackpad and hold it down**

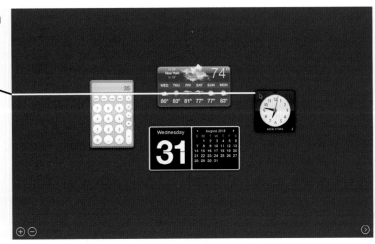

It is important that you keep the mouse button or the trackpad pressed as you drag the item:

 **Drag the clock to a position at the top right of your screen**

 **Release the mouse button/trackpad**

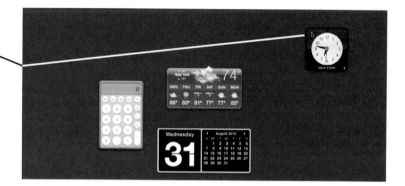

This is how you return to your desktop, from the *Dashboard*:

On the *Dashboard*, in the bottom right corner of the screen:

 **Click** ⊘

You will see the desktop again:

1.8 Sleep Mode

If you have not used your Mac for a couple of minutes, it appears to turn off, all by itself. This is when the Mac reverts to *sleep mode*. In this mode the device will save energy. You can put the Mac into sleep mode yourself, if you do not need to use the computer for a while. You do this using the menu bar at the top of your screen:

In the top left of the desktop:

☞ **Click**

A menu will appear with a list of various options:

To put the Mac into sleep mode:

☞ **Click Sleep**

Now the screen will turn dark and the Mac will appear to be completely turned off. To wake the Mac up from sleep mode:

☞ **Press the mouse button or the trackpad**

Or:

⌨ **Press a random key on the keyboard**

Or:

☞ **Briefly press the power button**

Tip

Close the cover
You can quickly put your MacBook, MacBook Pro or MacBook Air into sleep mode by simply closing the screen cover. The MacBook will wake up when you open the cover again.

1.9 Turn Off the Mac

If you do not intend to use the Mac for a longer period of time, it is better to turn the power off altogether. With an iMac, Mac Pro or Mac mini this will save energy. With a MacBook, MacBook Pro or Air this will prevent the battery from going dead. This is how you turn off the Mac:

In the top left of the screen:

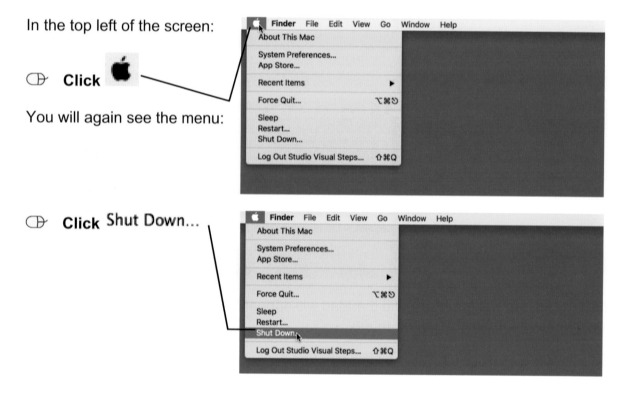

Click

You will again see the menu:

Click Shut Down...

Now you will be asked if you are sure you want to shut down your computer. You will have a minute to think about this. Use the `Cancel` button to prevent the Mac from turning off the power. If you do not do anything, the Mac will turn off after 60 seconds. You can practice turning off the computer right now:

☞ **Click** `Shut Down`

In future, you can always decide to put the Mac into sleep mode, or turn it off completely.

Are you sure you want to shut down your computer now?

If you do nothing, the computer will shut down automatically in 56 seconds.

☑ Reopen windows when logging back in

Cancel   Shut Down

In this chapter you have learned how to turn the Mac on and off and how to put it into sleep mode. You have also practiced some of the basic actions needed to allow a mouse or trackpad interact with items on the computer screen. In the following chapters you will get acquainted with some other actions, such as dragging files into folders.

In addition, you have learned about the desktop, the *Dock*, the *Launchpad* and the *Dashboard* programs. And you know how to use the widgets on the *Dashboard*. By performing the exercises on the next page you can repeat and practice these actions once more. For additional information, be sure to take a look at the *Tips* and the *Background Information* at the end of this chapter.

1.10 Exercises

The following exercises will help you master what you have just learned. Have you forgotten how to do something? Use the number beside the footsteps $\theta\theta^1$ to look it up in the appendix *How Do I Do That Again?* at the end of the book.

Exercise: Launchpad and Dashboard

☞ Turn on your Mac (and your screen, if necessary).

☞ If necessary, log in. $\theta\theta^1$

☞ Open *Launchpad.* $\theta\theta^2$

☞ Open the *Dashboard* program. $\theta\theta^3$

☞ Calculate this sum: `25 x 11 =` with the *Calculator* widget. $\theta\theta^4$

☞ Drag the *Calculator* widget to a position on the top left of the screen. $\theta\theta^5$

☞ Go back to the desktop. $\theta\theta^6$

Exercise: Sleep mode and Turn Off

☞ Put your Mac into sleep mode. $\theta\theta^7$

☞ Wake up the Mac again. $\theta\theta^8$

☞ Turn off the Mac. $\theta\theta^9$

1.11 Background Information

Dictionary

Apple	*Apple Inc.* is a US-based company founded in 1976. Its headquarters are in Cupertino, California. Well known *Apple* products include the Macintosh personal computer, the portable iPod music player, the iPhone, the iPad tablet, the *MacOS* operating system and the *iTunes* music program.
Apple ID	Combination of an email address and a password, also called *iTunes App Store Account*. You need to have an *Apple ID* in order to use some options on the Mac.
Click	Briefly press the mouse once (on a Magic Mouse), press the left mouse button (on a mouse with two buttons), or press the trackpad. By clicking something you can select the item or carry out a certain action or command.
Dashboard	A component of *MacOS* that contains mini software programs called *widgets*.
Desktop	The work area on a computer screen. When you open a program, it will appear on the desktop.
Desktop computer	A desktop computer is usually placed on a fixed spot on a table or desk.
Dock	A component of *MacOS* that lets you open various programs. The *Dock* is the horizontal bar of icons at the bottom of your screen. These icons actually represent shortcuts that will open folders or programs installed on the computer.
Drag	Move something on the screen by selecting the item and holding the mouse button or trackpad down while you move the pointer.
Icon	A small picture indicating a file, folder or program.
iMac	A type of *Apple* desktop computer, where the computer and the screen are integrated as a single unit. The iMac was first introduced in 1998.

- Continue on the next page -

iPad   A tablet computer designed and marketed by *Apple*. Instead of an actual keyboard or keypad, the iPad uses a Multi-Touch screen and a virtual keyboard with virtual keys and buttons.

iPhone   A combination of a cell phone, a multimedia player and a wireless Internet device, designed and marketed by *Apple*. Instead of a keyboard, the iPhone has a touchscreen that displays all the keys and buttons.

iPod   A line of portable media players designed by *Apple*.

Launchpad   A component of *MacOS* that provides instant access to Mac applications. *Launchpad* contains icons for all the programs installed on the Mac. Applications can be opened directly from the *Launchpad*.

Mac   An *Apple* computer, also called Macintosh computer.

MacBook Air   A very lightweight portable computer made by *Apple*. The first MacBook Air was introduced in 2008. The current editions have an 11 or 13 inch screen.

MacBook Pro   *Apple's* more powerful notebook, intended for business and professional use. The current editions have a 13 or 15 inch screen.

Macintosh   A type of personal computer made by *Apple* and first introduced in 1984. The Macintosh computer was the first commercially successful personal computer using a graphic user interface and a mouse, instead of the user having to type complicated commands.

MacOS   The operating system for the Macintosh computers.

Mac mini   A compact, portable and quiet desktop computer manufactured by *Apple*. The Mac mini is supplied without a monitor, keyboard, mouse or trackpad. These items must be purchased separately.

Mac Pro   The Mac Pro is the most powerful desktop computer from *Apple*. The Mac Pro is supplied without a monitor, keyboard, mouse or trackpad.

Magic Mouse   The first Multi-Touch mouse manufactured by *Apple*. With this mouse you not only can point and click with your finger, but use touch gestures such as swiping and scrolling.

Magic Trackpad   A separate trackpad made by *Apple* and equipped with the Multi-Touch technology. You can use the device by clicking it with your fingers or dragging your fingers across the device.

- Continue on the next page -

Menu, menu bar	A menu contains a list of options for a specific program. Menus will remain hidden until you click the titles on the menu bar. The menu bar is located in the top left of your screen. The menu bar will change and adjust itself according to the program that is currently active.
Multi-Touch	A method of interacting with a computer or another device by using a touch-sensitive surface. A trackpad, mouse or touchscreen that is equipped with the Multi-Touch technology will recognize multiple concurrent contacts made with the screen. These devices can interact with the screen using multiple fingers at once.
Notebook	A notebook or laptop computer is a portable computer that you can use anywhere you want. You can set it on your lap for instance or place it on a table or desk.
Program	A sequence of commands (instructions), used by a computer to execute a certain task. When you use a program, the computer will read the command you have typed and will execute it.
Sierra	The 2016 version of Apple's operating system for Macs is named *MacOS Sierra*.
Sleep mode	A mode where the screen of the computer has turned black and the disk unit has been turned off. When you put your computer in sleep mode, it will still be turned on, but will consume less power. If you use sleep mode, it takes less time to start up the computer.
Trackpad	A trackpad is also called a touchpad. It is a pointing device that consists of a special surface that can transfer the movement and position of the user's fingers into an onscreen movement or command.
USB port	A narrow, rectangular connector on a computer, to which you can connect a USB (Universal Serial Bus) device, such as a mouse.
Widget	A mini program in *Dashboard*. Widgets can be used for a multitude of tasks, such as keeping track of the stock market, viewing the weather forecast, looking up words in a dictionary, etcetera.

Source: Apple Dictionary, www.apple.com

1.12 Tips

 Tip

Quickly open the Dashboard

If you use the *Dashboard* often, there are several ways to open it more quickly. The first method is by using the keyboard:

 Press the F4 key

Depending on the type of keyboard you use it will look like this or .

If the F4 key isn't working, you can also use your Magic Mouse or trackpad and use your fingers. This is how you can use your Magic Mouse to switch from the desktop to the *Dashboard*:

 Swipe <u>two</u> fingers across your Magic Mouse, from left to right

Please note: swiping is a very gentle movement. You do not need to press the mouse.

With the trackpad on your MacBook, Macbook Pro or MacBook Air, and with the Magic Trackpad, it works like this:

 Swipe <u>three</u> or <u>four</u> fingers across your trackpad, from left to right

To return to the desktop you just need to repeat this movement, only this time from the right to the left.

Tip

Beach ball

Do you see a spinning disk or 'beach ball' instead of your regular pointer ↖ ?
This means your Mac is busy executing a task.

☞ **Wait until the beach ball has disappeared**

Afterwards you can continue working.

 Tip

Close the Launchpad
If you open a program through the *Launchpad*, the *Launchpad* will automatically be closed. But you can also close the *Launchpad* without opening a program:

☞ **Click a blank area on the screen**

Now you will see the desktop once again.

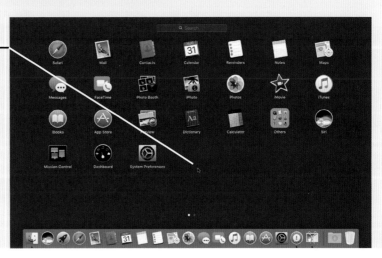

 Tip

Add and delete widgets
You can also add extra widgets to your *Dashboard*. You do that like this:

In the bottom left corner of the screen:

☞ **Click** ⊕

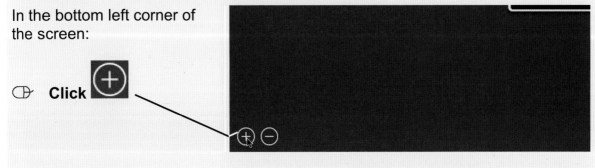

- Continue on the next page -

You will see various widgets. You can practice adding a widget by adding the *Tile Game* widget:

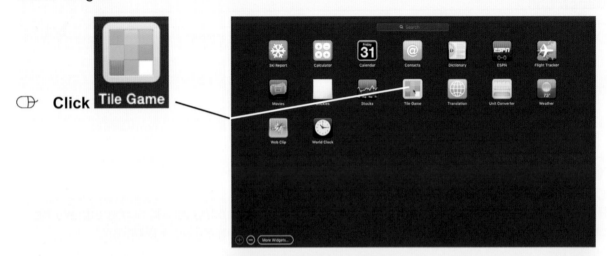

☞ **Click** Tile Game

The widget will be added:

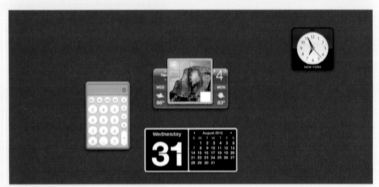

The *Tile Game* widget is a puzzle game. You will see an image in its completed form. First, shake the puzzle so the pieces are mixed up:

☞ **Click the puzzle**

You will see the pieces of the puzzle move around. To stop them moving around:

☞ **Click the puzzle**

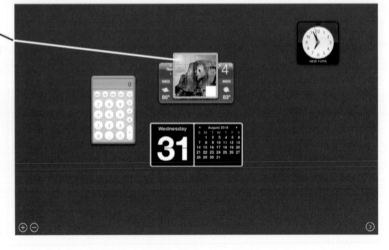

- Continue on the next page -

You can try to solve the puzzle by shifting around the pieces:

⮕ **Click the piece you want to move**

The block will move over to the blank area. This way you can solve the puzzle, step by step.

If you no longer want to use a widget, you can delete it. Here is how to do that:

In the bottom left corner of the screen:

⮕ **Click**

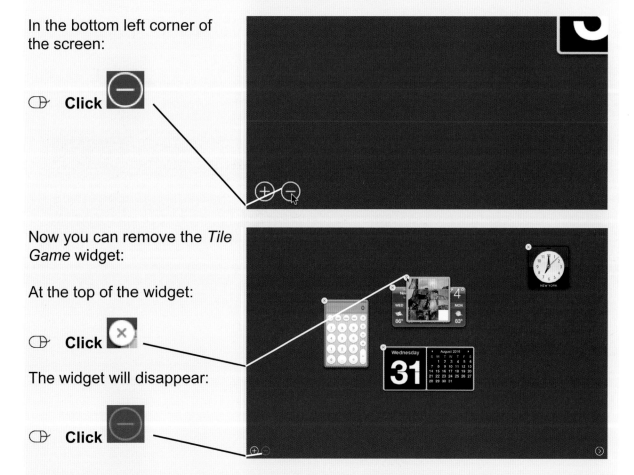

Now you can remove the *Tile Game* widget:

At the top of the widget:

⮕ **Click**

The widget will disappear:

⮕ **Click**

Please note: to use some of the widgets such as *Weather* and *Dictionary*, you will need to have an active Internet connection. If your computer is not connected to the Internet, you will see an error message when you try to use the widget or when the widget itself tries to retrieve new data.

Tip
Turning off the Mac with the power button

In this chapter you have seen how to turn off the Mac by using 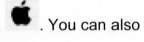. You can also
use the power button to turn the Mac off or to restart it.

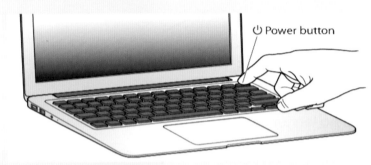 **Press the power
button and hold it
down for 2 seconds**

A window will open.

In the window you can
choose if you want to restart
or shut down the Mac. You
can also choose to put the
Mac to sleep:

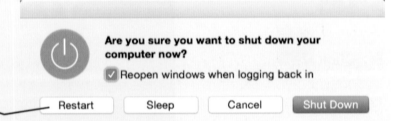

Please note: if you hold down the power button too long the computer will perform
the 'Force Quit' operation which turns the computer off. You may lose unsaved
documents if you force the computer to turn off in this manner.

You can also access this window by using the Control button and the power button:

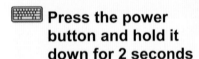 **Press** `control` **and the power button simultaneously**

2. Working with TextEdit

TextEdit is a simple and easy to use text editing program. It is one of the standard programs included in *MacOS*. You can use this program for most of your writing needs such as creating a letter, note or memo. The handy thing about using a computer to type your letters or other documents is that you can keep improving them. With the old fashioned typewriter it was much harder to fix mistakes. Starting over with a fresh new piece of paper was often the only way to go. Now, you can simply save your text and in the meantime do something else. At a later time, you can resume your work and continue further with the text.

You can also modify a document that you previously created. You can add a few alterations here and there to an existing letter and reuse it for a different situation.

Some of the techniques you learn in this chapter can be applied to other programs, such as when you write an email message. In this chapter you will get acquainted with *TextEdit* by creating a letter and using some of the basic formatting options. After that you will learn how to save and print your documents.

In this chapter you will learn how to:

- open the *TextEdit* program;
- minimize and maximize the window;
- write a letter;
- use bullets;
- save a letter;
- close *TextEdit* by using the menu bar;
- open a letter you saved by using the *Dock*;
- view the letter in print preview;
- print the letter;
- save changes.

2.1 Opening TextEdit

In this example you will be using the *Launchpad* to open the *TextEdit* program:

☞ **Open *Launchpad*** 👣²

You will see the programs that are installed on your computer. Some of the program icons are stored in a folder called *Other*. This is how you open *TextEdit*:

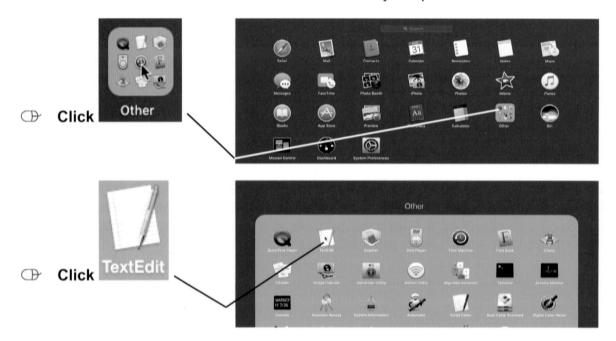

👆 **Click** **Other**

👆 **Click** **TextEdit**

✖ **HELP! I do not see the folder Other or the TextEdit icon.**
If you cannot find the program icon for *TextEdit* you can use the search box:

👆 **Click the search box**

⌨ **Type:** te

As soon as you start typing,
you will see the search
results appear:

👆 **Click** **TextEdit**

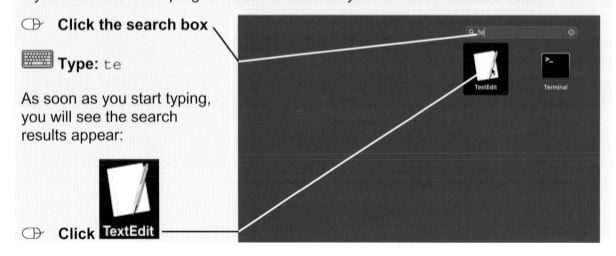

2. Working with TextEdit

TextEdit is a simple and easy to use text editing program. It is one of the standard programs included in *MacOS*. You can use this program for most of your writing needs such as creating a letter, note or memo. The handy thing about using a computer to type your letters or other documents is that you can keep improving them. With the old fashioned typewriter it was much harder to fix mistakes. Starting over with a fresh new piece of paper was often the only way to go. Now, you can simply save your text and in the meantime do something else. At a later time, you can resume your work and continue further with the text.

You can also modify a document that you previously created. You can add a few alterations here and there to an existing letter and reuse it for a different situation.

Some of the techniques you learn in this chapter can be applied to other programs, such as when you write an email message. In this chapter you will get acquainted with *TextEdit* by creating a letter and using some of the basic formatting options. After that you will learn how to save and print your documents.

In this chapter you will learn how to:

- open the *TextEdit* program;
- minimize and maximize the window;
- write a letter;
- use bullets;
- save a letter;
- close *TextEdit* by using the menu bar;
- open a letter you saved by using the *Dock*;
- view the letter in print preview;
- print the letter;
- save changes.

2.1 Opening TextEdit

In this example you will be using the *Launchpad* to open the *TextEdit* program:

☞ **Open *Launchpad*** 🐾**2**

You will see the programs that are installed on your computer. Some of the program icons are stored in a folder called *Other*. This is how you open *TextEdit*:

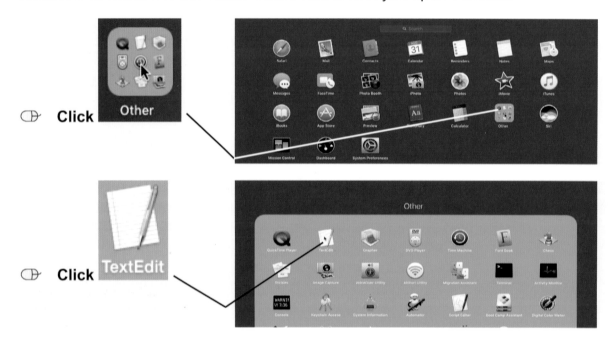

👆 **Click** Other

👆 **Click** TextEdit

🩹 **HELP! I do not see the folder Other or the TextEdit icon.**

If you cannot find the program icon for *TextEdit* you can use the search box:

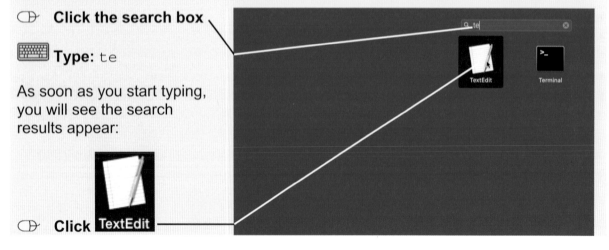

👆 **Click the search box**

⌨️ **Type:** te

As soon as you start typing, you will see the search results appear:

👆 **Click** TextEdit

The *TextEdit* program will be opened on the desktop in a new window:

The name of the program, **TextEdit** will now appear on the menu bar:

If you click *TextEdit* in the menu bar, you will see a list of available commands for the *TextEdit* program.

Notice that there is also now an icon for the *TextEdit* program in the *Dock*:

Below the [icon] icon you will see a dot ▇. This tells you that the program is active. If you look at the *Dock* carefully, you can easily see which programs are opened.

The *TextEdit* window consists of various elements:

Buttons for closing, minimizing and maximizing the window:

The toolbar with all sorts of tools for formatting the text:

The cursor:

The title bar:

The ruler:

The blank 'sheet' where you can type your text:

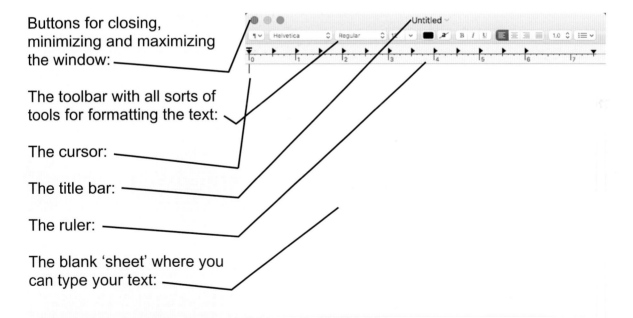

2.2 Maximizing and Minimizing a Window

By default, a window will always be displayed in the optimum size that is best suited to the program. But this does not mean that the size of the window is fixed. If you think the window is too small, you can display the window full screen, or 'maximize' it:

Click

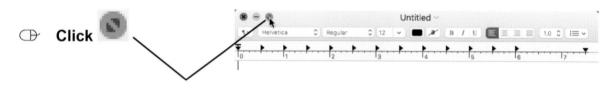

Now the *TextEdit* window will almost fill the entire screen:

The *Dock* and the menu bar has disappeared, they are revealed as soon as you place your mouse all the way to the top or bottom of your screen

If you think this screen is too big, you can return to the default window size, like this:

Position the pointer on the top left of your screen

Click

Now you will see the *TextEdit* program in its original window. You can also hide this window, without closing the program. This is called minimizing. It can be useful if you want to use a different program for a while and need working space on the desktop. Here is how to minimize a window:

Click

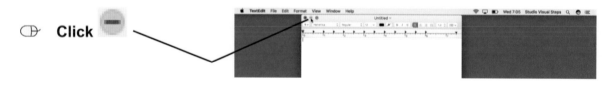

The *TextEdit* window will disappear. In the *Dock* you will see an extra icon. You can use click this icon to display the window once more:

☞ **Click**

 Tip
Different icon

You can also open this window by clicking the other *TextEdit* icon in the *Dock*.

Now you will see the *TextEdit* window once again. In the next section you will be writing a letter.

Please note:
Be sure to perform the following tasks. This practice letter will be used a number of times in later chapters of this book.

2.3 Writing a Letter

This book assumes that you are already acquainted with the keyboard. You should be able to do the following things:

Type letters, blank spaces and digits.

Type capital letters, punctuation marks and symbols with the Shift key.

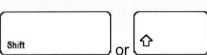

Delete a typo with the Delete or Backspace keys.

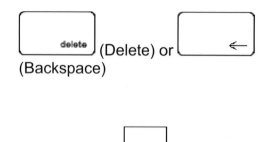 (Delete) or (Backspace)

Whether you have a Delete key or a Backspace key depends on the type of Mac you are using.

Start a new paragraph with the Enter/Return key.

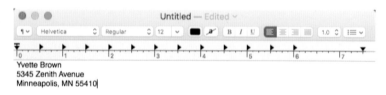 or

🢅 Please note:
There are many different types of keyboards. Some keys, such as the Shift key, will have a text written on them while others may show an image of an arrow.

🢅 Please note:
If you do not have a lot of experience using the keyboard, you can read the *Bonus Chapter Basic Text Editing Operations* and learn more about the basic operations. You can find this bonus chapter on the website that goes with this book:
www.visualsteps.com/macossierra
In *Appendix B Opening Bonus Chapters* you can read how to open the bonus chapter.

You can start by typing your own name and address information:

 Type your first and last name

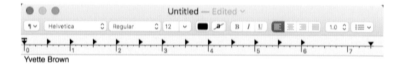

Yvette Brown

 Press 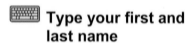 **(enter/return key)**

Now you can type your address:

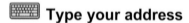 **Type your address**

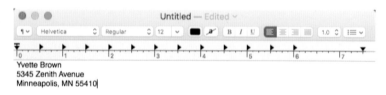

Yvette Brown
5345 Zenith Avenue
Minneapolis, MN 55410

Press

 **Type your city, state and the zip code (or postal code)**

Continue and enter the place and date:

 Press *[enter / return]* **twice**

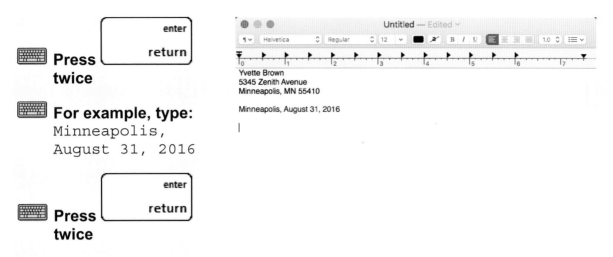

⌨️ **For example, type:**
Minneapolis,
August 31, 2016

Press *[enter / return]* **twice**

🩹 HELP! I am not a very good typist.

If you do not yet have much experience with typing on a keyboard, typing the text may take up a lot of time. If you want, you can make up a shorter text to type.

You have started by typing the sender and the date. Now you can enter the name and address of the recipient, the subject and the introductory phrase or header:

⌨️ **Type:**
William and Anne
Johnson
6455 Forest View Lane
Maple Grove, MN 55442

Subject: brunch

Dear William and Anne,

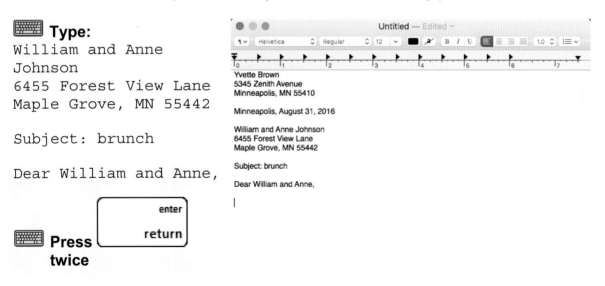

Press *[enter / return]* **twice**

Now you are going to continue typing the rest of the letter:

⌨ **Type:**

As you probably
already know, our aunt
and uncle Lynn and
Peter, will be
reaching their 50th
wedding anniversary.
They would like to
celebrate this event
with a brunch at the
Hilton Garden Inn
located in the
Minneapolis Maple
Grove area.

We would like to
select a date that
will fit everyone's
schedule. Can you let
me know which date
below would be best
for you?

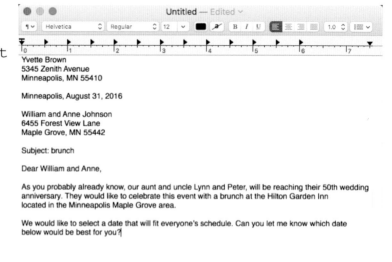

⌨ **Press** [enter / return] **twice**

2.4 Bullets

Now you can add a bulleted list of brunch dates:

🖱 **Click**

You will see a menu with
various bullet characters:

🖱 **Click** 🐑

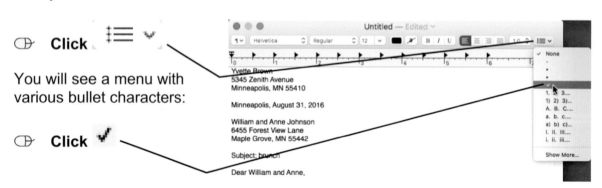

The first bullet will now appear in your letter:

⌨ **Type:** Saturday,
October 1

⌨ **Press** (enter/return)
[enter / return]

You will see a new bullet
character on the new line:

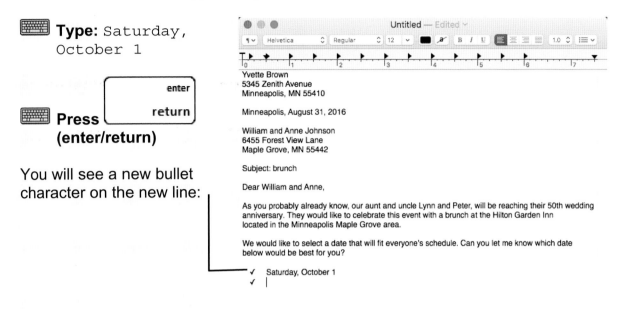

Now you can complete the list:

⌨ **Type:** Saturday,
October 8

⌨ **Press** [enter / return]

⌨ **Type:** Saturday,
October 15

⌨ **Press** [enter / return]

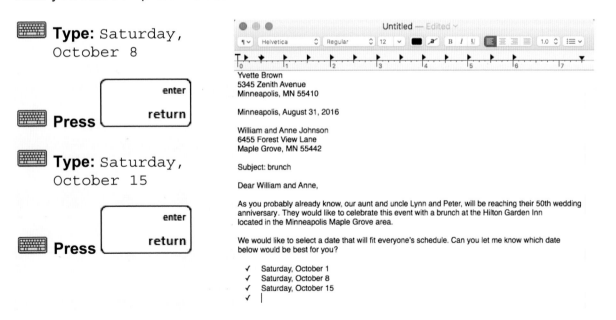

You have finished typing the list.

At the end of the list, a new bullet has been inserted. You do not need this bullet:

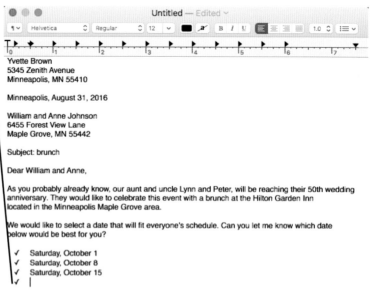

 **Press**

The bullet has been removed and the cursor is positioned at the beginning of the line:

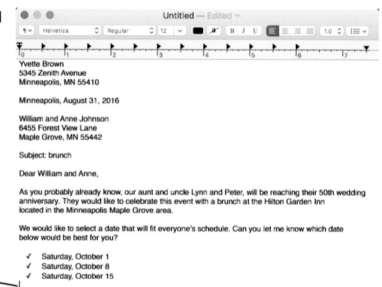

 **Press**

Just finish the letter:

⌨️ **Type:**
Thanks for your quick response.

Greetings,
Yvette

In the next section you will save the letter to your computer.

2.5 Saving a Document

Now you are going to save the letter, in other words, store it on your computer. By saving the document, you can open it again later on and continue with the editing. A document is also called a file. You can save the document by using the menu bar:

👆 **Click** File

You will see a menu:

👆 **Click** Save...

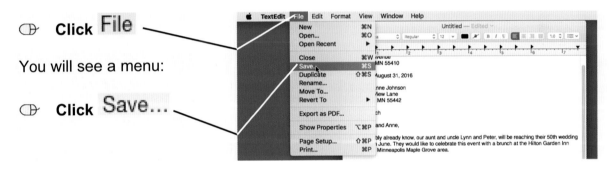

A new window will appear on top of the *TextEdit* window. You can enlarge this window so that you can view all the folders on your computer. Folders are locations on your computer where you can store files. You can read more about folders in *Chapter 3 Working with Folders and Files in Finder*.

When you save a file for the first time, you will see this small window. To see more files and folders:

👆 **Click**

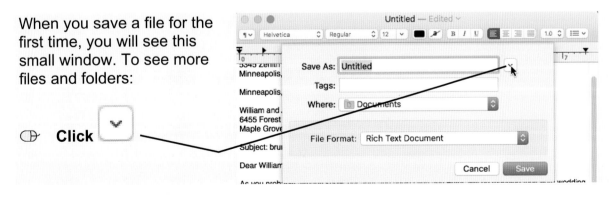

Now you will see a larger window:

By default, *TextEdit* will add the file name *Untitled*:

You will see the file name in the box next to **Save As:**:

By default, a new document is saved in the **Documents** folder:

You can change the document's name:

Type: brunch letter

Click **Save**

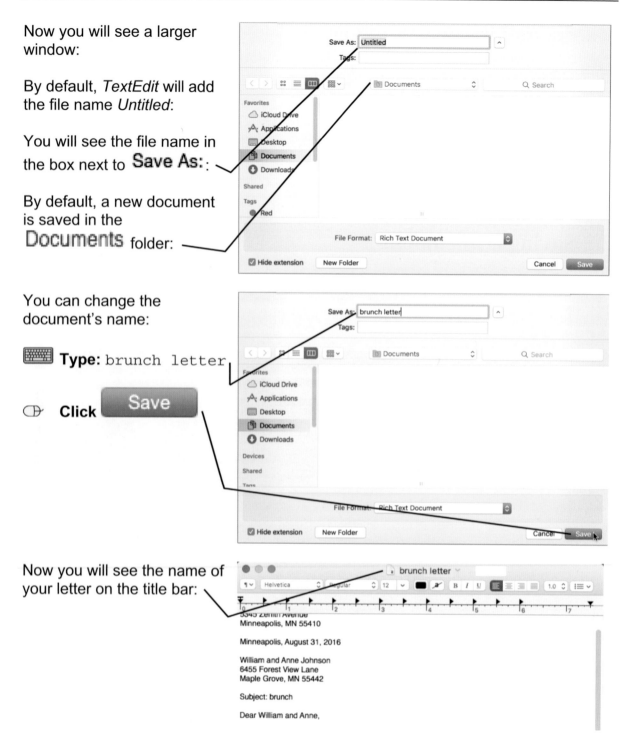

Now you will see the name of your letter on the title bar:

The letter has been saved in the *Documents* folder on your computer.

2.6 Closing TextEdit

In *MacOS* you can close most of the program windows in this way:

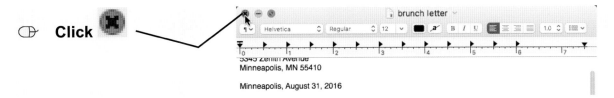

☞ **Click** [X]

Now the *TextEdit* window has disappeared. But the program itself is still open:

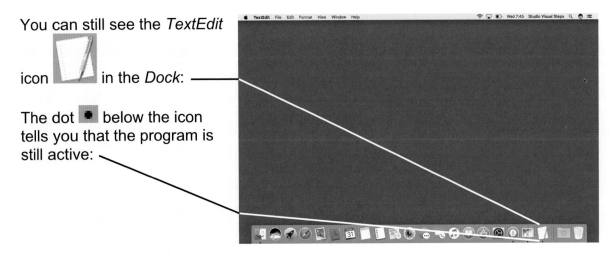

You can still see the *TextEdit* icon in the *Dock*:

The dot below the icon tells you that the program is still active:

You can open the window again by clicking the icon:

☞ **Click** [icon]

Now the *TextEdit* window will be opened once again:

You will see a blank
document:

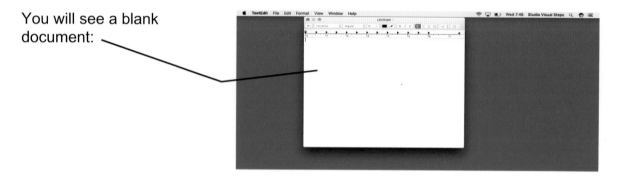

You can fully close the *TextEdit* program using the menu bar:

⊕ **Click** **TextEdit**

⊕ **Click** Quit TextEdit

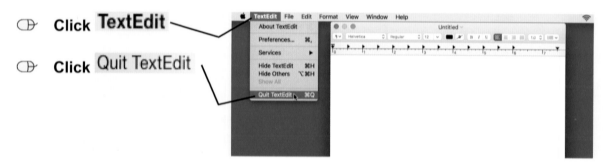

Now the *TextEdit* icon has
disappeared from the *Dock*:

You can open *TextEdit* again:

☞ **Open *TextEdit*** 👣10

You will see the *TextEdit* window. You can quickly open a recent document by using
the *File* option on the menu bar:

⊕ **Click** File

⊕ **Click** Open Recent

⊕ **Click** 📄 brunch letter

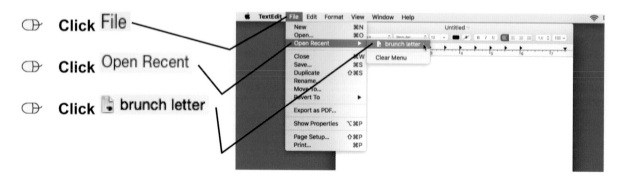

The letter will be opened in a
second window in *TextEdit*:

In the next section you will print the letter.

2.7 Printing a Letter

When you write a letter, most likely you will want to have it printed on paper. You can
practice doing this now.

 Please note:

In order to complete the following tasks, you will need to have a printer connected to
your Mac. If you do not have such a printer, just work through the next few steps
until you reach the point where you actually need to print, on page 63. If you are
using this book during a course, you can always ask your instructor for permission to
print the document.

You can print the letter by using the *File* option on the menu bar:

☞ **Click** File

☞ **Click** Print...

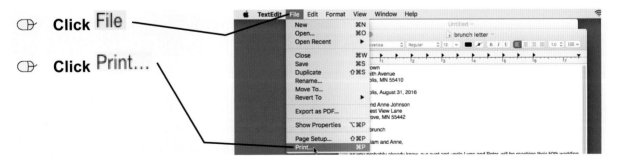

Now you will see a window
with a *print preview*, a
miniature rendering of what
the printed version of the
letter will look like:

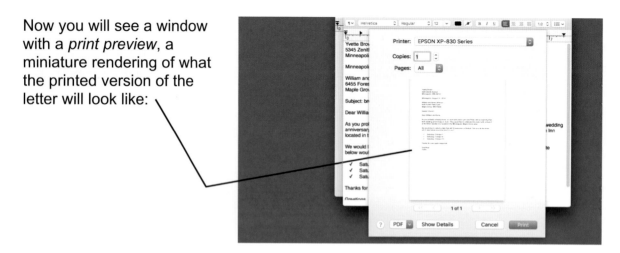

The text has not been evenly spaced across the length of the page. You can easily
solve this problem by inserting some blank lines. First, you need to close this window:

At the bottom of the window:

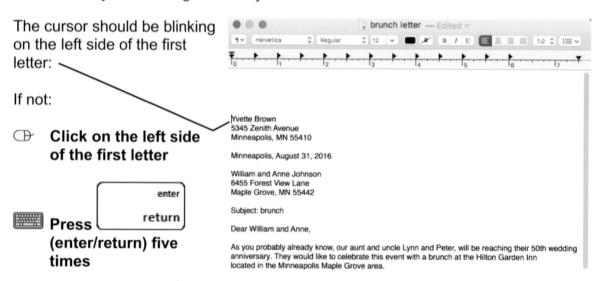

☞ **Click** Cancel

You will see your letter again. Now you can insert a few blank lines:

The cursor should be blinking
on the left side of the first
letter:

If not:

☞ **Click on the left side
of the first letter**

⌨ **Press** (enter/return) **five
times**

Yvette Brown
5345 Zenith Avenue
Minneapolis, MN 55410

Minneapolis, August 31, 2016

William and Anne Johnson
6455 Forest View Lane
Maple Grove, MN 55442

Subject: brunch

Dear William and Anne,

As you probably already know, our aunt and uncle Lynn and Peter, will be reaching their 50th wedding
anniversary. They would like to celebrate this event with a brunch at the Hilton Garden Inn
located in the Minneapolis Maple Grove area.

☞ **Insert a blank line between the address and the date** 🦶🦶11

☞ **Insert a blank line between the date and the recipient** 🦶🦶11

☞ **Insert a blank line between the recipient and the subject** 🦶🦶**11**

☞ **Insert a blank line between the subject and the header** 🦶🦶**11**

Take a look at the results in the print preview window:

⊕ **Click** File

⊕ **Click** Print...

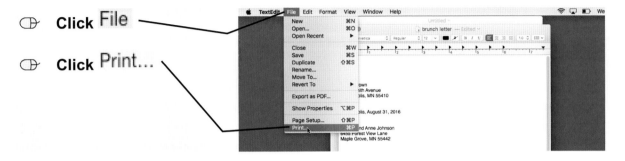

Now the text of the letter has been evenly divided across the page. Before you enter the print command:

☞ **Check to make sure the printer is turned on**

☞ **Make sure the printer contains enough paper**

Is the printer ready? Then you can enter the print command:

If you really want to print the letter:

⊕ **Click** Print

If you do not want to print the letter:

⊕ **Click** Cancel

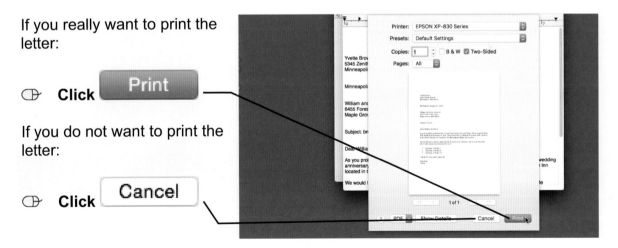

2.8 Save Changes

You have edited your letter in several places. If you need to work on your letter for a longer period of time, it is a good idea to save the document at regular intervals. Here is how you do that:

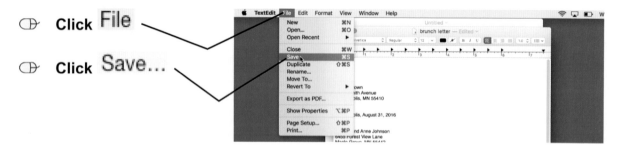

☞ **Click** File

☞ **Click** Save...

MacOS can also help you with the *Autosave* option: by default, the changes in your document are saved automatically every five minutes. When you close the *TextEdit* window, the final changes will also be saved. You can check this out for yourself. First, add some new text to the letter's subject:

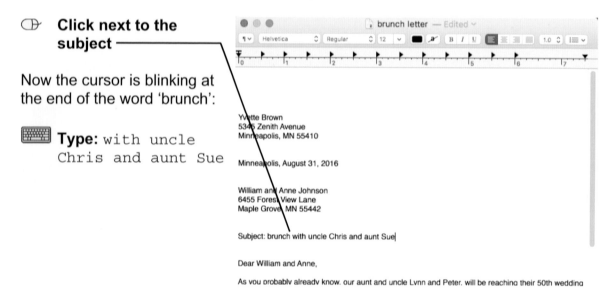

☞ **Click next to the subject**

Now the cursor is blinking at the end of the word 'brunch':

⌨ **Type:** with uncle Chris and aunt Sue

Now you are going to check to see if the new text is saved when you close the window:

☞ **Close the** *TextEdit* **window** ᐟᐟ12

In the *Dock*:

⊕ **Click**

👉 **Open the recently edited letter using the menu bar** 🐾¹³

You will see that the final
changes have been saved:

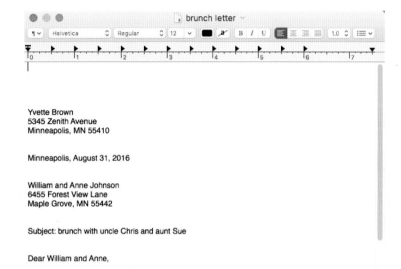

Yvette Brown
5345 Zenith Avenue
Minneapolis, MN 55410

Minneapolis, August 31, 2016

William and Anne Johnson
6455 Forest View Lane
Maple Grove, MN 55442

Subject: brunch with uncle Chris and aunt Sue

Dear William and Anne,

You can close the document. You can do this with the menu bar:

⊕ **Click** File

⊕ **Click** Close

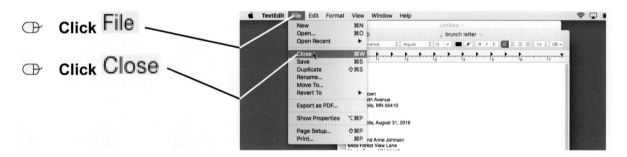

Now you can close the *TextEdit* program. On a Mac this is called quitting:

☞ **Click** **TextEdit**

☞ **Click** Quit TextEdit

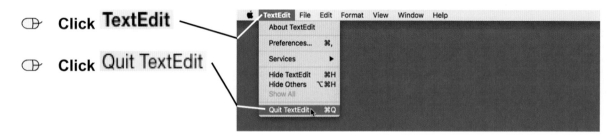

The *TextEdit* icon has disappeared from the *Dock*:

 Tip
Continue where you left off
Do you plan to edit the same document over the next few days? In that case, you do not need to close the document first, before quitting *TextEdit*. As soon as you open *TextEdit* again, you will immediately see the document you were working on.

This useful feature goes even further: you can also decide not to close *TextEdit* when you turn your computer off. In this way, the program and the document that was open when you turned the computer off will still be open when you turn your computer on again.

Because *MacOS* automatically saves your work, you do not need to worry about losing the most recent changes you have made.

In the following exercises you can repeat some of the actions we have discussed in this chapter.

2.9 Exercises

The following exercises will help you master what you have just learned. Have you forgotten how to do something? Use the number beside the footsteps 🐾¹ to look it up in the appendix *How Do I Do That Again?* at the end of the book.

Exercise: Minimize and Maximize

☞ Open the *TextEdit* program. 🐾¹⁰

☞ Minimize the window. 🐾¹⁴

☞ Open the minimized window by using the *Dock*. 🐾¹⁵

☞ Maximize the window. 🐾¹⁶

☞ Restore the maximized window to its original size. 🐾¹⁷

Exercise: Write and Save a Letter

☞ Type your own name and address, one below the other.

☞ Type the following text. If you do not have a lot of typing experience, you can make up your own text:

```
Atlanta, December 10, 2016

Tim and Sandra Smith
501 Main Street
Atlanta, GA 30507

Subject: garage sale

Dear Tim and Sandra,

On January 11 our local tennis club will hold its annual
garage sale. This year, the proceeds will be donated to the
Red Cross. Do you by any chance have some old things you would
like to get rid of for this garage sale? For instance:
```

☞ Start typing a bulleted list. ᵔᵔ**18**

☞ Type the list below. ᵔᵔ**19**

- books
- CDs
- toys
- old appliances

☞ Close the bulleted list. ᵔᵔ**20**

☞ Type the conclusion of the letter:

Please let me know if you have anything we can use. I will be
happy to come and collect it.

Thank you very much!

Kind regards,

Your name

☞ Save the letter in the *Documents* folder and name the file *garage sale letter*.
ᵔᵔ**21**

Exercise: Print a Letter

☞ View the print preview. ᵔᵔ**22**

☞ If possible, print the letter. ᵔᵔ**23**

Exercise: Close and Stop

☞ Close the *TextEdit* window. ᵔᵔ**12**

☞ Quit *TextEdit*. ᵔᵔ**24**

2.10 Background Information

Dictionary

Autosave	A function that saves changes in a document automatically at regular intervals.
Close	If you close a window, you will only close the open window. The program itself is still running (active). You will see a small indicator light appearing below the program's icon in the *Dock*.
Cursor	The blinking vertical line that indicates where the text will be inserted.
Documents	A folder where you can save your text files.
Maximize	Making a program window bigger, so it is displayed on a full screen. The *Dock* and the menu bar will still be visible after maximizing the window.
Minimize	Making a program window disappear from the screen, without quitting the program.
Open	A command for retrieving a document that is stored on a computer or other type of storage medium.
Print	A command for printing a document on paper, by means of a printer.
Print preview	A small preview of the letter, to show how it will look like on paper.
Save	A command for saving a document to the computer, or another type of storage medium.
Stop/Quit	Closing a program completely.
TextEdit	A text editing program included in the operating system.
Title bar	The horizontal bar at the top of a window. The options on the title bar will change in accordance to the program that is opened. In *TextEdit*, the title bar contains the name of the document you are editing.

Source: Apple Dictionary, www.apple.com

Printers

The printer most in use at home is the so-called *inkjet printer*. This type of printer prints letters by spraying tiny droplets of ink onto the paper.

A lot of these printers can also print in color. Such a printer is equipped with a black ink cartridge, as well as a three-color cartridge. By mixing up these colors on paper, a huge variety of colors can be created.

The containers with the ink are called *cartridges*. Each type of printer uses its own type of cartridges.

Inkjet printer

Inkjet printers can print on regular paper, but also on special types of paper, depending on the desired print quality. For example, you can buy special photographic paper for printing photos.

Laser printers operate according to a very different principle. A laser printer uses a very fine-grained powder, the so-called *toner*. The toner is used to melt the shape of the letters onto the paper, at very high temperatures.

The print quality of a laser printer is better than that of the inkjet. Laser printers are available as color printers or black and white printers.

Laser printer

Photo printers are printers that use a special process for printing digital photos on photographic paper.

According to the manufacturers, these printers can produce prints that approach the quality of professional printing services.

Most of these types of printers can be connected to the computer, but some models can also print photos directly from a digital camera's memory card, via a wireless internet connection (wi-fi) or a network.

Photo printer

2.11 Tips

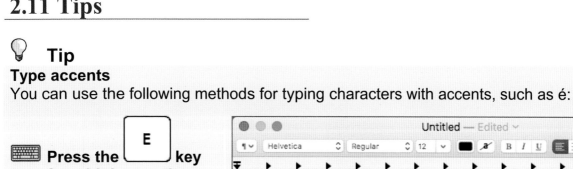

Type accents
You can use the following methods for typing characters with accents, such as é:

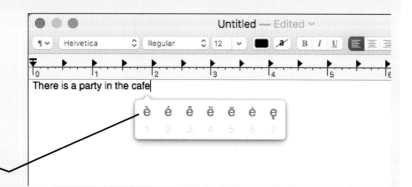

Press the [E] **key for a bit longer than usual**

A dialog box will appear displaying various forms of the accented character:

If you press the number of the desired accent on your keyboard, the letter with that accent will be inserted into the text. Number 2 stands for é:

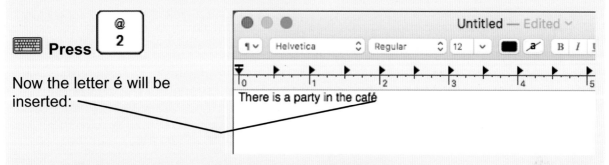

Press [@ 2]

Now the letter é will be inserted:

Do you want to know more about typing special characters? Then just read through the *Bonus Chapter Basic Text Editing Operations* and learn the basic operations. The bonus chapter can be found on the website that goes with this book:
www.visualsteps.com/macossierra
In *Appendix B Opening Bonus Chapters* you can read more about these bonus chapters.

Tip

Revert to the last saved version
Have you made changes to a document, but then decide you no longer want to keep them? You can easily undo the changes in programs where you have enabled the *Autosave* function.

As soon as you edit a document, you will see the word Edited in the title bar:

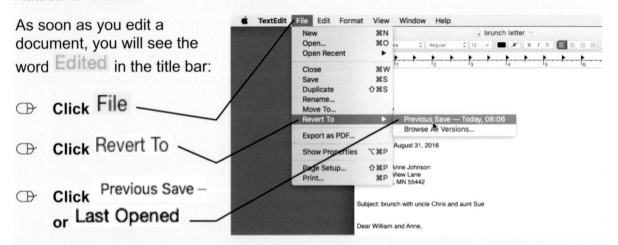

☞ **Click** File

☞ **Click** Revert To

☞ **Click** Previous Save – or Last Opened

The document will be restored to the state it was in when you last opened it.

 Tip

View different versions
MacOS does not just save the last opened version of a document, but you can retrieve all the versions that have been saved since the creation of the document. This is how you retrieve previously saved versions:

☞ **Click** File

☞ **Click** Revert To

☞ **Click** Browse All Versions...

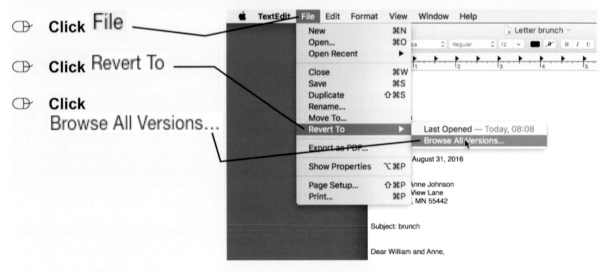

- Continue on the next page -

Here you see the document in its present state:

Here you see a stack of different versions of this document:

At the bottom of the version you will see the date and time of when the document was saved:

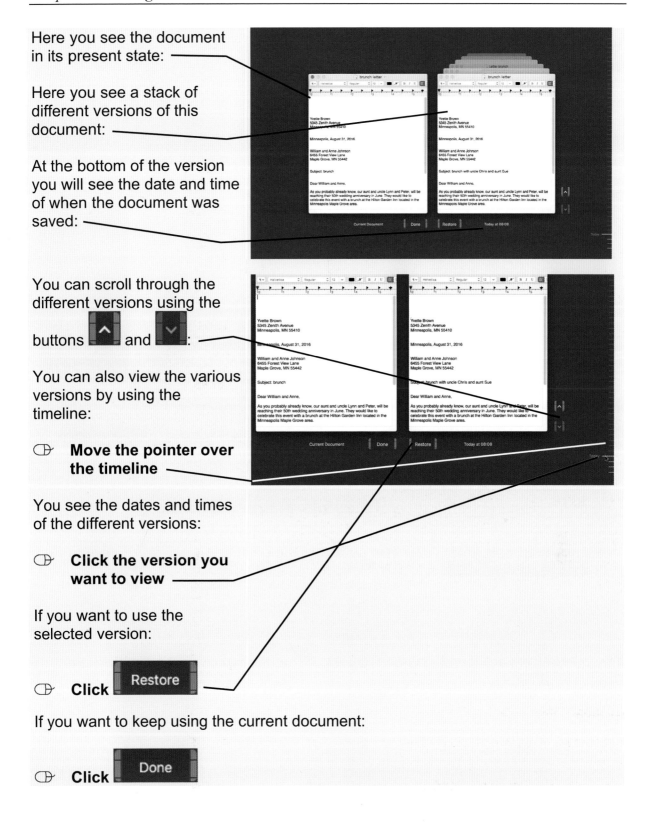

You can scroll through the different versions using the buttons ⌃ and ⌄:

You can also view the various versions by using the timeline:

🖰 **Move the pointer over the timeline**

You see the dates and times of the different versions:

🖰 **Click the version you want to view**

If you want to use the selected version:

🖰 **Click** **Restore**

If you want to keep using the current document:

🖰 **Click** **Done**

🔆 Tip
Spell check

You may have noticed a dotted red line appearing under some of the words. This means that the automatic spell checker has encountered a word that cannot be found in the *MacOS* dictionary. It may be a misspelled word, or a name that is not recognized by *MacOS*.

With the *Show Spelling and Grammar* function you can check for possible errors and correct them (or not). Here is how to do that:

☞ **Click** Edit

☞ **Click**
Spelling and Grammar

☞ **Click**
Show Spelling and Gramm

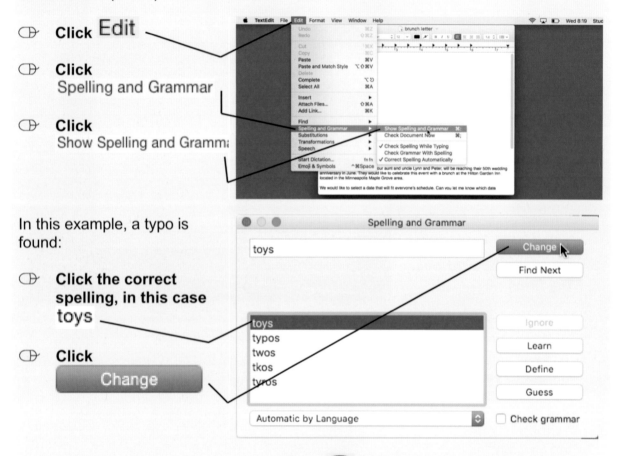

In this example, a typo is found:

☞ **Click the correct spelling, in this case** toys

☞ **Click**
Change

If no other errors are found, you can use the ⊗ button to close the *Spelling and Grammar* window.

Tip

Launchpad

If there are more programs installed on your Mac, they may no longer fit in a single *Launchpad* window. A new window will be created automatically. Once a second *Launchpad* window has been created, you will see two dots at the bottom of the

Launchpad window  :

In this example, a second window is present. This is how you switch to the second *Launchpad* window:

☞ **Click**

You can use the arrow keys to switch between programs in the *Launchpad* window. To return to the previous window:

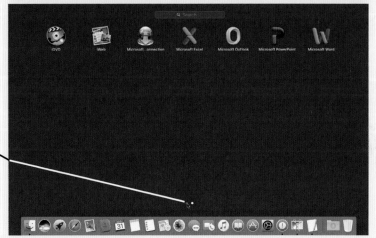

☞ **Click the first**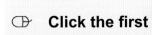

You will again see the first window.

You can also use the touch operations on your Magic Mouse or trackpad. This is how you return to the first *Launchpad* window with your Magic Mouse:

☞ **Swipe a single finger across your Magic Mouse, from left to right**

Please note: swiping is a very gentle movement; you do not need to press the mouse.

- Continue on the next page -

Here is how to do that with the trackpad on your MacBook, Macbook Pro or MacBook Air, and with the Magic Trackpad:

 Swipe two fingers across your trackpad, from left to right

To go back to the second window you need to repeat this movement, but now do it from right to left.

 Tip

Open programs
In this book, you mainly will use *Launchpad* to open programs. But there is also another method for opening programs:

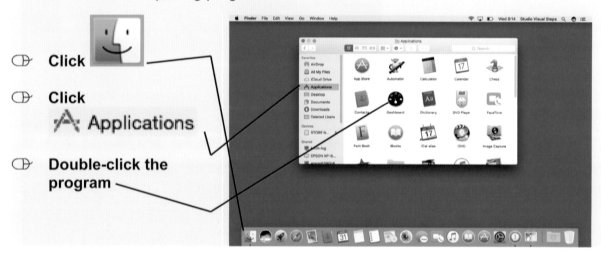

☞ **Click**

☞ **Click**
   ⚛ **Applications**

☞ **Double-click the program**

3. Working with Files and Folders in Finder

In this chapter you will learn how to work with the *files* and *folders* stored on your Mac. A file is a collective term for all the data stored on the computer. A file could be a program, a text document or a photo, for example. The basic actions you will learn to perform in this chapter can be applied to nearly every type of file.

The files on your computer are arranged in *folders* (also called *directories*). Folders may not only contain files, they can also contain other folders. A folder that is stored within another folder is called a *subfolder*. You can create as many subfolders as you want, and store as many files and new subfolders within these subfolders.

Fortunately, on your Mac, you do not need to arrange all these things yourself. In *MacOS*, a few folders have already been created for you. These standard folders include the *Documents* and *Downloads* folders. You can use these folders for arranging and ordering particular types of files. In the previous chapter you stored a file created with *TextEdit* in the *Documents* folder.

Finder is the name of the *MacOS* program that can be used to manage the folders and files on your computer. In *Finder* you can delete, copy, rename and move files and folders. You will be using the *Finder* window for example, each time you want to copy a text file or a photo to a USB stick.

In this chapter you will learn how to:

- open *Finder*;
- change the view of the *Finder* window;
- create a new folder;
- copy and move a file to a different folder;
- change a file name;
- delete a file;
- empty the *Trash*;
- copy a file to a USB stick;
- safely disconnect the USB stick.

3.1 Opening Finder

The *Finder* program has its own fixed place in the *Dock*. It is the only program that is always active. You cannot close *Finder*. You will always see a dot ▬■▬ below this

icon: . This is how you open the *Finder* window:

⊕ **Click**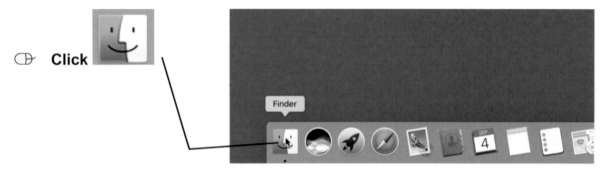

The *Finder* window will be opened:

By default, the
🗄 **All My Files** overview will
be opened:

This is the place where
MacOS collects all your files.
In the *Documents* folder you
will see the documents you
saved in the previous
chapter:

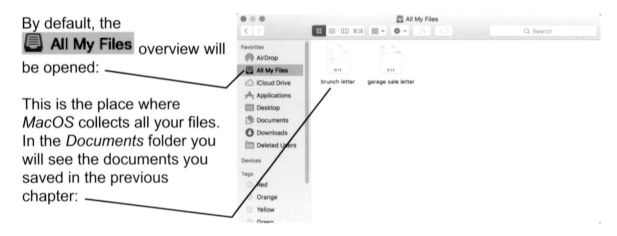

3.2 Changing the View for Finder

There are several ways of displaying the files and folders in *Finder*. Your screen may look a bit different at present.

In this example, the files are displayed as icons:

If you want to display the files in a list:

☞ **Click** ≡

You will see a list of all the files:

You can also display the files in columns:

☞ **Click** ⫼

Now the files are displayed in columns:

☞ **Click** 🗎 brunch letter

The file has been selected. In the right-hand column you will see a preview of this file:

Beneath the preview, you will see additional information about this file:

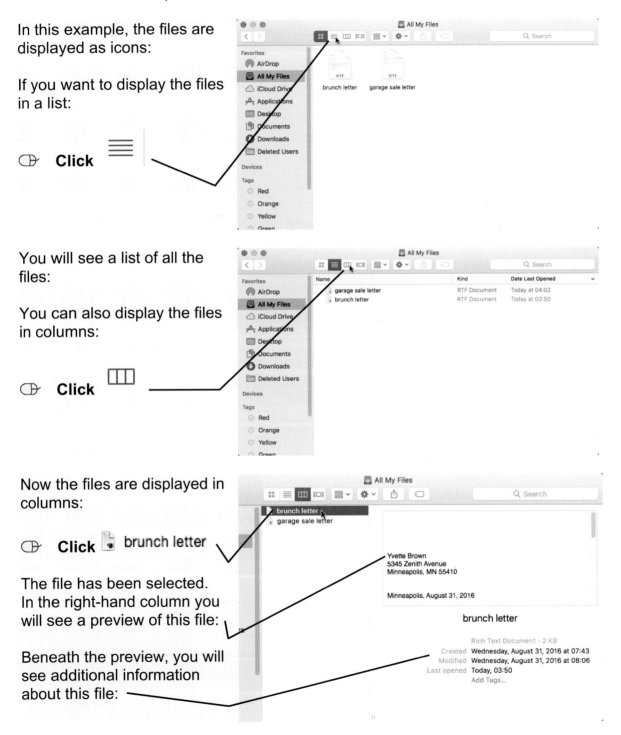

In the following examples, the *Symbols* view is used:

⊕ **Click**

There are even more settings you can use to modify the view of a window. For instance, you can display the *path bar* in the *Finder* window. Use the *View* option on the menu bar to do this:

⊕ **Click** View

⊕ **Click** Show Path Bar

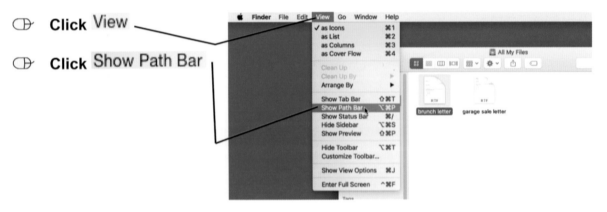

 HELP! I see a command called Hide Path Bar.

Does your menu contain the Hide Path Bar option? This means the path bar is already visible in *Finder*.

☞ **Just continue reading**

The path bar is displayed:

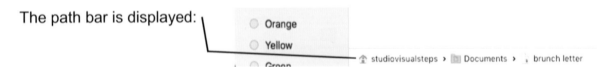

In the path bar, you can see at a glance in which folder a selected file or a selected folder is stored: ⌂ studiovisualsteps ▸ Documents ▸ brunch letter .

This means that the *brunch letter* has been stored in the *Documents* folder. The *Documents* folder is stored in the personal folder of the user called *studiovisualsteps*. On your own computer, there will be a different name for this folder.

You are going to check if your computer has the same settings for the *Finder* view as in these examples:

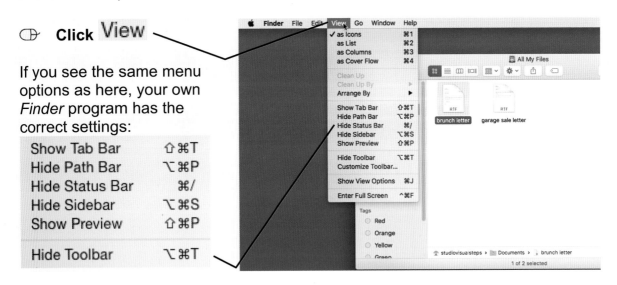

☞ **Click** View

If you see the same menu options as here, your own *Finder* program has the correct settings:

Show Tab Bar	⇧⌘T
Hide Path Bar	⌥⌘P
Hide Status Bar	⌘/
Hide Sidebar	⌥⌘S
Show Preview	⇧⌘P
Hide Toolbar	⌥⌘T

 HELP! My menu has a Show... option instead of a Hide... option.

If you see Show in a menu option, it means the component is hidden by *Finder*.

☞ **For example, click** Show Sidebar

Now this component will be displayed in *Finder*.

☞ **Make sure the path bar and the status bar are displayed, by changing the menu options in the same way as the example above**

In order to provide a good view of the files, it is useful to order them alphabetically, by their file name. You will need to set this up for each individual folder, like this:

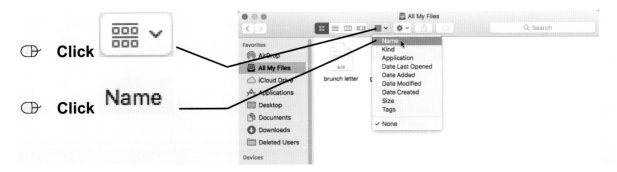

☞ **Click**

☞ **Click** Name

3.3 The Various Components in Finder

Finder does not just display the contents of a folder. The *Finder* window contains specific sections that will help you navigate through the folders on your computer. Take a closer look now at these components:

Navigation pane:
In this window pane you will see the folders that are most important:

The blue bar indicates which folder or view has been selected:

In the *file list*, the files in this folder are displayed as icons:

In the *path bar* you can view the location of a selected folder or file:

In the *status bar* you can see how many files are contained within a folder and how many files are selected:

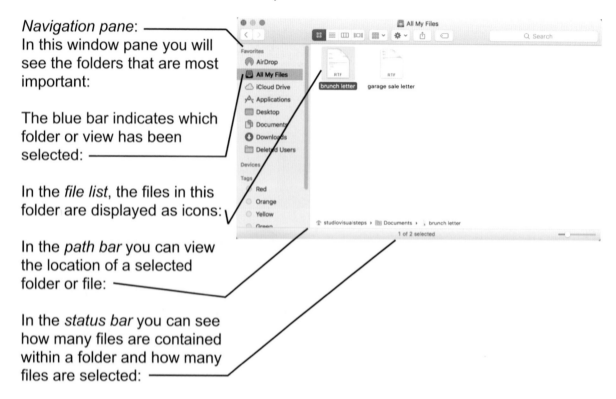

By using the *navigation pane* on the left-hand side, you can quickly open a folder on your computer. When you click a folder in the left *navigation pane*, the contents of this folder will be displayed on the right side, the *file list* part of *Finder*.

 Tip
Icons for files and folders
By default, *MacOS* will display a miniature preview of the file or folder in the icon that goes with this file or folder.

For example, this icon ___RTF___ for a text file.

In the case of a photo file, the preview is even more obvious: .

3.4 Creating a New Folder

You can use folders to arrange your files in an orderly way. Each file on your computer is stored in a folder. A folder may also contain another folder. A folder contained within another folder is called a *subfolder*.

You can create your own new folders. For example, it may be useful to separate your letters from other documents. To see how this is done, you are going to create a new subfolder in the  folder. First, you need to open the *Documents* folder:

👉 **Click**  **Documents**

You will see the contents of the *Documents* folder:

Your *Documents* folder will contain at least two files. These are the letters you have written in the previous chapter.

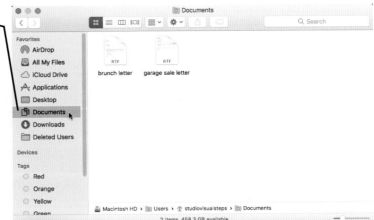

💡 **Tip**
Path bar
This is what you currently see in the path bar

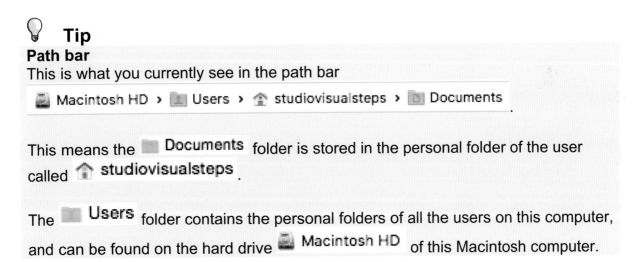

This means the ▫ Documents folder is stored in the personal folder of the user called 🏠 studiovisualsteps.

The ▫ Users folder contains the personal folders of all the users on this computer, and can be found on the hard drive 💾 Macintosh HD of this Macintosh computer.

You are also going to order the files in this folder alphabetically:

👉 **Let the program alphabetically order the files in the Documents folder by their names as well** 👣³⁷

Now you can create a new folder:

⊕ **Click** File

⊕ **Click** New Folder

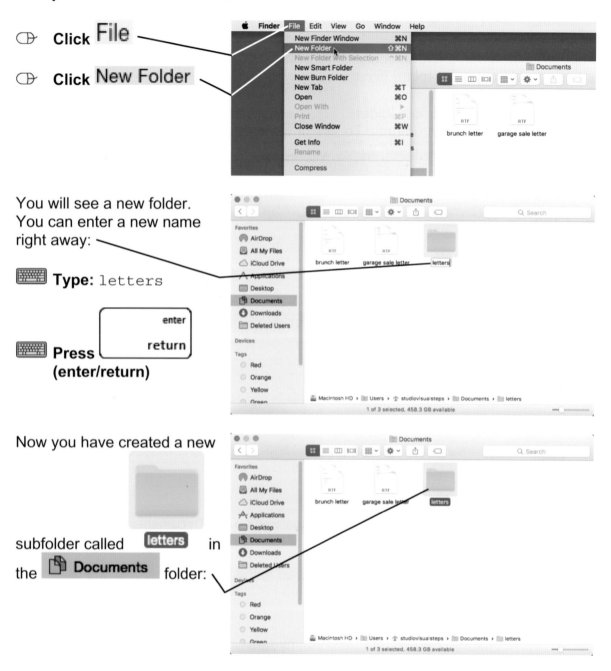

You will see a new folder.
You can enter a new name
right away:

⌨ **Type:** letters

⌨ **Press** (enter/return)

Now you have created a new

subfolder called letters in

the 🗂 **Documents** folder:

In the next section, you can use the *letters* folder to save a letter you will write in *TextEdit*. First, you are going to minimize the *Finder* window:

☞ **Minimize the *Finder* window** 👣14

3.5 Save in a Folder

You will be writing a letter in *TextEdit* and saving it in the new **letters** folder. The saving action can also be done in other programs in pretty much the same way.

☞ **Open** *TextEdit* ✂**10**

Type a short sentence:

⌨ **Type:** `Letter for saving`

☞ **Click** **File**

☞ **Click** **Save...**

First, enter a name for the new document:

⌨ **Type:** `letter`

You switch to a different view:

☞ **Click** ▥

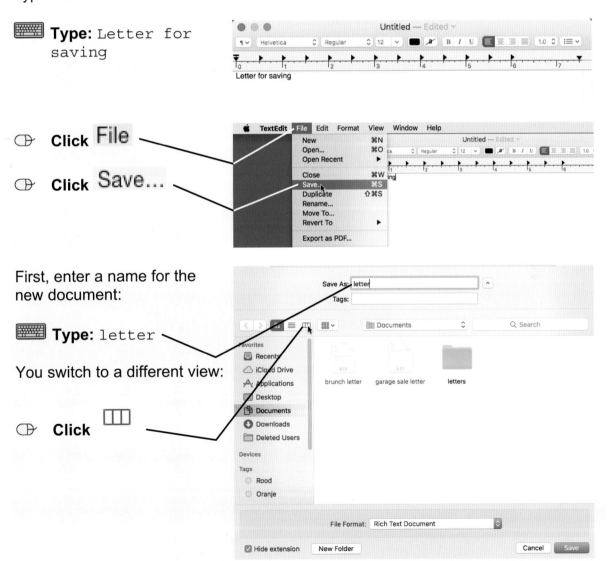

TextEdit will immediately assume that you want to save the new document in the *Documents* folder too. But now you are going to select the *letters* subfolder instead:

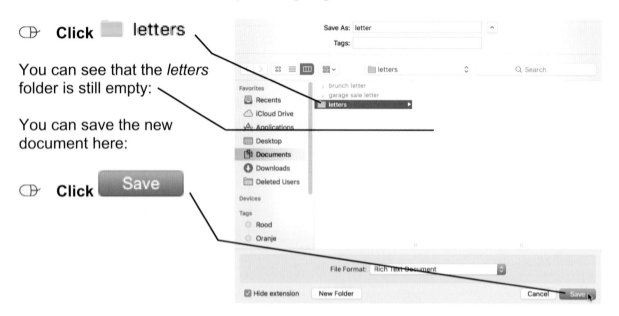

Click [ ] **letters**

You can see that the *letters* folder is still empty:

You can save the new document here:

Click [**Save**]

Now the file called *letter* has been saved in the *letters* folder.

📭 **Close the *TextEdit* window** 👣^{12}

📭 **Quit *TextEdit*** 👣^{24}

You can open *Finder* once again, to check whether your file has been saved in the *letters* folder. For this, you are going to use the *Dock*:

Click [ ]

You can quickly open the *letters* folder by *double-clicking*. Here is how to do that:

Click (**letters**) **twice in quick succession**

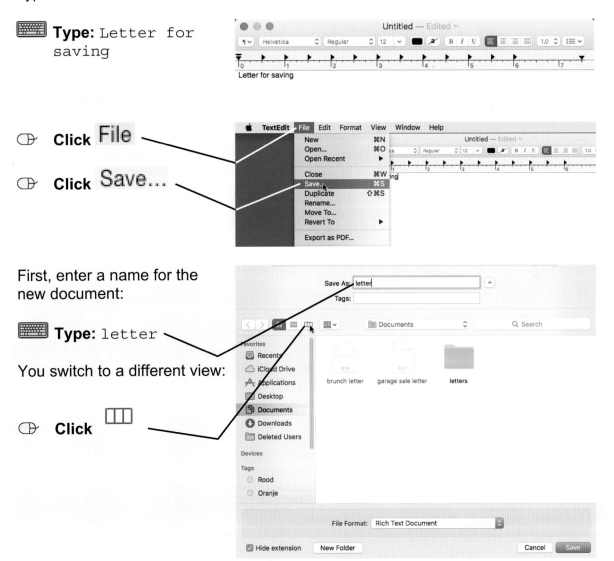

☞ **Click** letters **twice in quick succession**

In the title bar you can see that the *letters* folder has been opened: ———

In the file list you will see the document you saved: ———

You can go back to the *Documents* folder:

⊕ **Click** 📑 **Documents**

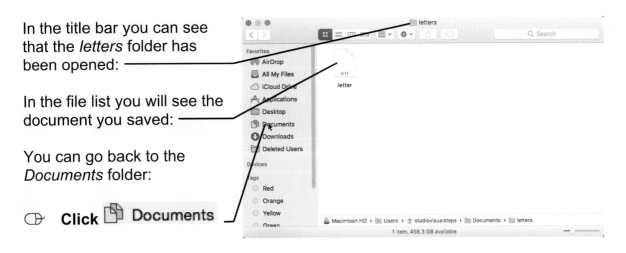

3.6 Copying a File

You can also copy files. For example, if you want to make a second copy of a letter, so that you can change a few things. As an exercise, you are going to copy the *brunch letter* file to the *letters* folder. Before you can copy the letter, you need to select it first:

⊕ **Click** brunch letter

The file icon will turn into

brunch letter. The blue color indicates that the file has been selected:

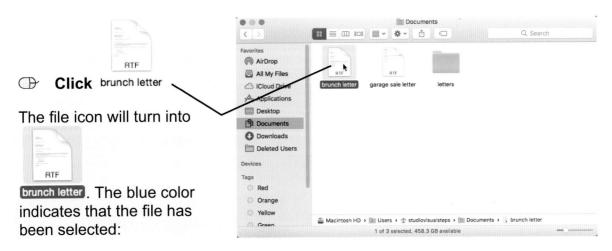

Now you can use the *Edit* option in the menu bar to copy the file:

⊕ **Click** Edit

⊕ **Click** Copy "brunch letter"

You will not see anything happen, but *MacOS* will know that you want to copy the file. Now you can paste the copied file into the *letters* folder:

First, open the *letters* folder:

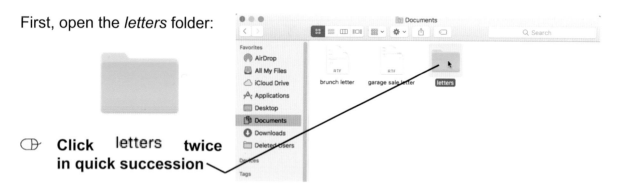

👆 **Click** letters **twice in quick succession**

 Please note:
From this point on in the book, the command 👆 **Click … twice in quick succession** will be shortened to 👆 **Double-click…**

❌ HELP! The name is displayed in a light-blue frame.

Do you see a light-blue frame around the name? Has the pointer turned into ⌶? For

example: letters   .

In that case you have clicked the name letters instead of the folder   .

👆 **Click a different area of the window further away from the icon**
☞ **Now try again to double-click the *letters* folder**

You will see the contents of the *letters* folder. Now you can paste the copied file into the folder:

👆 **Click** Edit

👆 **Click** Paste Item

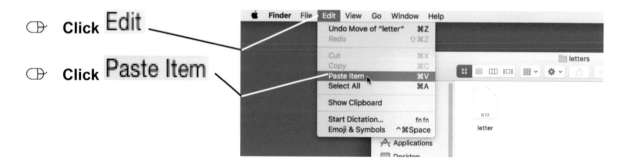

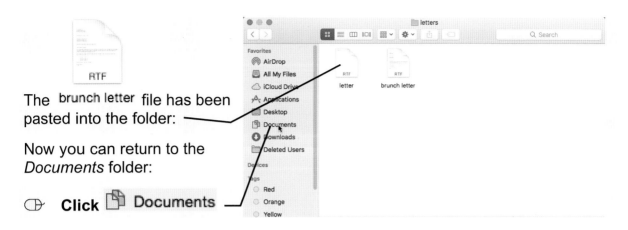

The `brunch letter` file has been pasted into the folder:

Now you can return to the *Documents* folder:

☞ **Click** 📑 **Documents**

3.7 Moving a File

In *Finder*, you can also move a file to a different folder. You can do this by dragging the file to another folder. Go ahead and try it:

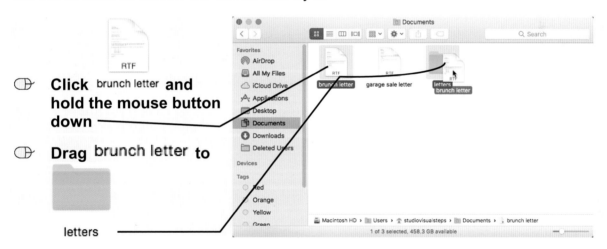

☞ **Click** `brunch letter` **and hold the mouse button down**

☞ **Drag** `brunch letter` **to**

letters

This is how you drag a file with a trackpad:

👉 **Position the pointer on** `brunch letter`

👉 **Press a fingertip on the trackpad and keep applying pressure**

👉 **Drag your fingertip across the trackpad, towards** `letters`

After a few seconds the *letters* folder will be opened:

In the folder, you will see the
file that you just moved:

⬭ **Release the mouse
    button/trackpad**

A small window appears. Previously, you had already copied the same file to the *letters* folder, but you cannot save two files with the exact same name in the same folder. In *MacOS* you can choose if you want to replace the first file by the file you are currently moving, or if you want to save both files in the same folder. You are going to save both files

⬭ **Click** [Keep Both]

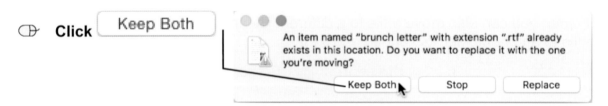

➥ **Please note:**

If the folder to which you are moving or copying a file does not already contain a file with the same name, you will not see this window. The file will simply be moved or copied to the folder right away.

You will see that the file you
moved has been called
brunch letter
      copy   :

Even if the content of both
files is exactly the same, they
still need to have different file
names. That is why the
system automatically adds
the word *copy* to the second
file.

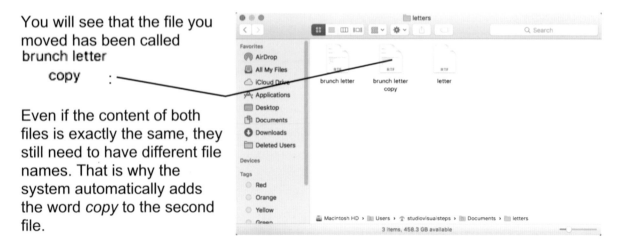

Now the files may be mixed up and not neatly ordered. That is why you need to order the files by their names:

☞ **Order the files by their names** ✂️³⁷

3.8 Selecting Multiple Files

You can also select multiple files at once and copy or move them. First, you need to select the files. Just try it:

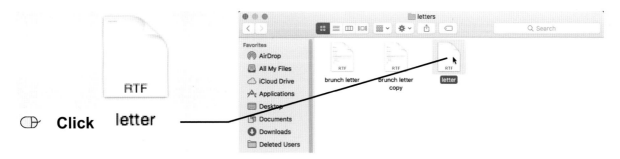

☞ **Click**   letter

Now the *letter* file has been selected.

☞ **Click** brunch letter copy

You will see that currently, the file called *brunch letter copy* has been selected, and the *letter* file is no longer selected. This is because you can only select a single file by clicking it. You can select more than one file by using the Command key:

The Command key always has the ⌘ sign on it:

You will find the Command key to the left and to the right of the space bar:

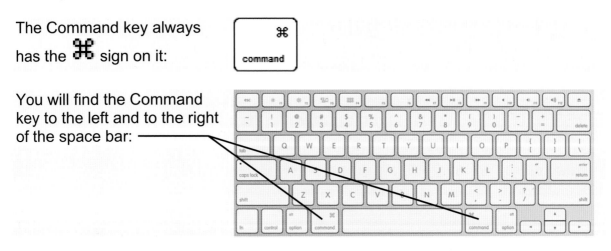

You use the Command key together with the mouse or the trackpad. The file called *brunch letter copy* is still selected:

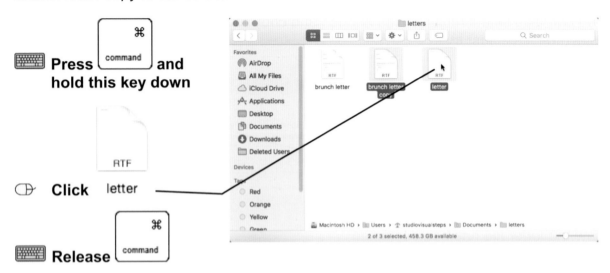

Press [⌘ command] **and hold this key down**

Click letter

Release [⌘ command]

Now both files have been selected. This is how you move the selected files to the *Documents* folder:

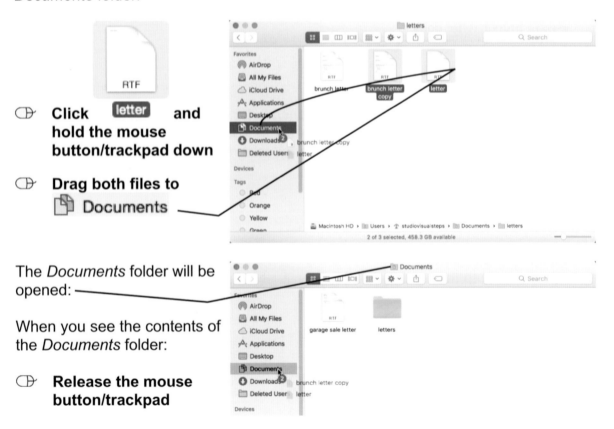

Click letter **and hold the mouse button/trackpad down**

Drag both files to 📄 **Documents**

The *Documents* folder will be opened:

When you see the contents of the *Documents* folder:

Release the mouse button/trackpad

Now both files have been moved to the *Documents* folder. You can undo this action:

☞ **Click** Edit

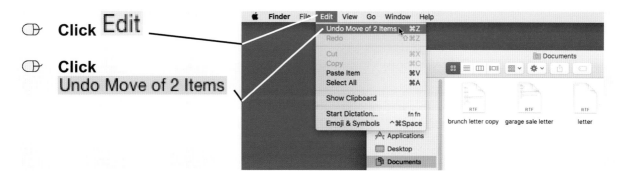

☞ **Click**
   Undo Move of 2 Items

The documents called *letter* and *brunch letter copy*, which you just moved, will now be removed from the *Documents* folder and will be stored in the *letters* folder once again.

☞ **Open the *letters* folder** 🦶²⁵

3.9 Changing the File Name

At some point, you may want to change the name of a file. For instance, when you have written several documents about the same topic and you want to be able to tell them apart. You can practice this now by renaming the *brunch letter copy* file:

☞ **Click the name**
   brunch letter copy

Now the name
brunch letter copy is dark blue:

☞ **Click**
   brunch letter copy
   once more

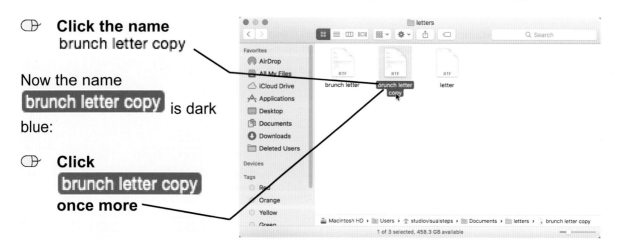

The file name has been selected: brunch letter copy.

HELP! I see a different window.

Do you see the *TextEdit* window now? Then you have double-clicked the file and have inadvertently opened the program. This is easy to remedy, just:

☞ **Close the** *TextEdit* **window** &096;12

☞ **Quit** *TextEdit* &096;24

☞ **Try again**

⌨ **Type the new name:**
  copy can be
  deleted

⌨ **Press**
  (enter/return)

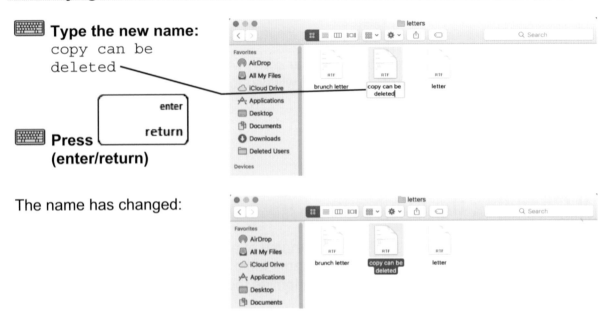

The name has changed:

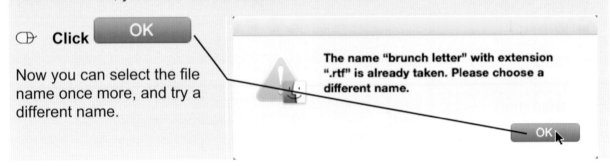

 HELP! Name already in use.

A folder cannot contain files with exactly the same name. If you try to use an existing name for a file, you will see this window:

🖱 **Click** OK

Now you can select the file name once more, and try a different name.

The name "brunch letter" with extension ".rtf" is already taken. Please choose a different name.

OK

 Tip
Folder
You can rename a folder in the same way you rename a file.

3.10 Deleting a File

It is a good idea to delete files you no longer use. This way, you will keep your folders orderly and well-arranged. In *MacOS* you use the *Trash* to delete files. You are going to move the file you just renamed to the *Trash*:

The file called *copy can be deleted* is still selected:

 Click File

 Click Move to Trash

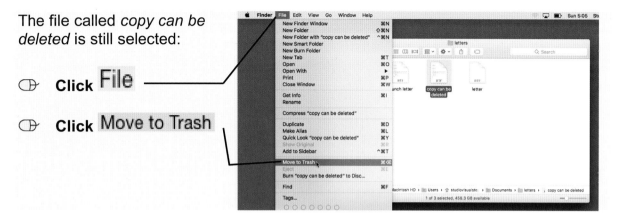

Now you will hear the sound of a wad of paper being tossed into the waste-paper basket. The *copy can be deleted* file has been removed from the *letters* folder. But the files you have moved to the *Trash* have not yet completely disappeared. Once you empty the *Trash,* the file will be permanently deleted. As long as a file is stored in the *Trash*, you can still retrieve it, if you want.

➡ Please note:

Be careful in deleting files. **Only delete the files you have created yourself.** If you did not create a file yourself, you may not be able to delete it because it is locked and you do not have permission to modify it.

💡 Tip

Move multiple files to the Trash at once

You can also move multiple files to the *Trash*, all at once. First, you need to select these files by clicking them, while you hold the Command key [⌘ command] down. Afterwards, you can move them to the *Trash*.

💡 Tip

Delete an entire folder

You can also delete an entire folder . You select a folder by clicking it. After that, you can move the folder to the *Trash*.

Tip

Drag
Another method is to drag the desired files and folders from *Finder* to the *Trash* in the *Dock*.

3.11 The Trash

Now you are going to take a look at the contents of the *Trash*. You can open the *Trash* by using the *Dock*:

☞ **Click**

You will see the *Trash* window, containing the deleted file called *copy can be deleted*. Now you can empty the *Trash*:

☞ **Click** Empty

Just to be sure, you will be asked to confirm this operation:

☞ **Click**
  Empty Trash

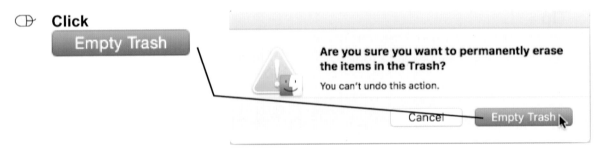

Now the file has been permanently deleted. You cannot retrieve it anymore.

☞ **If necessary, close the *Trash* window** ℭℭ**12**

Tip

Recover file from Trash
Have you accidentally moved the wrong file to the *Trash*? Or have you changed your mind and do you want to retrieve the file you deleted? Then you need to do this:

👆 **Click the file you want to recover**

👆 **Click**

👆 **Click** Put Back

If you select multiple files at once, you can recover all these files in the same way as described above.

 Tip

Does the Trash contain any items?
You can tell if there is anything in the *Trash,* by looking at the *Dock*. The icon in the *Dock* will change:

full   empty

 Tip

When do you need to empty the Trash?
You do not always need to empty the *Trash*, whenever you delete a file. If you empty the *Trash* every once in a while, this will be sufficient.

3.12 Copying to a USB Stick

If you want to copy a file to another computer, or make a safety copy (backup copy) and save it on a different medium, you can copy the file to a USB stick. A USB stick is also called a USB memory stick or memory stick. In the following steps you will be saving a copy of the *brunch letter* file to a USB stick.

Please note:

To work through this exercise, you will need to have a
USB stick. A USB stick is a small device that can be
connected to your computer's USB port. You can also
use an external hard drive. This is an external storage
device that is connected to your computer through a
USB cable. A USB stick or an external hard drive is a
medium for storing information, just like on your
computer's hard drive. Only, it is much easier to transfer
data to other computers by using a mobile storage
device.

If you do not own a USB stick or an external hard drive,
you can just read through this section. In this example
we will save the file on a USB stick. The same method
can be used to save a file to an external hard drive.

First, you need to insert your USB stick into the USB port on your computer.

The iMac has four USB ports
on the back of the monitor:

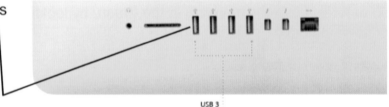

Source: iMac Quick Start Guide

The Mac mini and Mac Pro
have four USB ports on the
back of the case:

Source: Mac mini Quick Start Guide

The MacBook Air has a USB
port on both sides of the
notebook case:

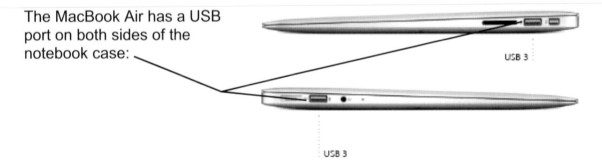

The MacBook and MacBook
Pro has two USB ports:

USB 3

USB 3

☞ **Insert the USB stick carefully into a USB port**

It does not seem to go in?

☞ **Turn over the USB stick (half-turn) and try again**

As soon as the USB stick is recognized, it will appear in the *Finder's Navigation
pane*, under Devices:

In this example, the USB stick
is called ▢ USB STICK :

Your own USB stick will
probably have a different
name.

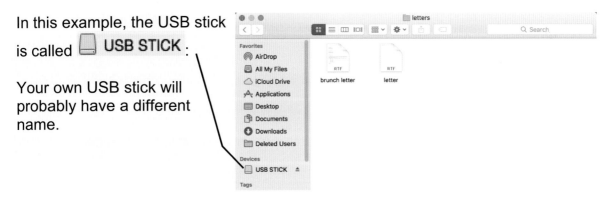

You can copy a file to the USB stick by dragging it to the stick. The *letters* folder is
still open:

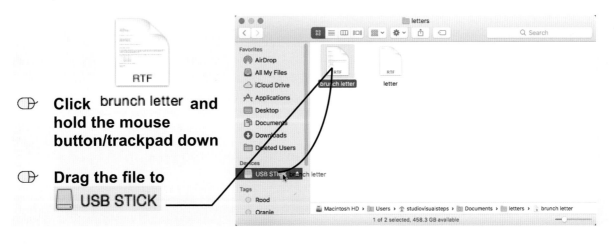

👆 **Click** brunch letter **and
hold the mouse
button/trackpad down**

👆 **Drag the file to
▢ USB STICK**

The USB stick will be opened:

In this example, the USB stick does not yet contain any files:

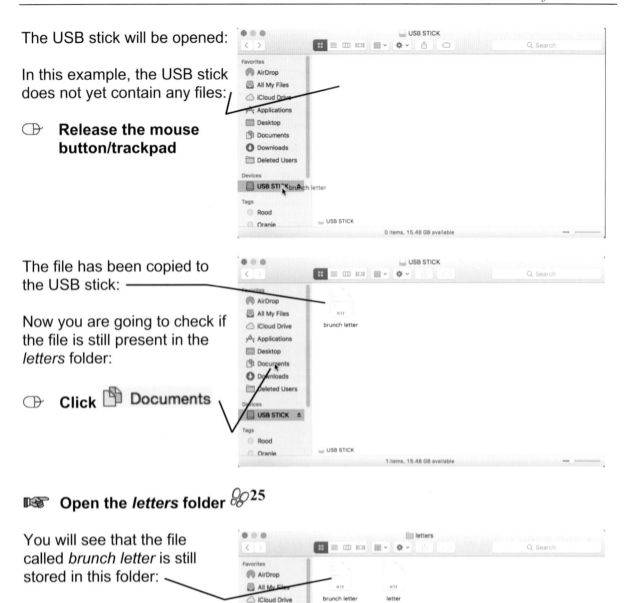

☞ **Release the mouse button/trackpad**

The file has been copied to the USB stick:

Now you are going to check if the file is still present in the *letters* folder:

☞ **Click**  **Documents**

☞ **Open the *letters* folder** ∂∂25

You will see that the file called *brunch letter* is still stored in this folder:

This means the file has been copied to the USB stick, not moved.

➥ **Please note:**

If you drag a file (or folder) to another folder on the same hard drive (on your own computer), the file (or folder) will be **moved** to this folder.

If you drag a file (or folder) to a folder on a different hard drive or USB stick, the file (or folder) will be **copied** to the folder on the other hard drive or USB stick.

3.13 Safely Disconnect the USB Stick

Whenever you want to remove storage devices, such as USB sticks, you always need to check whether the computer has finished storing the information. This is how you can safely disconnect the USB stick:

☞ **By ▢ USB STICK ,**
click ⏏

The USB stick has disappeared from the *navigation pane*. It is now safe to remove it from the computer:

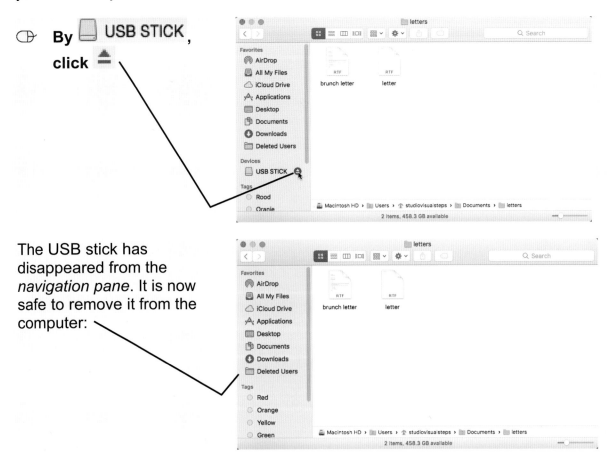

☞ **Remove the USB stick from the computer**

☞ **Close the *Finder* window** 𝄞**12**

You can also use *tabs* in *Finder*. Tabs allow you to quickly switch between folders. You can read more about this in the *Tips* at the end of this chapter.

In this chapter you have learned how to work with files and folders in *Finder*. You have practiced moving, deleting, copying and renaming files as well as dragging files to a USB stick. In the following exercises you can repeat these actions.

3.14 Exercises

The following exercises will help you master what you have just learned. Have you forgotten how to do something? Use the number beside the footsteps ﴾1﴿ to look it up in the appendix *How Do I Do That Again?* at the end of the book.

Exercise: Copy a File

☞ Open *Finder*. ﴾26﴿

☞ Open the *Documents* folder. ﴾27﴿

☞ Open the *letters* folder. ﴾25﴿

☞ Copy the file called *brunch letter* to the *Documents* folder. ﴾28﴿

Exercise: Move a File to a New Folder

☞ If necessary, open the *Documents* folder. ﴾27﴿

☞ Create a new folder and call it *practice*. ﴾29﴿

☞ Move the *brunch letter* file to the *practice* folder. ﴾30﴿

Exercise: Rename a File

☞ If necessary, open the *practice* folder. ﴾25﴿

☞ Change the name of the *brunch letter* file and call it *practice letter*. ﴾31﴿

☞ Close *Finder*. ﴾12﴿

Exercise: The Trash

☞ Open *Finder*. ⅋⅋²⁶

☞ Open the *Documents* folder. ⅋⅋²⁷

☞ Open the *practice* folder. ⅋⅋²⁵

☞ Move the file called *practice letter* to the *Trash*. ⅋⅋³²

☞ Move the *practice* folder to the *Trash*. ⅋⅋³²

☞ Open the *Trash*. ⅋⅋³³

☞ Empty the *Trash*. ⅋⅋³⁴

☞ If necessary, close the *Trash* window. ⅋⅋¹²

☞ Close *Finder*. ⅋⅋¹²

Exercise: Copy a File to a USB Stick

☞ Open *Finder*. ⅋⅋²⁶

☞ Open the *Documents* folder. ⅋⅋²⁷

☞ Open the *letters* folder. ⅋⅋²⁵

☞ Insert the USB stick into the computer.

☞ Copy the *letter* file to the USB stick by dragging it. ⅋⅋³⁵

☞ Safely disconnect the USB stick. ⅋⅋³⁶

☞ Remove the USB stick from the computer.

☞ If necessary, close *Finder*. ⅋⅋¹²

3.15 Background Information

Dictionary

All my files	An option in the *Finder* navigation pane, which provides a clear overview of all your files. Only the files you open in a regular way will be displayed, such as documents, pictures and videos. System files will remain hidden.
Contextual menu	A menu that is displayed when you right-click an item in *MacOS*. You will see different menu options, depending on the item you have right-clicked.
Double-click	Press the mouse twice, in rapid succession (on a Magic Mouse), press the left mouse button (on a regular mouse), or press the (Magic) trackpad. If you double-click a folder's icon in *Finder*, you will open the folder.
File	The collective name for all the data stored on your computer. A file can be a program, a data file containing several names, a text file written by you, or a photo. A file consists of a name and a file extension. An extension is a series of characters that come after the dot at the end of a file name, for instance: photo.jpg.
File list	The contents of an open folder are displayed in a file list.
Finder	Component of *MacOS*. *Finder* provides an orderly view of the files and folders stored on your computer and stored on drives and devices connected to your computer. Also, you can use *Finder* to search for/manage information on drives and devices.
Folder	You can use a folder to arrange your files. On your computer, each file is stored in a folder. A folder can also contain other folders (subfolders).
Hard drive	A storage medium where you can store your programs and files.
Navigation pane	This pane displays the list of folders that can be opened in the folder pane.

- Continue on the next page -

Path bar	The path bar is displayed beneath the *file list*. In the path bar you can see which folder has been opened in the folder pane, and the exact location of this folder on the computer.
PDF file	PDF stands for *Portable Document Format*. This file format is often used for information you can download, such as product manuals and brochures.
Right-click	Another name for a *secondary click*.
Secondary clicking	Also called *right-clicking*. This is a method of clicking which opens a contextual menu. Remember that for some mouse types, such as the Magic Mouse, the secondary clicking option still needs to be activated in *MacOS*, in the *System Preferences*.
Select	A mouse action with which you can mark part of a document.
Spotlight	A search technology that is built-in in the Macintosh computers. *Spotlight* builds a database with information on all the files stored on the computer. When you type a keyword in the *Spotlight* search box, the database will be searched for files that match this keyword. A list with the search results will be displayed.
Status bar	In the status bar you can view the number of files stored in a specific folder, the amount of remaining free disk space and the number of files that have been selected. The status bar will be displayed below the path bar.
Subfolder	A folder that is stored within another folder.
Trash	When you delete a file or a folder, it will be moved to the *Trash*. As long a file resides in the *Trash*, you can still recover it. But when you empty the *Trash*, the contents will be lost once and for all.
USB port	A narrow, rectangular connector on a computer, to which you can connect a USB (Universal Serial Bus) device, such as a USB stick.
USB stick	A small device on which you can store data. A USB stick is connected to the USB port on your computer. *Finder* will display the USB stick in the navigation pane, under the *Devices* header.

Source: Apple Dictionary, www.apple.com

Store on your computer

A computer contains a certain amount of *working memory*. Your work is temporarily saved in this working memory. When you turn your computer off, the contents of this working memory will be erased. That is why you need to save your work regularly.

There are several kinds of storage media: for example, the computer's hard drive or an external hard drive, but USB sticks and writable CD and DVD disks are also called storage media.

Hard drive   USB memory   External hard drive   Writable   Blu-Ray   SD-Card
                          stick   CD/DVD   disk

Hard drive

When you are using your computer, you will mostly save your work on the computer's hard drive. This is a tightly sealed, built-in box in your computer.

Hard drive   Mac Mini computer case

Within this box, a small disk is revolving. This is a magnetic disk, which enables it to record information.

You can decide what to store on your hard drive. For instance, you can save text, photos, or computer programs on this drive.

Each item that is stored on a hard drive is called a *file*. This may be a text, but it can also be a program or a digital photo.

As you have learned in this chapter, you can copy, move, rename and delete files on this hard drive.

3.16 Tips

 Tip

Cover Flow
Apart from the icons, the list and the panes, *Finder* contains another special feature for viewing the contents of the computer. This graphical user interface is called the *Cover Flow*. With *Cover Flow* you can flip through your files and folders in 3D (three-dimensional view). This is how you can change the view of the *Finder* to *Cover Flow*:

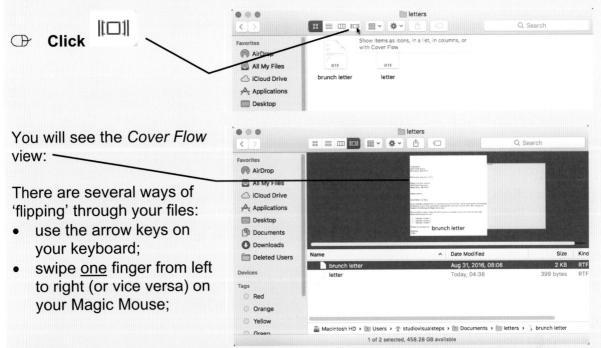

Click

You will see the *Cover Flow* view:

There are several ways of 'flipping' through your files:
- use the arrow keys on your keyboard;
- swipe <u>one</u> finger from left to right (or vice versa) on your Magic Mouse;

- swipe <u>two</u> fingers from left to right (or vice versa) across your trackpad.

Please note: if you use the touch operations on the Magic Mouse or the trackpad, the pointer needs to be positioned on the *Cover Flow* and not on the file list.

 Tip

Quick copy with the contextual menu
Instead of using the menu bar, you can also use the *contextual menu* to copy files and folders. The menu will appear when you click an item while holding the Control

key [control] down. This menu contains the same list of options that can be found on the menu bar.

- Continue on the next page -

This is how you copy a file using the contextual menu:

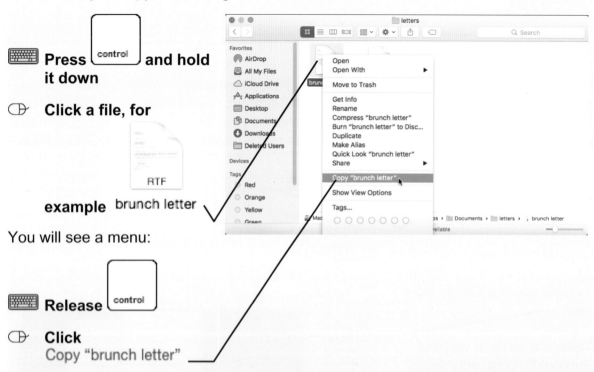

Press control **and hold it down**

Click a file, for example brunch letter

You will see a menu:

Release control

Click Copy "brunch letter"

Now the letter has been copied. You can also paste a file using the contextual menu:

👉 **Open the *Documents* folder** ⌘27

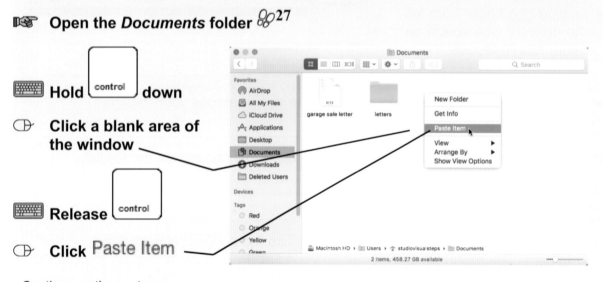

Hold control **down**

Click a blank area of the window

Release control

Click Paste Item

- Continue on the next page -

Now the letter has been copied:

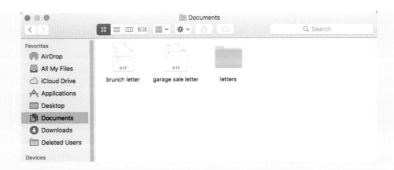

You can also use the contextual menus by *secondary* clicking. This is also called *right-clicking*. For some mouse types, such as the Magic Mouse, the setting in *MacOS* needs to be adjusted. In the tip below you can read how to do this.

 Tip

Secondary clicking

You can use the contextual menus by right-clicking (secondary clicking) with your mouse or trackpad. In order to do this, you may need to modify a setting in *MacOS*. In the *Dock* you will find the *System Preferences* icon:

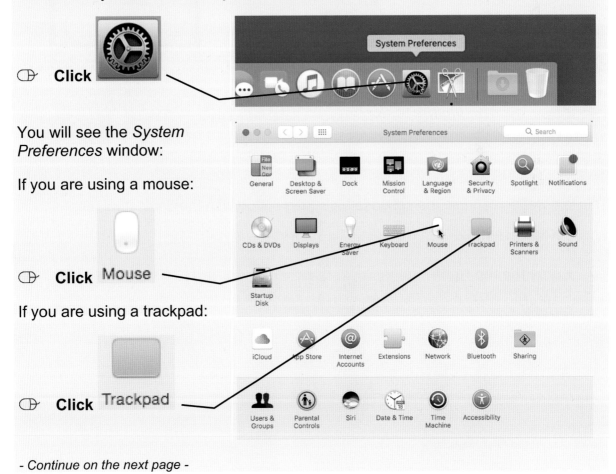

You will see the *System Preferences* window:

If you are using a mouse:

☞ **Click** Mouse

If you are using a trackpad:

☞ **Click** Trackpad

- Continue on the next page -

This is how you change the
mouse settings:

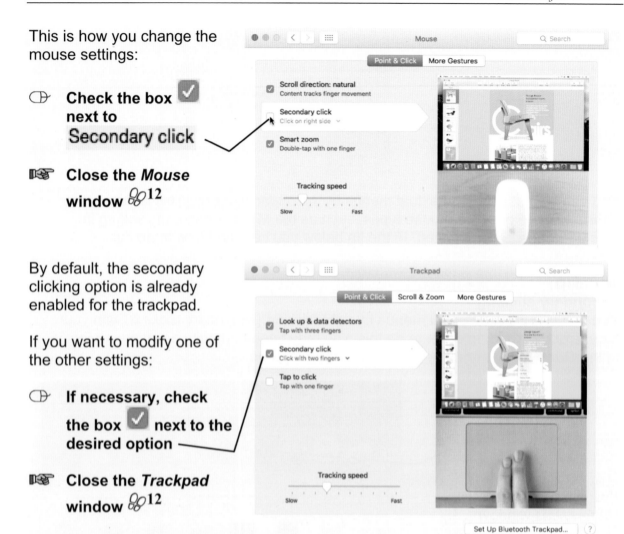

⊕ **Check the box** ✅
    next to
    Secondary click

☞ **Close the** *Mouse*
    window ⌘12

By default, the secondary
clicking option is already
enabled for the trackpad.

If you want to modify one of
the other settings:

⊕ **If necessary, check**
    the box ✅ **next to the**
    desired option

☞ **Close the** *Trackpad*
    window ⌘12

This is how you can use the secondary clicking option with the contextual menus:

With the Magic Mouse:

⊕ **Press the top right-**
    hand corner of the
    mouse

- Continue on the next page -

With a regular mouse:

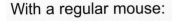 **Press the right mouse button**

With the (Magic) trackpad:

 Simultaneously press two fingers on the trackpad

It does not matter on which part of the trackpad you press.

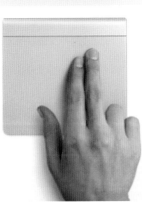

💡 Tip

Opening a folder through the menu bar

In this chapter you have seen how to open a folder via the window of *Finder*. You can also use the menu bar. Here is how you do that:

On the menu bar:

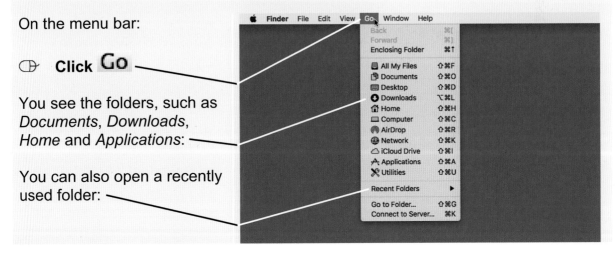

⊕ **Click Go**

You see the folders, such as *Documents*, *Downloads*, *Home* and *Applications*:

You can also open a recently used folder:

🔆 Tip

Search box in Finder

With the *Finder* search box you can quickly find a document or any other type of file:

👆 **Click** 📄 **All My Files**

👆 **Click the search box**

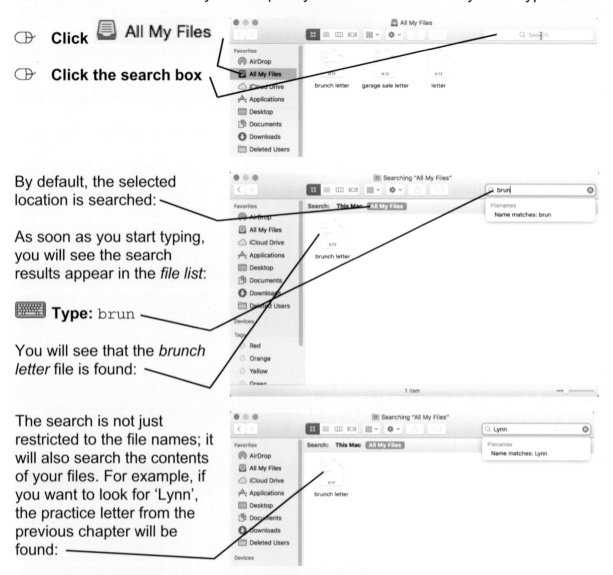

By default, the selected location is searched:

As soon as you start typing, you will see the search results appear in the *file list*:

⌨️ **Type:** brun

You will see that the *brunch letter* file is found:

The search is not just restricted to the file names; it will also search the contents of your files. For example, if you want to look for 'Lynn', the practice letter from the previous chapter will be found:

You do not need to know the exact file name to be able to retrieve a document. *Finder* uses the *Spotlight* search technology of *MacOS*. In the next tip you can read how to use *Spotlight* directly.

Tip

Search with Spotlight

Spotlight is the powerful search function in *MacOS*. You do not need to open *Finder* to use *Spotlight*. You can start a *Spotlight* search right from your desktop:

In the top right corner of the screen:

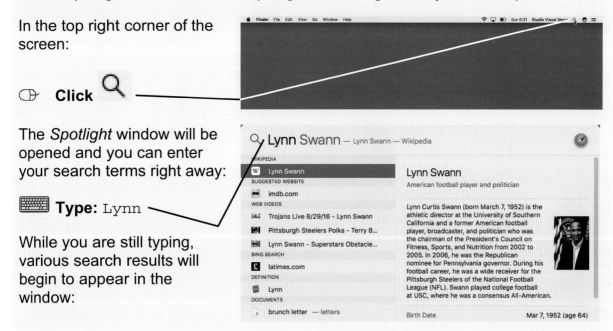

☞ **Click** 🔍

The *Spotlight* window will be opened and you can enter your search terms right away:

⌨ **Type:** Lynn

While you are still typing, various search results will begin to appear in the window:

Spotlight does not only search the files and folders on your Mac, it also searches the internet.

In *Spotlight* you can easily view a preview of a file:

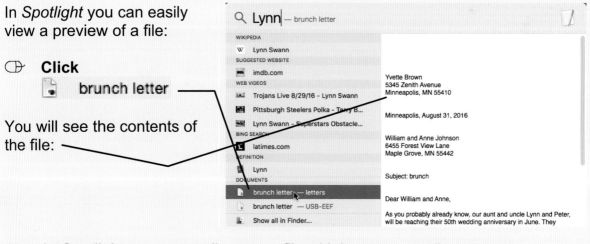

☞ **Click**
 brunch letter

You will see the contents of the file:

Also, in *Spotlight* you can easily open a file with its corresponding program:

☞ **Double-click**  brunch letter

The letter will be opened in *TextEdit*.

Tip

Quickly create a new folder with the files just selected
With the *New Folder with Selection* option in *MacOS*, you can quickly create a new folder containing a number of selected files.

☞ **Select a couple of files** ✂38

In this example we have selected two files:

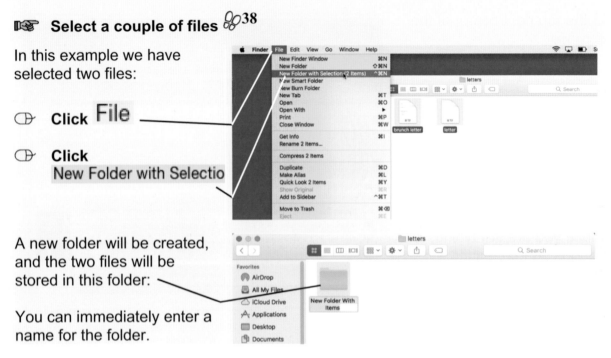

☞ **Click** File

☞ **Click**
New Folder with Selectio

A new folder will be created, and the two files will be stored in this folder:

You can immediately enter a name for the folder.

 Tip

Sort files in Finder
If you have a great deal of files stored in the same folder, it may get a little confusing and it becomes harder to find a particular file. The useful sorting option in *Finder* will help you get a better view. You can sort your files in different ways. For instance, alphabetically, by file name, creation date, size, or corresponding software program. This is how to view the various sorting options in *MacOS*:

☞ **Click**

You will see a menu with all the sorting options:

To select a sorting method, click the desired method.

You can set a different sorting method for each individual folder.

Tip

Using tags

If you have a lot of files on your Mac, you can organize them using *tags*. A tag is a colored label you add to a file that gives you more information about that file. For example, you can add tags like 'family', 'work', 'tennis' etc.

By default, *Finder* comes with a set of predefined colored tags:

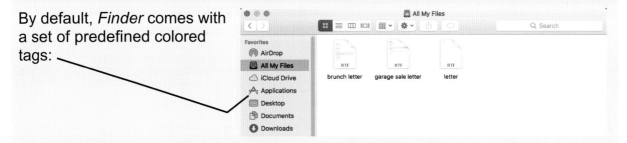

You can rename a tag like this using the contextual menu:

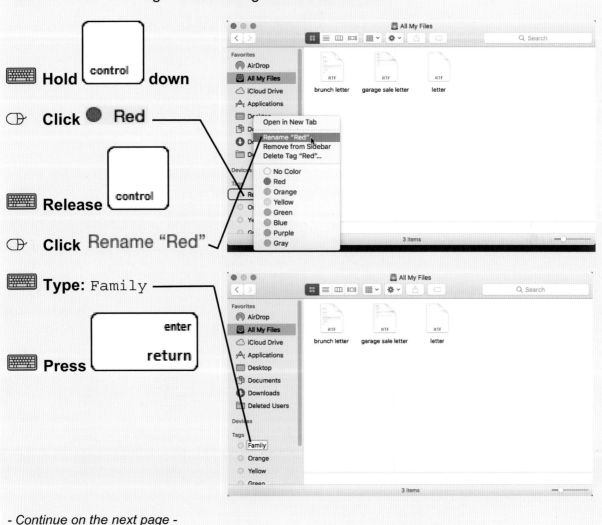

Hold `control` **down**

Click ● **Red**

Release `control`

Click Rename "Red"

Type: Family

Press `enter` `return`

- Continue on the next page -

You can add a tag to a file like this:

☞ **Click a file**

☞ **Click** ⚙ ⌄

☞ **Click the tag, for example** ⬤

When you position the mouse pointer on the tag, you see **Add Tag "Family"** .

A red dot has been added to the file name:

⬤ **brunch letter**

You can also add tags when you save a file in *TextEdit*:

☞ **Click the box by Tags:**

☞ **Click the desired tag, for example** ⬤ **Family**

☞ **Click** **Save**

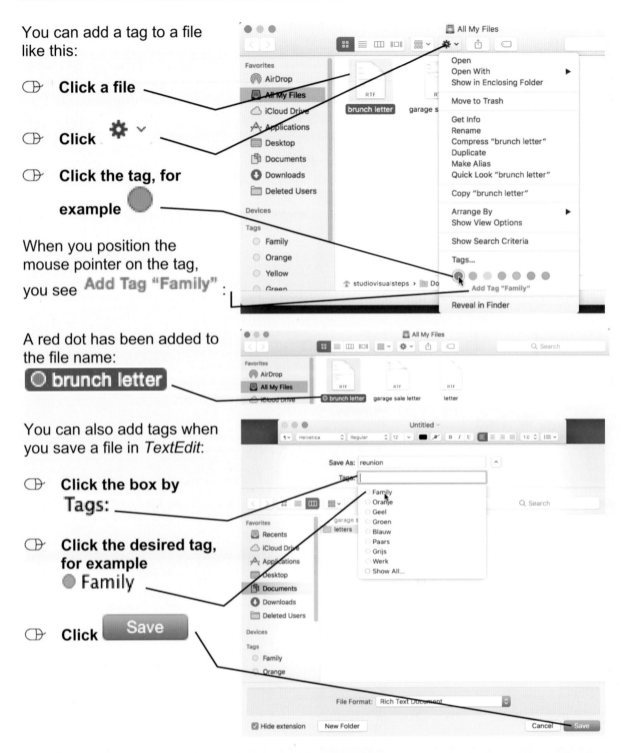

If necessary, you can use the methods described above to add multiple tags to a file. For example, a letter about a family tennis tournament at your tennis club, can get both the 'tennis' and 'family' tags.

- Continue on the next page -

You can use the tags to
quickly filter a group of files:

⊕ **Click** ● **Family**

You see all files you have
given this tag: ⟶

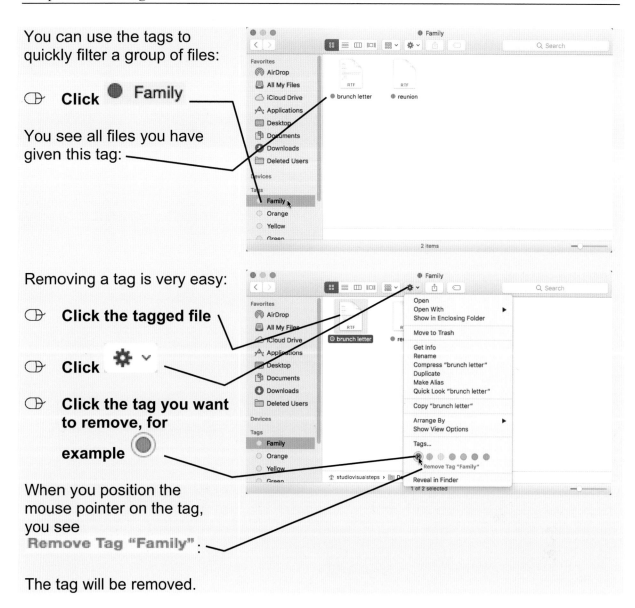

Removing a tag is very easy:

⊕ **Click the tagged file**

⊕ **Click** ⚙ ⌄

⊕ **Click the tag you want
to remove, for**

example ◎

When you position the
mouse pointer on the tag,
you see
Remove Tag "Family":

The tag will be removed.

 Tip
Finder Tabs
Finder includes *tabs*. Tabs allow you to quickly switch between folders or tags in
Finder. You can display the tab bar like this:

⊕ **Click** View, Show Tab Bar

- Continue on the next page -

Here you see the tab bar:

There is only one tab. It has the same name as the folder you are viewing, in this example Documents :

You can add a new tab like this:

👆 **Click** ➕

The new tab has been added:

By default, the new tab will display All My Files . You can view a different folder on this tab:

👆 **Click** 📄 **Documents**

👉 **Open the *letters* folder** ✂️25

The second tab displays the contents of the *letters* folder:

You can go back to the other tab like this:

👆 **Click the Documents tab**

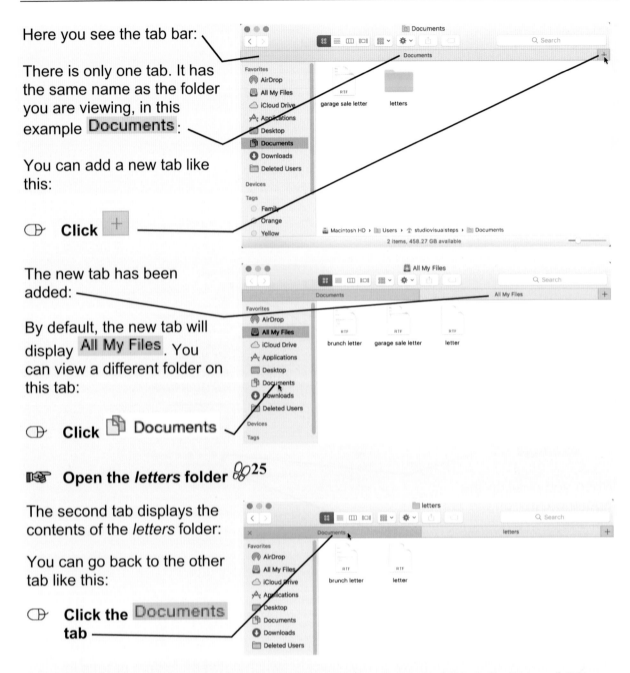

You can move items between tabs the same way you moved items between folders.

To close a tab:

👆 **Place the mouse pointer on the tab**

👆 **Click** ❌

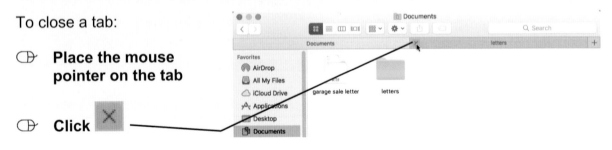

4. Surfing with Safari

The Internet is a worldwide network of computers that are connected to each other. There is a seemingly endless array of information or data available on this massive combination of millions of personal, business, and governmental computers. You can use your own computer to view information on the Internet. To do this, you need to use a program called an *Internet browser* or a *browser*. *Browsing* is much the same as browsing through a newspaper or a magazine, but instead of your hands, you use a mouse, touchpad or short-cut keys to flip through the pages of information. *Safari* is the name of the Internet browser used by *Apple*.

The information stored on the Internet can be viewed on websites. Usually, a website consists of multiple web pages. You can jump (or navigate) from one web page to the other or to another website, by clicking a link (also called hyperlink) on the page. This is called *surfing*.

In this chapter you will learn how to open a web page, and how to zoom in, zoom out and scroll. If you are using a (Magic) trackpad, you can use various touch gestures for these actions. We will also discuss how to open a link on a web page and how to save web pages on the *Favorites toolbar*. And finally you will learn how to set the homepage.

In this chapter you will learn how to:

- open *Safari*;
- open a web page;
- zoom in and zoom out;
- scroll;
- open a link on a web page;
- open a link in a new tab;
- switch between open tabs;
- close a tab;
- go to the previous or next page;
- add a bookmark or a folder to the favorites bar;
- use *Top Sites*;
- change the settings for the homepage;
- search;
- quit *Safari*.

4.1 Opening Safari

Here is how to open *Safari*, the program that lets you surf the Internet:

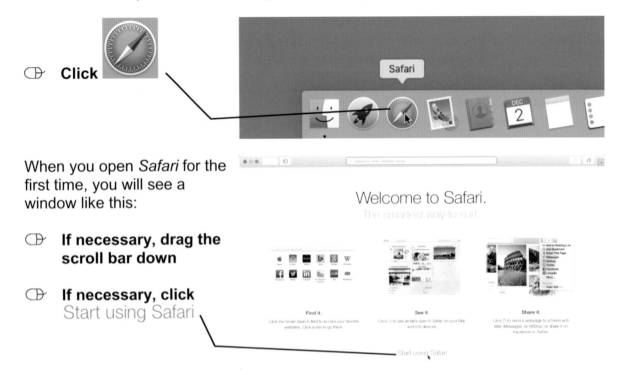

⟶ **Click**

When you open *Safari* for the
first time, you will see a
window like this:

⟶ **If necessary, drag the
scroll bar down**

⟶ **If necessary, click
Start using Safari**

Now you see *Favorites* window. This page contains icons that link to web pages you
want to visit more often. If you have not yet added any favorites yourself, you will see
the default favorites:

This page may look different
on your own screen, but this
will not affect the following
tasks you are going to do. A
little further on, you will learn
how to add favorites yourself.

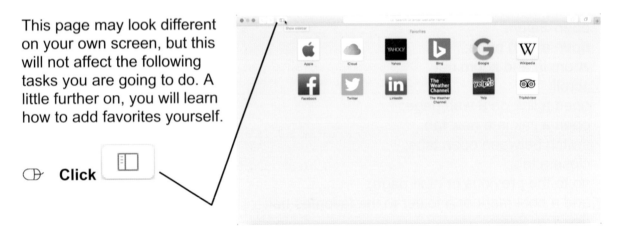

⟶ **Click**

Now you see *Favorites*, which displays thumbnails that link to the websites:

Here you see the address bar, which in *Safari* is also a search box. Here you can type a web address or keyword:

On the left you see the sidebar where you can access your bookmarks or reading list:

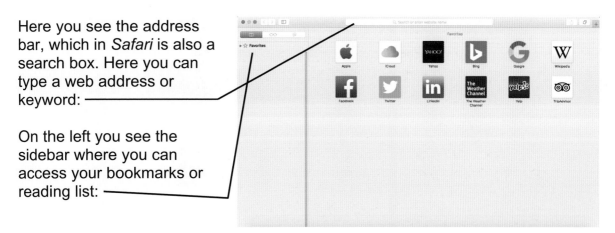

You can change the view of the *Safari* program by closing the sidebar and adding two extra toolbars:

☞ **Click**

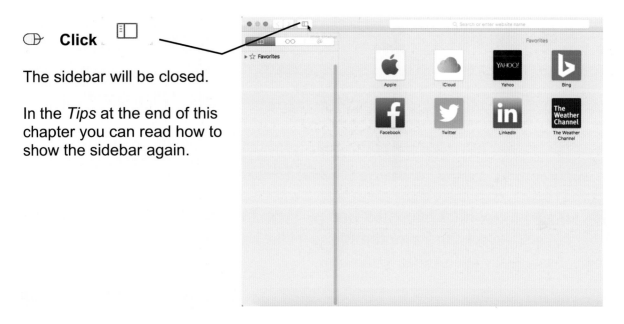

The sidebar will be closed.

In the *Tips* at the end of this chapter you can read how to show the sidebar again.

You also add the tab bar and the favorites bar:

☞ **Click** View

☞ **Click**
Show Favorites Bar

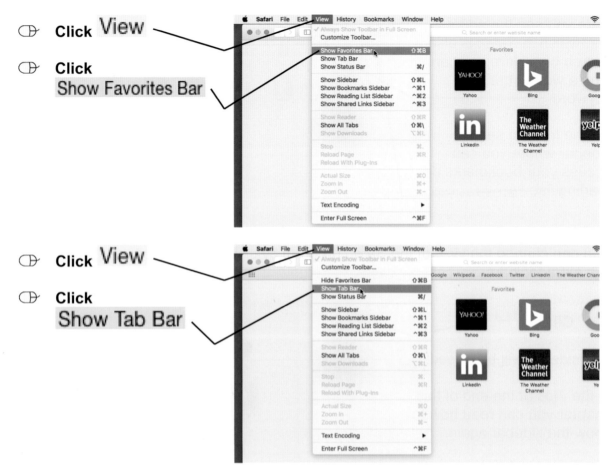

☞ **Click** View

☞ **Click**
Show Tab Bar

HELP! I see Hide Favorites Bar **or** Hide Tab Bar .

If you see the option Hide Favorites Bar or Hide Tab Bar in the menu, the toolbar has already been added to the view.

Here you will see the favorites bar containing links to favorite websites:

Below the favorites bar you will see the Favorites tab:

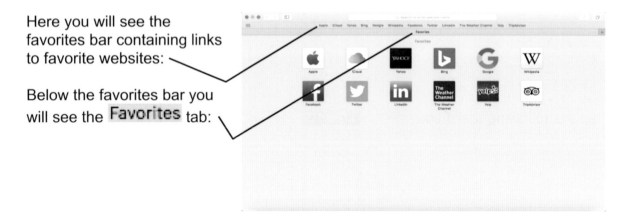

4.2 Opening a Web Page

You can open a web page by entering the web address in the address bar:

⊕ **Click the address bar**

Now you can type the web address:

⌨ **Type:**
www.visualsteps.
com

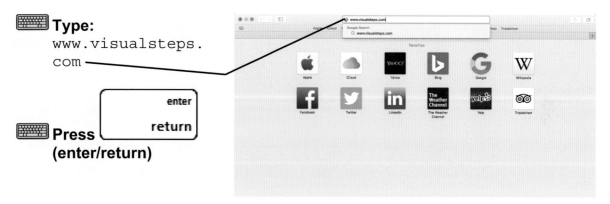

```
enter
return
```

⌨ **Press**
(enter/return)

🖐**Please note:**

If you copy a web address from a newspaper or a magazine, it is important to type the dots and slashes (/) in the right places. Otherwise, the web page will not be found by the browser.

Does the web address start with http://www...? Then you do not need to type the prefix http://.

Now you will see the Visual Steps website:

The page may look a bit different now, but this will not affect the following tasks you are going to do.

4.3 Zooming In

If you think the letters and images on a website are a bit small, you can zoom in and enlarge them. First, we will show you how to do this with the Magic Mouse and the (Magic) trackpad. For the Magic Mouse you may need to adjust a setting first:

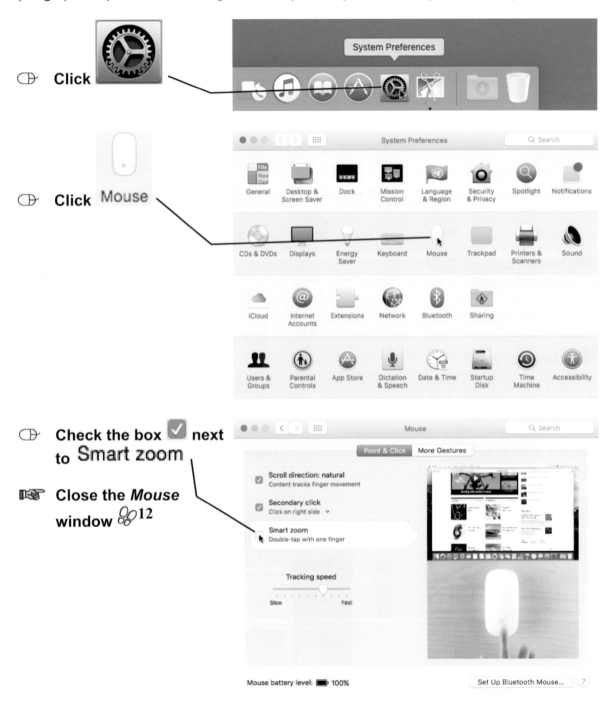

Click

Click Mouse

Check the box ☑ next to Smart zoom

Close the *Mouse* window ✂️ 12

Now you can quickly zoom in by tapping the Magic Mouse with one finger:

☞ **Position the pointer next to**
Now Available!

☞ **Tap the Magic Mouse twice, in rapid succession**

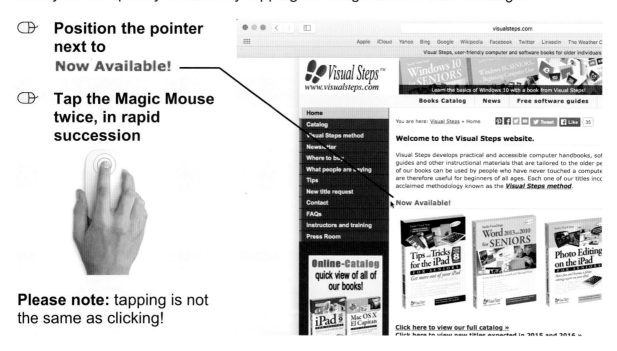

Please note: tapping is not the same as clicking!

If you are using a (Magic) trackpad, you can zoom in by tapping with two fingers:

☞ **Position the pointer next to**
Now Available!

☞ **Tap the (Magic) trackpad twice in rapid succession with two fingers**

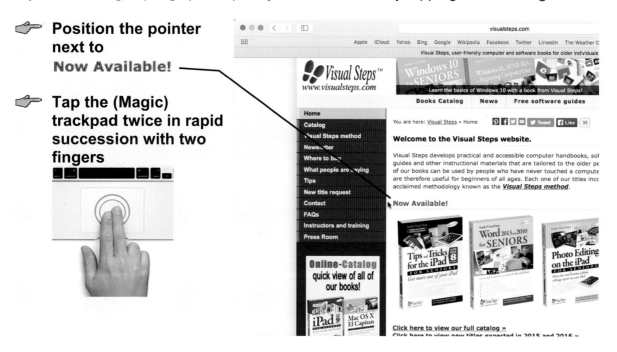

If you cannot zoom in while following these instructions, you can try another method for zooming in. In the *Tips* at the end of this chapter you can read more about this.

HELP! A different web page is opened.

If another web page is opened, you have been clicking instead of tapping.

In the top left of the window:

 **Click**

☞ **Try it again**

You will see that the web page is displayed in a much larger size:

If you do not use a Magic Mouse or a (Magic) trackpad, you can use the key combination Command and + to gradually zoom in:

⊕ **Position the pointer next to** Now Available!

⌨ **Simultaneously press** ⌘ command **and** + =

You will zoom in on the page, but not as closely as with the Magic Mouse or the (Magic) trackpad.

☞ **Zoom in on the dark blue menu on the left three more times** ℰ℘**39**

Now the letters and images have become much larger:

4.4 Scrolling

Scrolling is useful when you cannot see the entire web page at once on your screen. Most of the time you will want to move up and down through the page, but sometimes you may need to scroll from side to side. This is how you do it with a Magic Mouse:

☞ **Drag your finger upwards a bit, on the Magic Mouse**

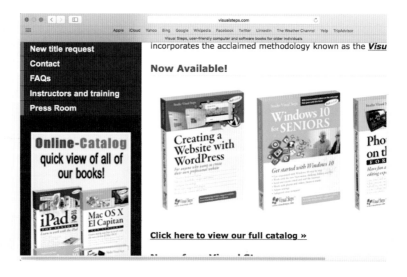

You will see that you are scrolling towards the bottom of the page:

This is how you scroll upwards:

☞ **Drag your finger downwards a bit, on the Magic Mouse**

If you are using a (Magic) trackpad you need to scroll with two fingers:

 Drag two fingers upwards a bit, on the trackpad

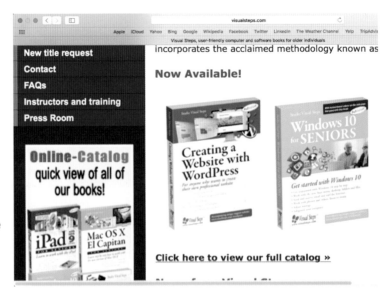

Now you will see that you are scrolling downwards on the page:

This is how you scroll in an upward direction:

 Drag two fingers downwards a bit, on the (Magic) trackpad

 Tip
Scrolling sideways
If the web page is wider than the *Safari* window, you can also scroll from side to side. You do this by moving your finger(s) from right to left or from left to right across the surface of your Magic Mouse or (Magic) trackpad.

If you are using a regular mouse with a scroll wheel, you can scroll downwards by spinning the scroll wheel. The scroll wheel is located between the left and right mouse buttons:

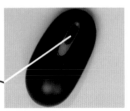

This is how you scroll downwards:

⊕ **Spin the wheel towards yourself**

Scrolling upwards is just the other way round:

☞ **Spin the wheel away from yourself**

You can also scroll by using the scroll bars to the right and at the bottom of the window. These scroll bars are only displayed when you start spinning the scroll wheel or start scrolling by dragging your fingers on the (Magic) Mouse or the (Magic) trackpad.

This is how you scroll sideways:

☞ **Position the pointer on the scroll bar** ——

☞ **Press the mouse button/trackpad and hold it pressed down**

☞ **Drag the scroll bar to the right**

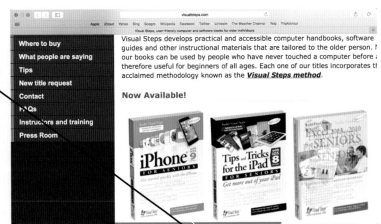

4.5 Zooming Out

If you want to view the web page from a distance again, you can zoom out. The letters and images will then become smaller. This is how you zoom out with the Magic Mouse:

☞ **Tap the Magic Mouse twice, in rapid succession**

Please note: tapping is not clicking!

This is how you zoom out with the (Magic) trackpad:

 Tap the (Magic) trackpad twice, with two fingers, in rapid succession

If you cannot zoom out by rapidly tapping twice, you can use a different method for zooming out with the trackpad. In the *Tips* at the end of this chapter you can read more about this.

If you do not use a Magic Mouse or a (Magic) trackpad, you can use the key combination Command and – to gradually zoom out:

Press $\mathcal{H}$ command **and** – **simultaneously**

☞ **Repeat the same action until the web page is displayed in the desired size**

Now you will see the Visual Steps website again in its original size.

After you have zoomed in, you can also quickly revert to the website's actual size. You can read how to do this in the *Tips* at the end of this chapter.

4.6 Opening a Link on a Web Page

You can jump from one web page to another by clicking a link (also called hyperlink) on the page. A link refers to a different web page. Just try it:

☞ **Position the pointer on Where to buy**

The pointer turns into a hand 🖑 and the menu item changes color:

By this you can tell that the pointer is pointing at a link.

☞ **Click Where to buy**

You will see the web page with information on where to find the Visual Steps books:

4.7 Working with Tabs

A link can also be opened in a new tab. You can do this by using the Command key:

Press ⌘ command and hold it down

Click **Visual Steps method**

Release ⌘ command

The link will be opened in a new tab. This is how you go to this tab:

Click the **The Visual Steps Method** tab

You will see the page with information about the Visual Steps Method. This is how you return to the first tab:

Click the **Where to find our product** tab

Now you will again see the first tab. You can close the second tab:

Position the pointer on the second tab

On the second tab, click ✕

Now there is just one open tab:

In *section 4.12 Top Sites* you can read how to open a tab without having to click a link.

4.8 Go to a Previous or Next Page

After you have opened a link, you can quickly return to the page you previously visited. Just try it:

Click

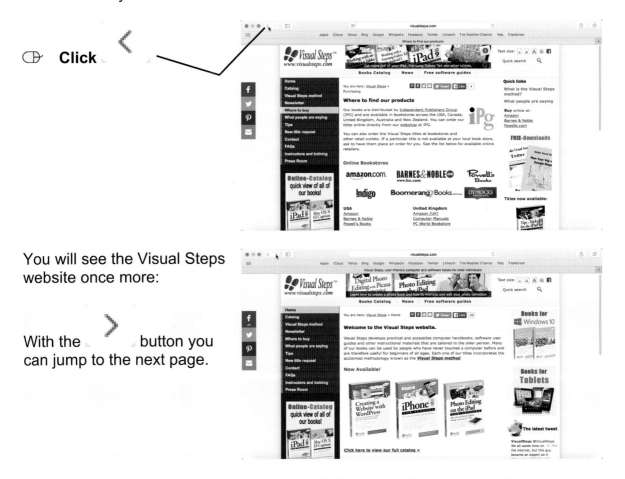

You will see the Visual Steps website once more:

With the   button you can jump to the next page.

In the *Tips* at the end of this chapter you will find an additional tip for flipping through the web pages you just visited.

4.9 The Favorites Bar

In *Safari* you can add a button to the favorites bar for the websites you regularly visit. In this way, you can quickly access these websites whenever you want. Just take a look at the buttons that are already in place on the favorites bar:

You will see buttons for websites like *Apple*, *iCloud*, *Google*, *Facebook*, *Twitter*, and *Wikipedia*:

These buttons are called bookmarks.

☞ **Click** Wikipedia ——

You will see the *Wikipedia* homepage:

Wikipedia is an online encyclopedia, maintained and edited by Internet users.

4.10 Adding a Bookmark to the Favorites Bar

You can also add a new button to the favorites bar yourself. You can practice doing this by adding a bookmark for the Visual Steps website:

☞ **Return to the Visual Steps website** ℬ℘**40**

🖱 **Click** ⬆

🖱 **Click**

📖 Add Bookmark

You will see a window where you can select the location for this bookmark:

By default, the
📖 Favorites has been
selected:

If the names of the bookmarks on the favorites bar are very long, you will not be able to fit a lot of bookmarks on the bar. The name of the website has already been selected, so you can type a new name right away:

⌨ **Type:** Visual Steps

🖱 **Click** Add

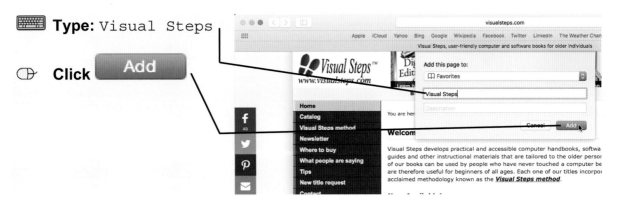

Now the Visual Steps
bookmark has been added to
the favorites bar:

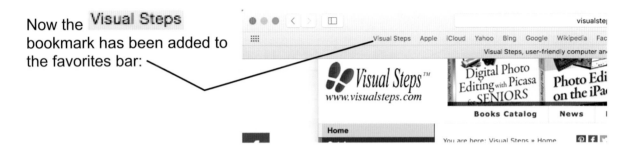

4.11 Adding a Folder to the Favorites Bar

You can also add an entire folder to the favorites bar. The bookmarks in this folder
will be displayed on the bar as a menu. This is how you create a new folder:

☞ **Click** Bookmarks

☞ **Click** Edit Bookmarks

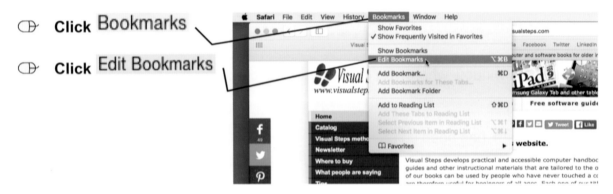

Now the bookmarks editor will be opened. This is a page in which you can edit, view
and arrange your bookmarks.

☞ **Double-click**
   ☐ Favorites

You will see an overview of
the bookmarks currently
placed on the favorites bar:

You can add a new folder:

☞ **Click** New Folder

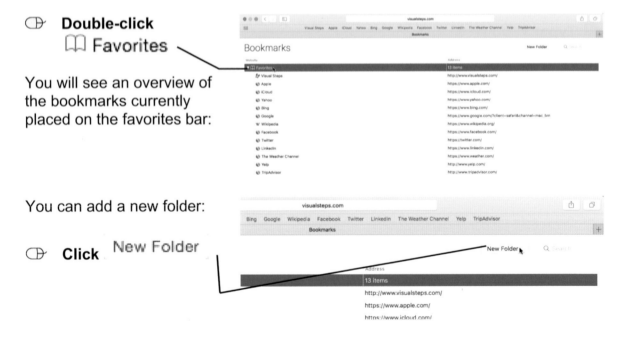

A new folder will be added. You can enter a name for the folder right away:

Type: `Example`

Press (enter/return)

The folder is ready for use. Now you are going to move the bookmark for the Visual Steps website to this folder:

☞ **Click 👣 Visual Steps and hold the mouse button/trackpad down**

☞ **Drag 👣 Visual Steps to ▢ Example**

☞ **Release the mouse button/trackpad**

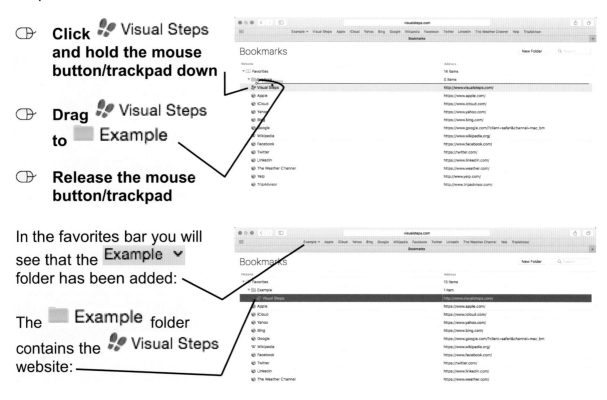

In the favorites bar you will see that the Example ⌄ folder has been added:

The ▢ Example folder contains the 👣 Visual Steps website:

Now you can close the bookmarks editor and return to the website:

☞ **Click Bookmarks**

☞ **Click Hide Bookmarks Editor**

You will see the Visual Steps homepage once again.

 Tip

Remove a bookmark or a folder from the favorites bar
You can quickly remove the buttons you do not use very often from the favorites bar:

☞ **Click**

☞ **If necessary, click**

☞ **Click the bookmark or folder you want to remove**

⌨ **Press** [←] **(Backspace)**

Now the bookmark or folder has been removed from the favorites bar.

If the bookmark you want to remove has been placed in a folder:

☞ **Double-click the folder**

☞ **Click the bookmark you want to remove**

⌨ **Press** [←] **(Backspace)**

4.12 Top Sites

Safari keeps track of your favorite websites, by monitoring your surfing behavior. These websites will be added to the *Top Sites* page. If you want to take a quick look at one of your favorite websites while reading something on another website, you can open *Top Sites* in a new tab. The default setting is to open *Favorites* when you add a new tab. You set up *Top Sites* like this:

☞ **Click Safari**

☞ **Click Preferences...**

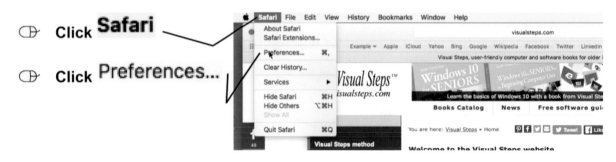

$\oplus$ **Click** [↕] **by**
New tabs open with:

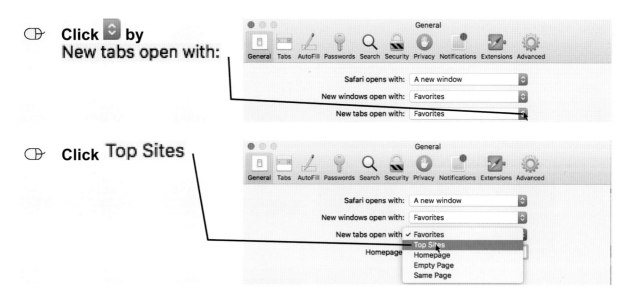

$\oplus$ **Click** Top Sites

☞ **Close the** *General* **window** ✂12

$\oplus$ **Click** [+]

Top Sites will be opened in a new tab: ———

The page on your screen will look different than the one shown here in the screenshot. Most likely you will see some of your own frequently visited websites.

If you have not done a lot of surfing yet, *Safari* will show default popular websites such as *Facebook*, *The Weather Channel* and *Tripadivor*. When you start surfing a bit more, these websites will be replaced by the other websites you visit.

This is how you open a website from the *Top Sites*:

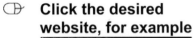 **Click the desired website, for example**

In this example you will see the www.yahoo.com website:

It has a search engine and links to many other topics. It is updated frequently. What you see on your screen will look different than what you see here in the example.

This will not affect the following actions.

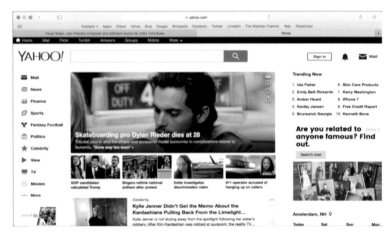

You can open *Top Sites* also like this:

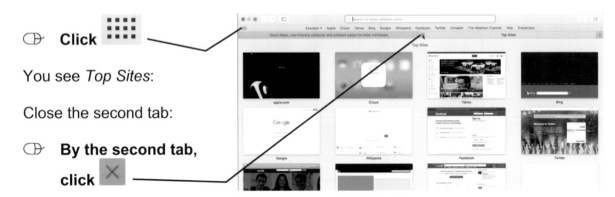

Click

You see *Top Sites*:

Close the second tab:

By the second tab, click

4.13 Set a Homepage

The homepage is the website you first see when you open *Safari*. By default, you will see *Favorites*. But you can also change the settings and set your own favorite website as your homepage.

Double-click the address bar

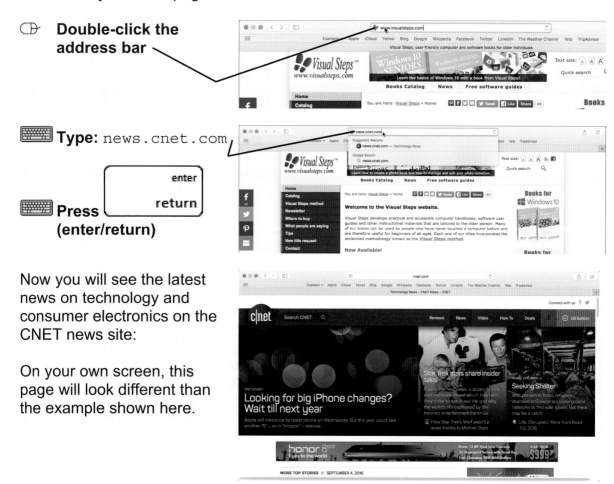

Type: news.cnet.com

Press (enter/return)
enter
return

Now you will see the latest news on technology and consumer electronics on the CNET news site:

On your own screen, this page will look different than the example shown here.

On the menu bar, you can set this website as a homepage:

Click Safari

Click Preferences...

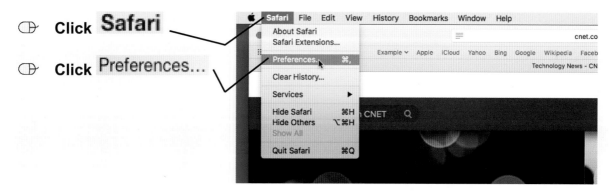

Here you can add a web
address for your homepage:

If you want to use the current
web page:

⊕ **Click**

 Set to Current Page

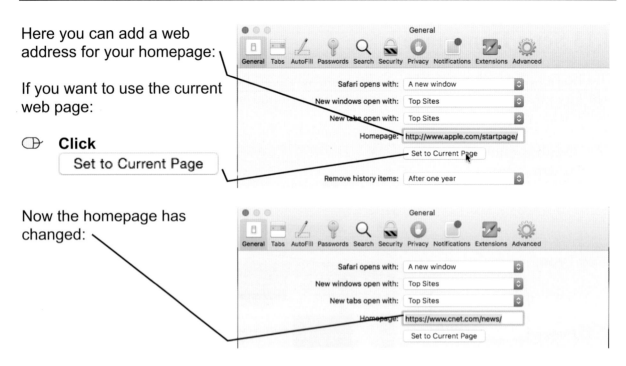

Now the homepage has
changed:

You need to change a setting to make sure that new windows will open with this
homepage instead of *Top Sites*:

⊕ **By**
New windows open with:,

click ⬍

⊕ **Click** Homepage

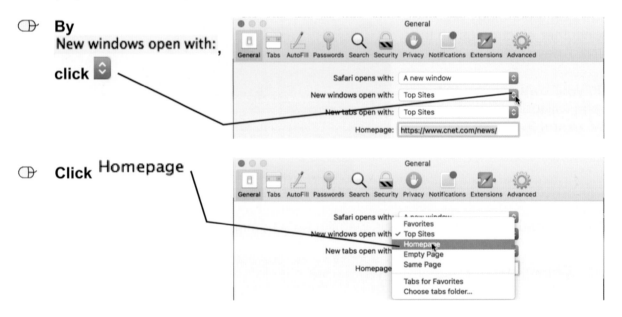

You can close this window:

☞ **Close the *General* window** ⅋¹²

Now you can check to see if *Safari* opens the correct homepage. Start by opening a different website:

☞ **Open the www.visualsteps.com website** ℮℮**41**

You will see the Visual Steps website again. Now you can close *Safari*:

☞ **Close the *Safari* window** ℮℮**12**

At present, *Safari* is still active. If you open the *Safari* window again from the *Dock*, the new homepage will be displayed. Check to verify that now:

⊕ **Click**

You will see the CNET website once again:

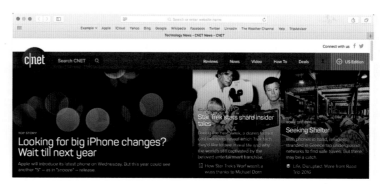

4.14 Searching

The *Safari* program contains a useful search box to help you quickly find information on all sorts of subjects. This is how you use it:

⊕ **Click the address bar**

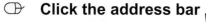

Now you can type a keyword:

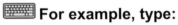 **For example, type:**
`magic mouse`

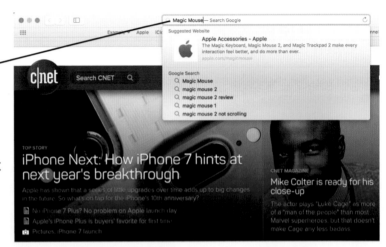

You will immediately see several suggestions for relevant keywords:

You can select a keyword by clicking it. For now, this is not necessary.

To use your own keyword:

 **Press** [enter / return]
(enter/return)

Here you see the search results:

To view a search result, just click the link. For now, this is not necessary.

4.15 Quitting Safari

In *MacOS Sierra*, to close an application completely, you need to explicitly tell it to quit. It is not enough to simply close a window. This may take some getting used to, if you are a previous *Windows* user. This is how you quit *Safari*:

☞ **Click** **Safari**

☞ **Click** Quit Safari

Now the *Safari* program is no longer running.

In this chapter you have learned how to use *Safari* to surf the Internet. You can use the following exercises to practice these skills once more.

4.16 Exercises

The following exercises will help you master what you have just learned. Have you forgotten how to do something? Use the number beside the footsteps $\mathscr{S}^1$ to look it up in the appendix *How Do I Do That Again?* at the end of the book.

Exercise: View a Web Page

In this exercise you will be viewing a web page in *Safari*.

☞   Open *Safari*. $\mathscr{S}^{42}$

☞   Open the website at www.nytimes.com $\mathscr{S}^{41}$

☞   Zoom in on the web page. $\mathscr{S}^{43}$

☞   Scroll downwards to the end of the web page. $\mathscr{S}^{44}$

☞   Scroll upwards to the beginning of the web page. $\mathscr{S}^{45}$

☞   Zoom out again. $\mathscr{S}^{46}$

Exercise: Links and Tabs

In this exercise you will practice the actions needed to work with links and tabs.

☞   If necessary, open the www.nytimes.com website. $\mathscr{S}^{41}$

☞   Open a link to an interesting news item. $\mathscr{S}^{47}$

☞   Return to the previous page. $\mathscr{S}^{40}$

☞   Open a link in a new tab. $\mathscr{S}^{48}$

☞   Display the new tab. $\mathscr{S}^{49}$

☞   Return to the first tab. $\mathscr{S}^{49}$

☞ Close the second tab. ⌘**50**

Exercise: Add a Bookmark

In this exercise you will be adding a bookmark to the favorites bar.

☞   Add the current www.nytimes.com web page to the favorites bar.
Shorten the name of the page to *ny.com* ⌘**51**

☞   Add a new folder called *Practice* to the favorites bar. ⌘**52**

☞   Move the bookmark for *ny.com* to the *Practice* folder. ⌘**53**

☞   Delete the *Practice* folder. ⌘**54**

☞   Close the bookmarks page. ⌘**55**

Exercise: Top Sites

In this exercise you will be taking another look at your *Top Sites*.

☞   Open *Top Sites*. ⌘**56**

☞   Open one of the websites. ⌘**57**

☞   Return to the previous page. ⌘**40**

☞   Close the *Safari* window. ⌘**12**

☞   Open *Safari*. ⌘**42**

☞   Quit *Safari*. ⌘**58**

4.17 Background Information

Dictionary

Bing	Search engine developed by *Microsoft*.
Bookmark	A web address that is stored in a list will give you quick access to the website in the future.
Bookmarks editor	A window in which you can edit, view and arrange bookmarks.
Browser	A computer program that can display web pages. A few examples are *Safari, Chrome, Firefox, Edge* and *Internet Explorer.*
DuckDuckGo	Internet search engine that emphasizes protecting searchers' privacy. *DuckDuckGo* distinguishes itself from other search engines by not profiling its users and by deliberately showing all users the same search results for a given search term.
Favorites bar	A toolbar that contains links to your favorite websites.
Google	A company that has developed a large number of computer applications, such as the *Google* search engine, *Google Maps* and *Google Earth.*
Homepage	The starting or landing page of a website. The web page that is opened when you open *Safari* is also called a homepage.
Hyperlink	Also called a link.
Internet	A worldwide network of millions of computers that are connected on the basis of a general set of communication protocols. Most people are familiar with its Internet section, called the World Wide Web (usually called the Web).
Link	A link is a navigational tool on a web page that automatically leads the user to the information when clicked. A link can be displayed as text or as an image, such as a picture, a button or an icon. Also called a hyperlink.
Maps	An app where you can view maps and satellite photos, search for locations and plan trips.

- Continue on the next page -

Reading list	A feature that helps you save web pages and links for you to read later, even when you are not connected to the internet.
Safari	A browser application made by *Apple*.
Safari Reader	An option in *Safari* that lets you display an article without any distracting advertising banners. This makes it easier to focus on the content of the article.
Scroll	Moving a web page upwards, downwards, or from side to side.
Scroll bar, scroll block	A horizontal or vertical bar that appears whenever the content on a web page is greater than the size of the browser window. You can drag the scroll bar up or down, or from side to side to display the parts of the web page not in view.
Sidebar	Bar or pane on the left side of the *Safari* window where you can access your bookmarks or reading list.
Surf	Displaying one web page after the other by clicking links (hyperlinks).
Top Sites	A feature in *Safari*. *Top Sites* remembers which websites you visit the most. You can open the websites from the *Top Sites* page with just one click.
Web address	Each web page has its own unique address. This address is called the Uniform Resource Locator (URL). For example, the URL for the Visual Steps homepage is **http://www.visualsteps.com**
Web page	A web page is a source of information on the World Wide Web. It can be viewed in a browser application.
Website	A website is a collection of web pages linked together.
Wikipedia	An online encyclopedia, maintained and edited by Internet users.
WWW	(World Wide Web) A large network of computers connected to millions of other smaller networks located all over the world. This huge network contains an infinite number of web pages.
Yahoo!	A portal with a variety of web based services including search.
Zoom in	View an item more closely; the letters and images will become larger.
Zoom out	View an item from a distance; the letters and images will become smaller.

Source: Apple website, Wikipedia

4.18 Tips

 Tip
Add a bookmark to a folder on the favorites bar
You can add a new bookmark directly to a folder on the favorites bar:

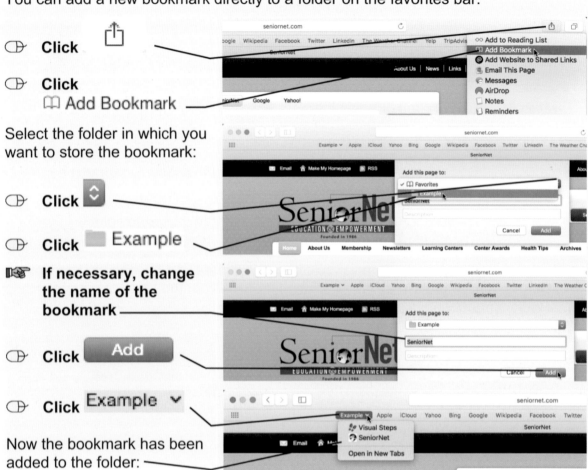

⊕ **Click**

⊕ **Click**
📖 Add Bookmark

Select the folder in which you
want to store the bookmark:

⊕ **Click**

⊕ **Click** 📁 Example

☞ **If necessary, change
the name of the
bookmark**

⊕ **Click** Add

⊕ **Click** Example ⌄

Now the bookmark has been
added to the folder:

 Tip
Zoom in and zoom out with touch gestures
If you are using a (Magic) trackpad on a MacBook Pro, you can zoom in and out on
websites by using touch gestures. This is how you zoom with the (Magic) trackpad:

 **Move your thumb and
index finger away
from each other on
the (Magic) trackpad**

To zoom out again, move your thumb and index finger towards each other (pinch).

Tip
Quickly revert to original size
After you have zoomed in, you can quickly revert to the website's actual size, like this:

☞ **Click** View

☞ **Click** Actual Size

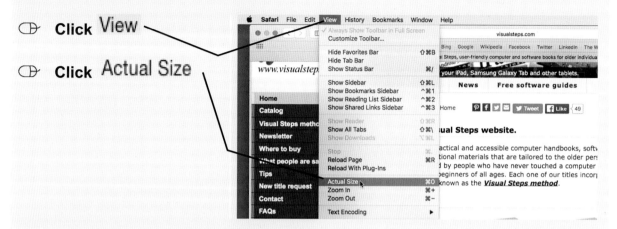

The same thing can be done with the short-cut key combination Command and 0 (zero):

⌨ **Press** ⌘ command and 0) **simultaneously**

 Tip
Add a new bookmark directly to Top Sites
When you create a new bookmark, you can also add this bookmark to *Top Sites*, instead of to the favorites bar. Next to the address bar:

☞ **Click** ⬆️
☞ **Click** 📖 Add Bookmark

Now you can select where to add the bookmark:

☞ **Click** 🔽

☞ **Click** ⊞ Top Sites

☞ **Click** Add

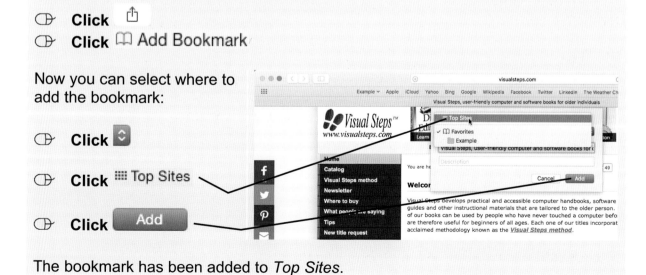

The bookmark has been added to *Top Sites*.

Tip

Settings for a new tab

If you have followed all the steps in this chapter, *Top Sites* will be displayed when you open a new tab. If you do not want this, you can change the settings and select a different event for opening a new tab.

👆 Click **Safari**, Preferences...

👆 By New tabs open with: click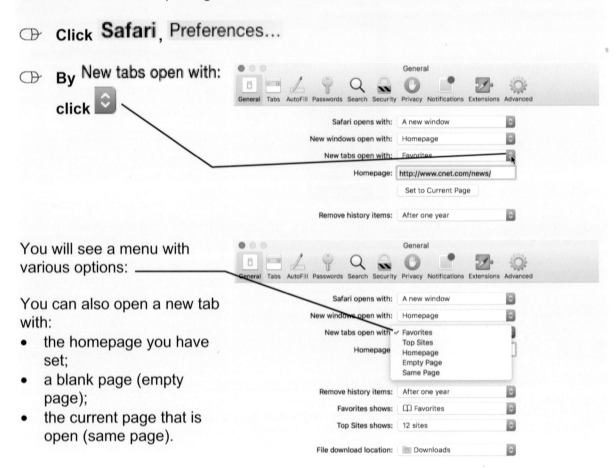

You will see a menu with various options:

You can also open a new tab with:

- the homepage you have set;
- a blank page (empty page);
- the current page that is open (same page).

Tip

Quickly scroll through a long page

If you want to quickly move through a very long page, you can use a swiping movement to scroll. With the Magic Mouse, you do that like this:

👆 **Quickly swipe upwards with one finger, over the Magic Mouse**

With a (Magic) trackpad:

 Quickly swipe upwards with two fingers, over the (Magic) trackpad

To quickly scroll downwards, make the same movement, but in the opposite direction.

Tip

Flip through pages with touch gestures
If you are using a Magic Mouse or a (Magic) trackpad, you can also use touch gestures to quickly flip through the pages you have visited, one after the other. You need to change a setting for the Magic Mouse first:

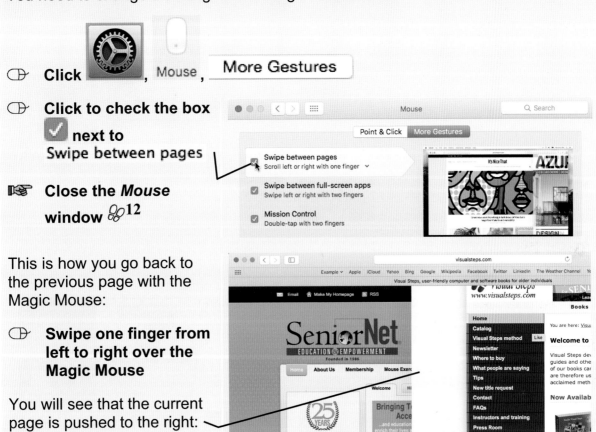

Click ⚙, Mouse, More Gestures

Click to check the box ☑ next to Swipe between pages

☞ Close the *Mouse* window ✂12

This is how you go back to the previous page with the Magic Mouse:

Swipe one finger from left to right over the Magic Mouse

You will see that the current page is pushed to the right:

With the (Magic) trackpad:

 Swipe two fingers from left to right over the (Magic) trackpad

If you have zoomed in on the page, these touch gestures will result in displaying the left side of the page first. By repeating the same movement once again, you will return to the previous page. To be effective, the swiping must be done very gently.

Tip

Mark a web page as a permanent Top Site

The pages that are displayed in *Top Sites* are constantly changing, as a result of your surfing behavior on the Internet. You can mark a web page as a permanent *Top Site*, which means it will always be displayed when you open *Top Sites*.

☞ **Click** ⠿

☞ **Place the mouse pointer on a thumbnail**

You will see the ⊠ 📌 buttons appear:

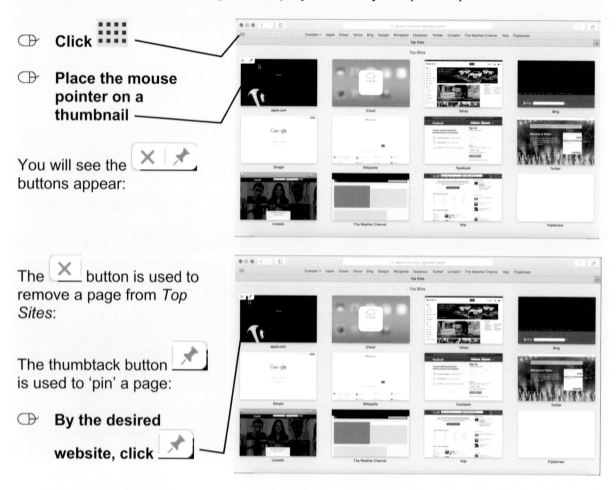

The ⊠ button is used to remove a page from *Top Sites*:

The thumbtack button 📌 is used to 'pin' a page:

☞ **By the desired website, click** 📌

- Continue on the next page -

The thumbtack button will now change into a blue

button :

Now the website will always be visible as a *Top Site*, even if you do not visit this site for a while.

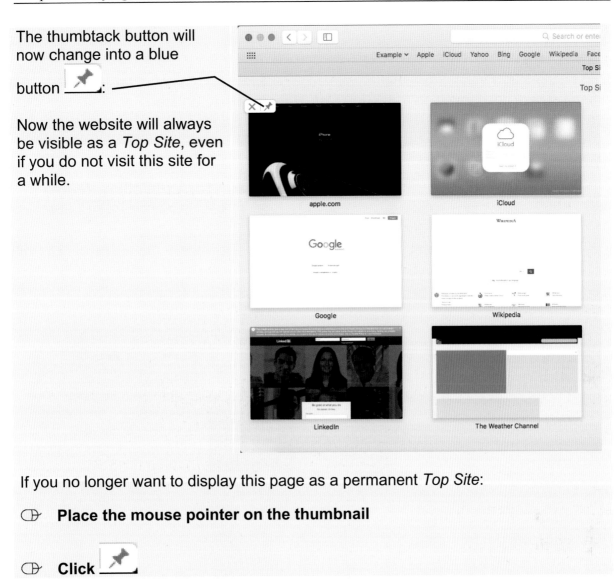

If you no longer want to display this page as a permanent *Top Site*:

Place the mouse pointer on the thumbnail

Click

Tip

Reading List

The *Reading List* is a feature that helps you save web pages to read later, even when you are not connected to the internet. Here is how to do that:

☞ **Position the pointer on the address bar**

☞ **Click** ⊕

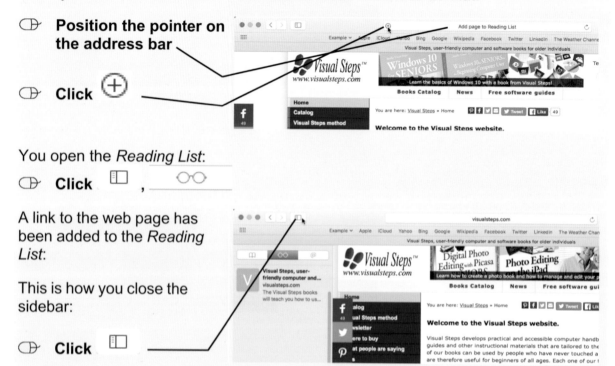

You open the *Reading List*:

☞ **Click** ▯ , ∞

A link to the web page has been added to the *Reading List*:

This is how you close the sidebar:

☞ **Click** ▯

This is how you open a page that has been added to the *Reading List*:

☞ **Click** ▯ , ∞
☞ **Click the desired page**

The advantage of the *Reading List* is that you can also view the saved pages when you are offline. Keep in mind that only the web page that is on screen will be stored. It is not possible to follow a link on a web page when you are offline. If you want to, you can store the linked page in the *Reading List* separately.

If the *Reading List* becomes too long, you can also delete some of the links:

☞ **Position the pointer on the desired link**

☞ **Right click the link**

☞ **Click** Remove Item

Tip

Select a different search engine

By default, *Safari* uses the well-known *Google* search engine. But you can also use the *Yahoo!*, *Bing* and *DuckDuckGo* search engines. First you will need to clear the address bar:

☞ **Click the address bar**

🖮 **Press** [⟵]

The web address is removed.

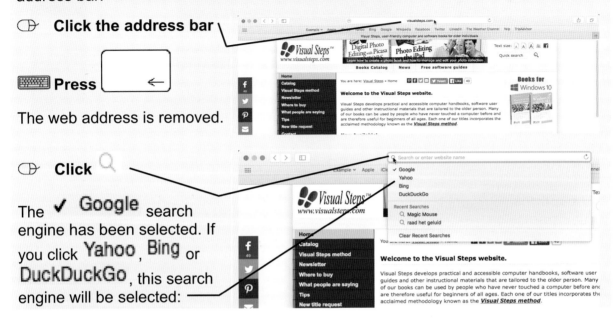

☞ **Click** 🔍

The ✔ **Google** search engine has been selected. If you click **Yahoo**, **Bing** or **DuckDuckGo**, this search engine will be selected:

 Tip

Show all tabs

If you have many tabs open at once, it will be difficult to quickly find that one tab you need. *Safari* has a solution for that:

☞ **Click** 🗗

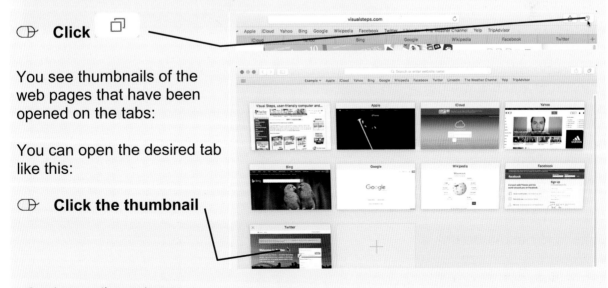

You see thumbnails of the web pages that have been opened on the tabs:

You can open the desired tab like this:

☞ **Click the thumbnail**

- Continue on the next page -

You see the tab:

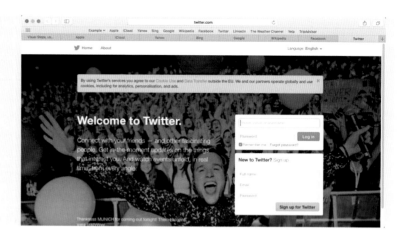

 Tip

Safari Reader

Safari Reader removes all advertisements and other distracting elements from the online articles you want to read. This option will only be visible when a web page contains articles.

In this example, you will see all sorts of animated advertising banners above and next to the article:

Safari has identified an article on this web page. You can tell this by the button in the address bar:

 Click

The article will be opened in a separate window without the advertisements:

Now you can quietly read the article without being distracted.

You can use the ᴬ A buttons to decrease or increase the font size:

- Continue on the next page -

When you increase or decrease the font size, *Safari* will remember this. Next time you open an article in *Safari Reader*, the font size will automatically be adjusted.

To close *Safari Reader*:

 Click

 **Tip**

Maps

Safari is very useful to plan trips and find information about and directions to landmarks, hotels and restaurants. But the *Maps* app can help you with that as well. This is how you open the *Maps* app:

Click

You might see a window that *Maps* is not authorized to access your location. In that case:

Click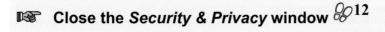

Click

Check the box ✅ **by**  **Maps**

☞ **Close the** *Security & Privacy* **window** ✂️[12]

- Continue on the next page -

The app is opened and you see a map:

You can search for an address or landmark like this:

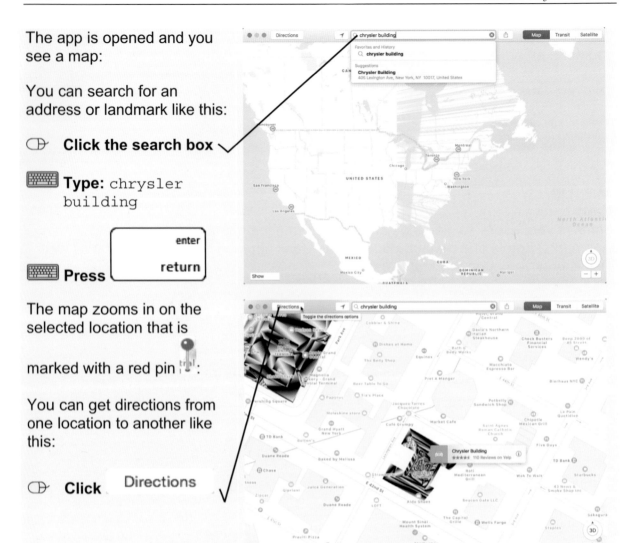

👆 **Click the search box**

⌨️ **Type:** `chrysler building`

⌨️ **Press** [enter / return]

The map zooms in on the selected location that is marked with a red pin 📍:

You can get directions from one location to another like this:

👆 **Click** 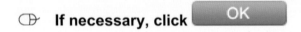 Directions

You might see a *Safety Warning* window:

👆 **If necessary, click** OK

- Continue on the next page -

You enter your start point:

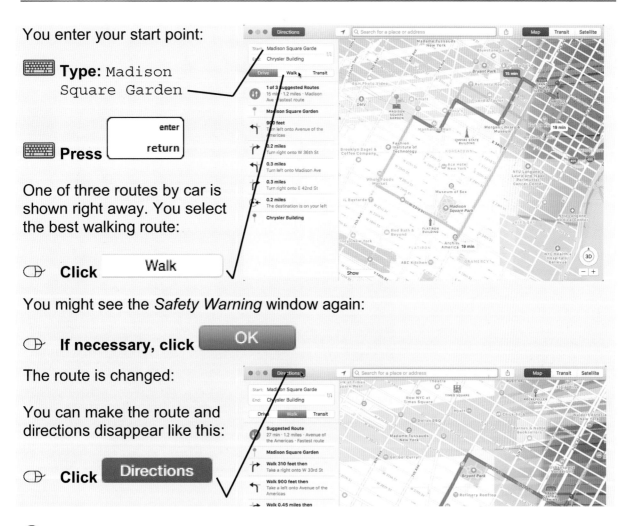

Type: Madison Square Garden

Press [enter return]

One of three routes by car is shown right away. You select the best walking route:

Click [Walk]

You might see the *Safety Warning* window again:

If necessary, click [OK]

The route is changed:

You can make the route and directions disappear like this:

Click [Directions]

Tip

Flyover

A very interesting feature of the *Maps* app is *flyover*, a photo-realistic, interactive 3D experience that lets you soar high above selected cities. First you search for a location:

Click the search box

Type: Eiffel tower

Press [enter return]

- Continue on the next page -

The map zooms in on the
selected location. You can
switch to satellite view like
this:

☞ **Click**   Satellite

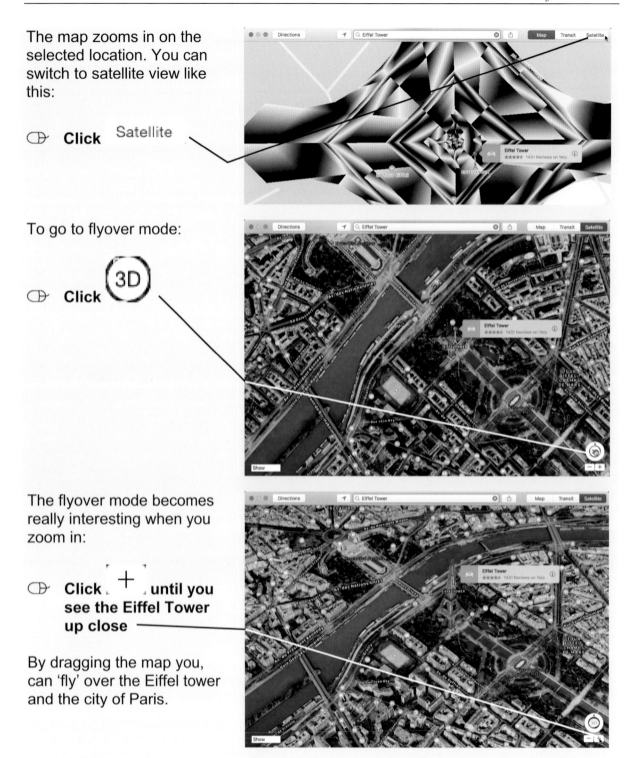

To go to flyover mode:

☞ **Click** (3D)

The flyover mode becomes
really interesting when you
zoom in:

☞ **Click** + **until you
see the Eiffel Tower
up close**

By dragging the map you,
can 'fly' over the Eiffel tower
and the city of Paris.

To go back to the regular map view:

☞ **Click** (3D) ,   Map

Tip

Pinned sites

In *Safari*, there is even another option for quickly accessing your favorite website; this is the so-called Pinned sites option on the tab bar. This is how you pin a website to the tab bar:

☞ **Right-click the tab**

☞ **Click** Pin Tab

You will see a small cube on the left-hand side of your tab. In this case, the cube contains a 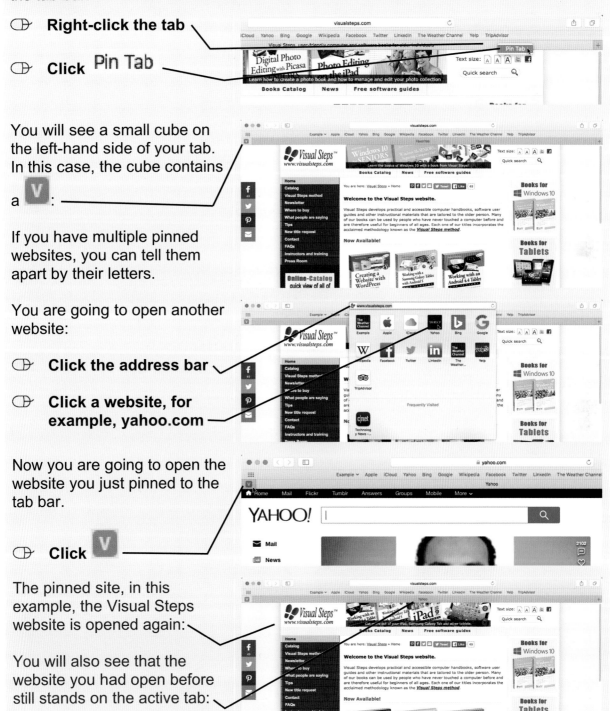 :

If you have multiple pinned websites, you can tell them apart by their letters.

You are going to open another website:

☞ **Click the address bar**

☞ **Click a website, for example, yahoo.com**

Now you are going to open the website you just pinned to the tab bar.

☞ **Click** V

The pinned site, in this example, the Visual Steps website is opened again:

You will also see that the website you had open before still stands on the active tab:

Notes

Write your notes down here.

5. Sending Emails with Mail

One of the most useful and frequently used applications on the Internet is electronic mail or *email*. You simply type your message on the computer and have it sent over the Internet to someone else.

MacOS contains a simple email program called *Mail* that lets you quickly and easily send and receive email messages. In this chapter you will learn how to set up your email account in *Mail*. We will show you how to configure an email account from Internet providers such as AOL or Verizon as well as from web-based email services such as *Outlook, Hotmail* or *Gmail*. *Outlook* accounts, for example, are email addresses that end with hotmail.com, live.com or outlook.com. If you use multiple email accounts, you can set them all up in *Mail*.

In this chapter we will explain the basics of how to send and receive an email message. You will also learn how to add the email address from a sender to your *Contacts* so that the next time you send this person a message you will no longer need to type the email address.

The fun thing about email is that you can send all sorts of things along with your email message. For example, a text file or a picture you just made. The items you send with your email message are called *attachments*. In this chapter you will also learn how to add an attachment to an email and how to view and save an attachment that you have received.

In this chapter you will learn how to:

- set up your email account;
- open *Mail*;
- write, send, receive and read an email;
- add an email address to *Contacts*;
- send, view and save an attachment;
- delete an email message;
- stop *Mail*.

 Please note:

To work through this chapter, you will need to have your own email address, including a user name and a password. Your email provider has probably supplied this information. You may have also saved the data yourself, while creating a *Outlook* or *Gmail* account.

5.1 Setting Up an Email Account

Before you can start sending emails, you need to set up an email account. In this section you will learn how to do that with an account from your Internet Service Provider (ISP), such as AOL or Verizon. But you can also use another account, like an account from work. You will need to have the data provided by the provider on hand. This includes your user name and password.
You can also add a web-based email account (also called webmail) to *Mail*, for example an *Outlook.com*, *Hotmail* or *Gmail* account. *Outlook.com*, *Hotmail* and *Gmail* are popular email services that can be accessed via an Internet browser, such as *Safari*. You can send and retrieve your email messages from any location in the world, as long as you are connected to the Internet.

If you have both an email account from an ISP as well as a webmail account, it still can be useful to set up your webmail account in *Mail*. In that way, you can retrieve your email messages in the email program installed on your computer without having to log in to the website of the email service. In the *Tips* at the end of this chapter you can read how to add a webmail account to *Mail*.

➥ Please note:

If you have an email account already set up, just continue reading until *section 5.2 Sending an Email*. You can continue with the steps again from that point on.

In the next few steps you will be setting up an account with an Internet Service Provider (ISP). First, you open the *System Preferences* in *MacOS*.

☞ **Click**

Open the Internet Accounts settings:

☞ **Click** Internet Accounts

You can choose from various pre-set templates for providers of email accounts. These templates only require that you enter your user name and password. In this example, we will set up an email address with an Internet Service Provider. In most cases, you will then need to select the **Add Other Account...** option:

Drag the scroll bar down

Click
Add Other Account...

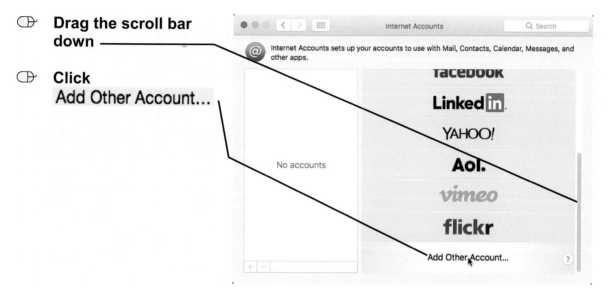

You will see a window where you can select the type of account you want to add:

Click
@ Mail account

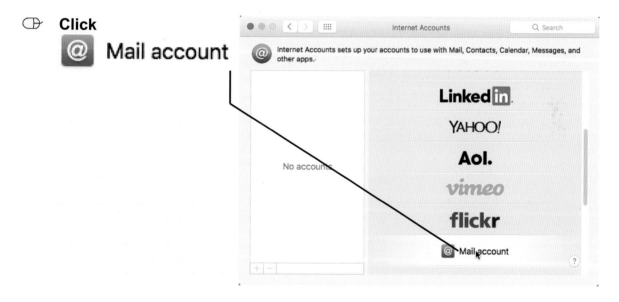

In the next window you need to enter some basic information about your email account:

If necessary, type your name ——————

By Email Address:, type your email address

By Password:, type the password ——————

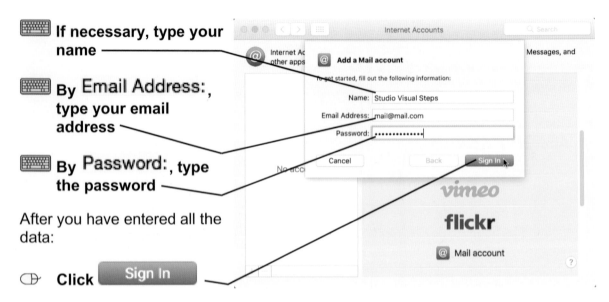

After you have entered all the data:

☞ **Click** Sign In ——————

The settings for your email account may be found automatically and you only have to click on the *Done* button.

If that does not happen, you will need to configure your account manually:

In this case you will see this error message: ——————

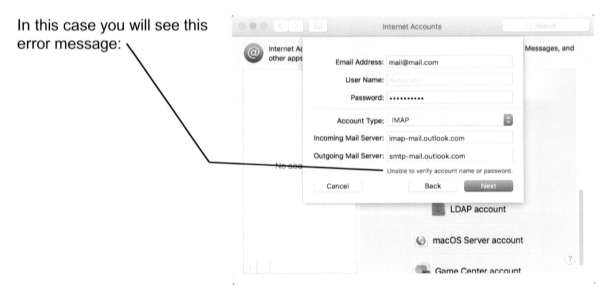

You can choose whether to set up your email account as an *IMAP* or *POP* account:

- IMAP stands for *Internet Message Access Protocol*. This means that you will manage your messages on the mail server. This server is a central storage medium owned by your email provider. The messages you have read will be saved on the mail server, until you delete them.
  IMAP is useful if you want to view, send and manage your emails on multiple computers or devices, such as an iPad or tablet. Your email folders (mailboxes) will look the same on each device. If you create new folders for storing your email messages, these folders will appear on each computer.
  If you want to use IMAP, you will need to set up your email account as an IMAP account. This will need to be done for each computer or device you use. Check with your email provider to see if they offer the IMAP functionality.
- POP stands for *Post Office Protocol*, which is the traditional way of managing email messages. As soon as you retrieve your messages, most email programs will delete the messages from the server and only store the messages on your local computer.
  However, the default setting for POP accounts in *Mail* is to save a copy of the message on the server, even after you have retrieved the message. This means that you can also retrieve this message on a different computer or device. In the *Tips* at the end of this chapter you can read how to modify these settings.

In this example we will set up a POP account. The procedure for setting up an IMAP account is very similar:

By **Account Type:**

click

Click **POP**

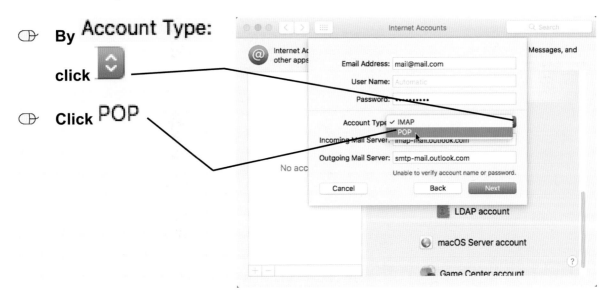

Type your user name. You can find this name among the data sent to you by your email provider.

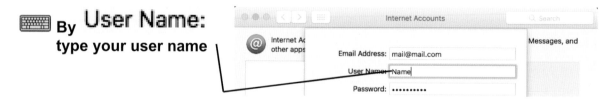

By **User Name:**
type your user name

The data for the servers for incoming and outgoing email have been sent to you by your Internet provider:

Type the address of the Incoming Mail Se in the box

Type the address of the Outgoing Mail Se in the box

Click **Sign In**

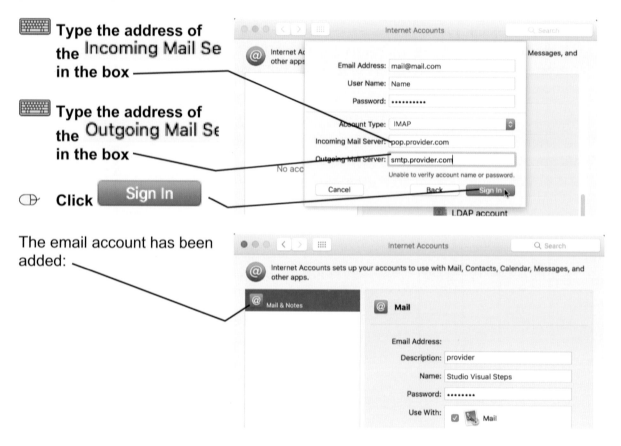

The email account has been added:

 Close the *Internet Accounts* window &❦12

✖ HELP! It does not work.

Many providers such as AOL and Verizon have posted instructions on their websites for setting up an email account in *MacOS*. Look for 'email settings Mac' or 'email settings Apple mail' on your provider's website and follow the instructions that are given.

5.2 Sending an Email

Just for practice, you are going to write and send yourself an email. First, you open the *Mail* program:

☞ **Click**

The program will check for new messages right away. In this example there are no new messages found, but in your own email program, it is possible that a few new messages have arrived. Now you will start a new, blank mail:

☞ **Click**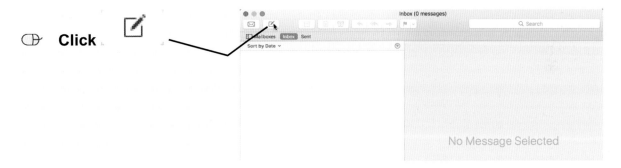

The new message window is opened. First, you need to add the recipient. In this example the recipient is yourself, so you will be adding your own email address:

⌨ **By** To: **, type your own email address**

Each email message has a subject:

☞ **Click next to** Subject:

⌨ **Type:** Test

Now you can type your message:

⊕ **Click the blank space where you want to type your message**

⌨ **Type:**
This is a test.

Continue on a new line:

⌨ **Press**

MacOS contains a dictionary which will help you while you are typing. Just see what happens when you deliberately make a spelling mistake:

⌨ **Type:** Togeter

A small window with a suggestion for the correct spelling appears under the misspelled word

Together ✕ :

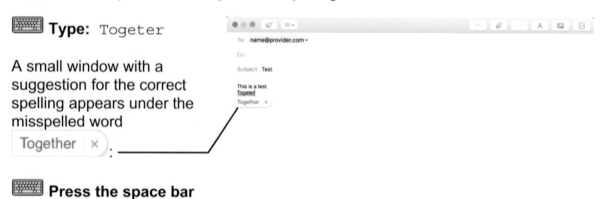

⌨ **Press the space bar**

The suggestion is accepted:

You may not even notice that a word is corrected while you are typing. The blue dotted line below the word Together shows you that the word has been corrected:

Tip

Suggested correction

The suggested correction 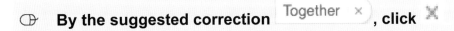 will be accepted automatically when you type a space, comma, period or other punctuation sign.

You can also refuse a suggested correction like this:

 By the suggested correction `Together  ×` **, click** ✖

You need to do this before you type a space, period, comma or other punctuation sign, otherwise the correction will be accepted.

 Tip

Disable Autocorrection

In the *Tips* at the end of this chapter you can read how to disable the autocorrection function during typing.

Please note: if you do disable the autocorrection function, this will become the setting for all the other programs that allow you to type text.

 Tip

Multiple suggestions

When there are multiple possibilities to correct the misspelled word, it will not be corrected automatically. A red dotted line **Mistike** will appear below the word instead. In that case you can correct a misspelled word like this:

 Right-click the word

Or:

⌨ **Hold** `control` **down**

 Click the word

 Click a suggested word that appears in the list

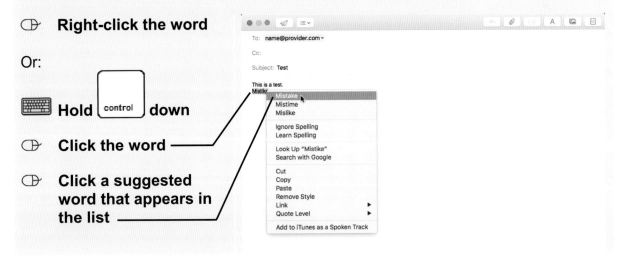

Now you can send your test email:

☞ **Click**

Your email message has
been sent. If the sound on
your Mac is on, you will hear
a sound signal.

5.3 Receiving an Email

Your message will be received shortly after you have sent it. You will hear a second
sound signal. If you do not receive a message right away, you can retrieve your new
messages in the following way:

☞ **Click**

Your email message will be received and you will hear a second sound signal.

☞ **If necessary, click**
Inbox (1)

HELP! I have not received anything.

Just wait a few minutes and click once more.

The number on the **Inbox (1)** button indicates the number of new messages. In this example there is only one new message, but you may have received multiple new messages on your own computer:

An unread message is marked by a blue dot ● next to the email message:

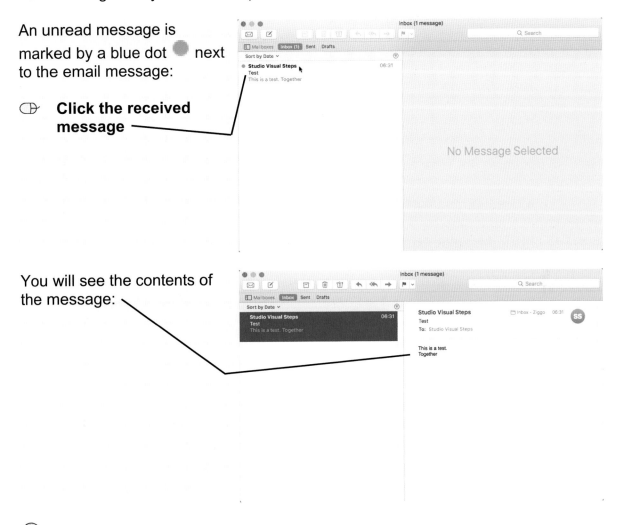

☞ **Click the received message**

You will see the contents of the message:

You will see the main window again in *Mail*. There is a toolbar at the top containing several buttons:

The list below explains what these buttons can do:

⊠   Retrieve new messages for all accounts.

✐   Compose a new message.

🗄   Archive the selected message.

🗑   Move the message to the *Trash*.

🗑   Mark the selected message as unwanted (or junk) email.

↩   Reply to the selected message. A return email message will be created with the recipient's email address already entered. The original message will be sent with it. You can start typing your reply message at the top of the screen.

⪻   If there are multiple recipients, all recipients of the selected message will receive a reply. A return email message will be created. Each recipient's email address is already entered. The original message will be sent with it. You can start typing your reply message at the top of the screen.

➡   Forward the selected message. The original email message will be converted into a new email message, which you can send to someone else. If you wish you can start typing your reply message at the top of the screen.

⚑ ⌄   Mark the selected message with a colored flag.

➷ Please note:

By default, there is no descriptive caption below the buttons in *MacOS*, but if you move your pointer over any of the buttons, a small pop-up message will be displayed with information. You can also add text to the icons. In the *Tips* at the end of this chapter you can read more about this feature.

5.4 Adding a Sender to Contacts

If you add the sender of an email message you received to your *Contacts* you will not need to type the address of this person every time you want to send a new email. You can simply select the address from your *Contacts*. The email you just sent to yourself is still selected. This is how you add your own address to your *Contacts*:

☞ **Click** Message

☞ **Click** Add Sender to Conta

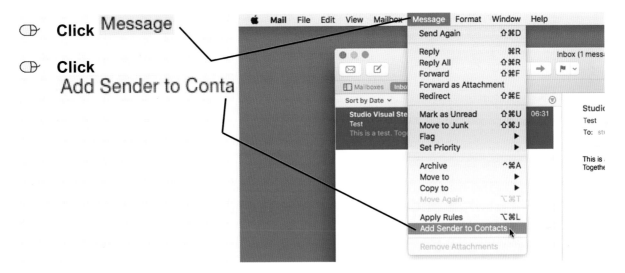

The email address will be added to the contacts. In the next section you will use the email address from *Contacts* to send a new email.

5.5 Sending an Email with an Attachment

The nice thing about email is that you can send all sorts of items along with your email message. For example, you can send a photo, drawing or a document. An item that is sent along with an email message is called an *attachment*. In the following step you will create a new message and add an attachment to it:

☞ **Open a new email message** ⁀⁀⁵⁹

You can add the email address you added to your *Contacts* like this:

☞ **Click** ⊕

A window containing the contacts on your Mac will be opened. This window is also known as the address panel. You will see your own address if you have added this in the previous section. Select your own email address:

In the address panel:

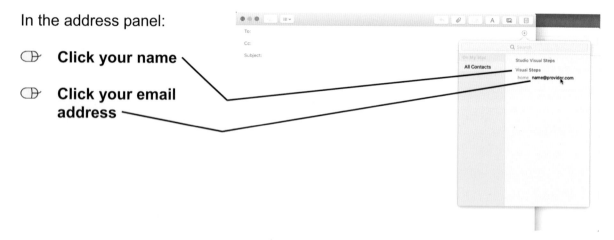

  Click your name

  Click your email address

![bandage icon] **HELP! I cannot click my name or email address.**

If you cannot click your name or email address, type your email address by To: .
See page 171.

The email address will be entered in the new message:

You will only see the name of the recipient:

Add a subject:

🖎 **Add this subject:** Test with attachment ✂️**60**

Type a short message:

🖎 **Add the following text** ✂️**61**

Dear Donna,

Here is the letter about the brunch.

Best regards,
(Your name)

To add an attachment to your email, you can use the button with the paperclip icon:

☐➔ **Click** [paperclip icon]

By default, the *Documents* folder will be opened. You can add one of the letters you created as you worked through the previous chapters. First you will need to open the *letters* folder:

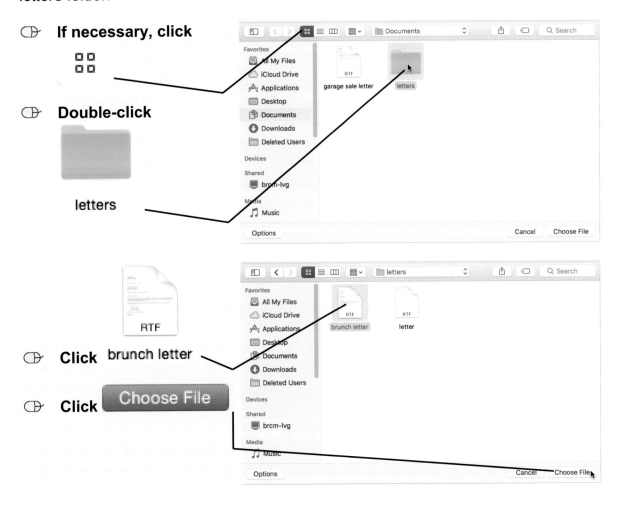

☐➔ **If necessary, click** [view icon]

☐➔ **Double-click** [folder] **letters**

☐➔ **Click** **brunch letter**

☐➔ **Click** **Choose File**

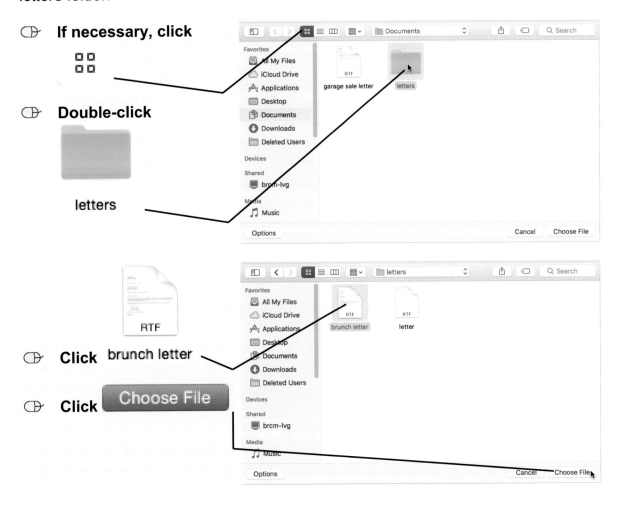

🩹 HELP! I do not have this file.

If you have not saved the file named *brunch letter.rtf*, you can also select a different document. For this exercise it does not matter which document you choose.

You will see that the attachment is inserted at the spot where the cursor is:

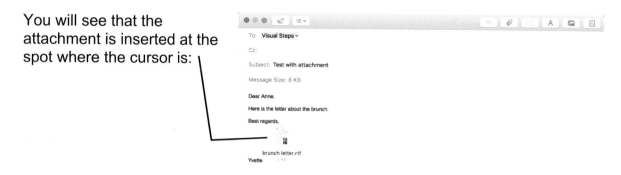

It is better to insert a blank line first. This looks a bit tidier:

👆 **Click between your name and the attachment**

⌨️ **Press** [enter / return] **twice**

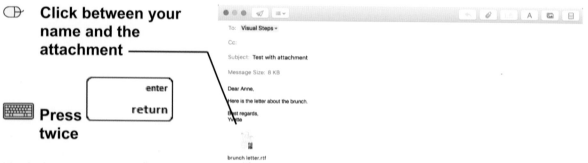

Now the attachment is placed a little lower in the message:

You can send the email:

☞ **Send the email** ⍉⍉62

5.6 Opening and Saving an Attachment

You may receive the email right away. If this is not the case:

☞ **Retrieve your new messages** ⚯⁶³

The email with the attachment is received:

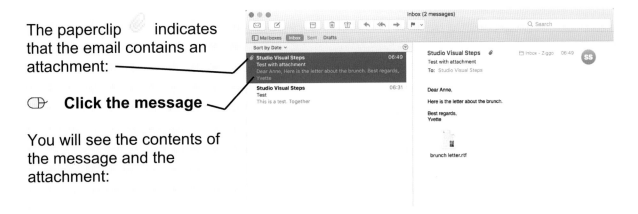

The paperclip 📎 indicates that the email contains an attachment: ——

👆 **Click the message** ⟍

You will see the contents of the message and the attachment:

This is how you can quickly view the attachment:

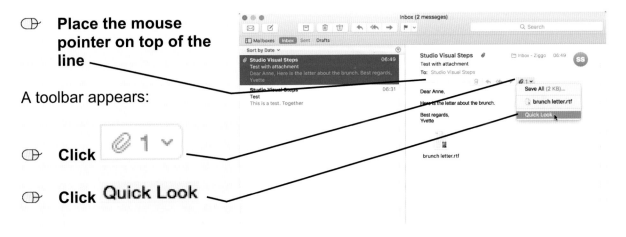

👆 **Place the mouse pointer on top of the line** ⟍

A toolbar appears:

👆 **Click** 📎 1 ˅

👆 **Click** Quick Look ⟍

You will see the contents of the attachment:

You can close this window:

☞   **Click** ❌

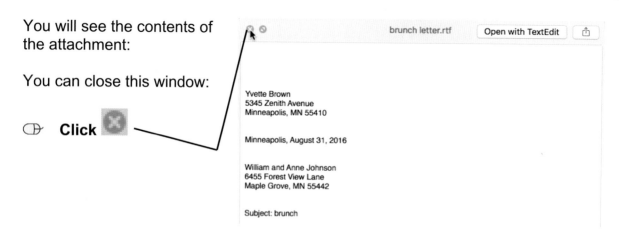

If you want to save the attachment:

☞   **Place the mouse pointer on top of the line** ——————

The toolbar appears again:

☞   **Click** 📎 1 ⌄

☞   **Click**
       📄 **brunch letter.rtf**

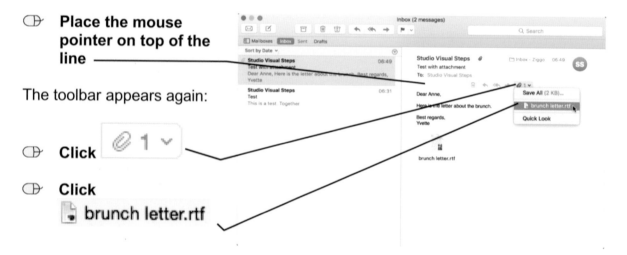

Now you can rename the attachment and select the folder where you want to save the file:

⌨   **Type:**
       `attachment.rtf`

☞   **Click** ⬍

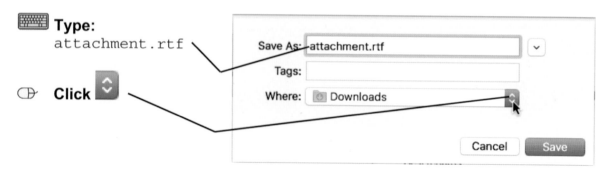

In the list displayed, select the *Documents* folder to save the attachment:

☞ **Click   Documents**

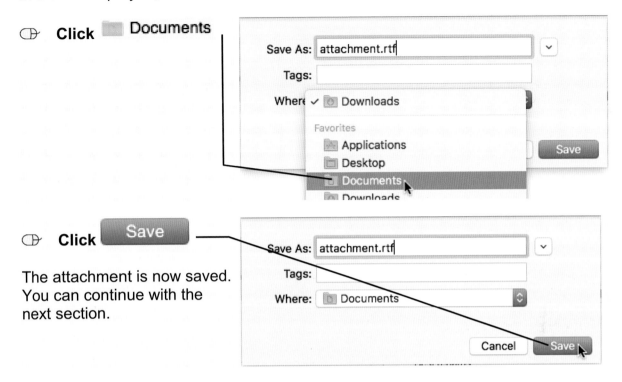

☞ **Click   Save**

The attachment is now saved.
You can continue with the
next section.

5.7 Deleting an Email

If you want to keep your *Inbox* tidy, you can delete all the old messages you no
longer need. You can try that now:

☞ **If necessary, click the
    message with the
    attachment again**

☞ **Click**

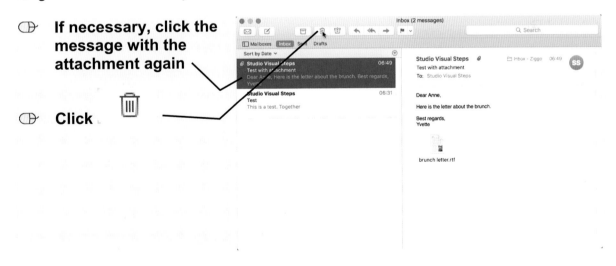

The message has been moved to the *Trash* mailbox:

In this example there is still one message left in the *Inbox*: ──

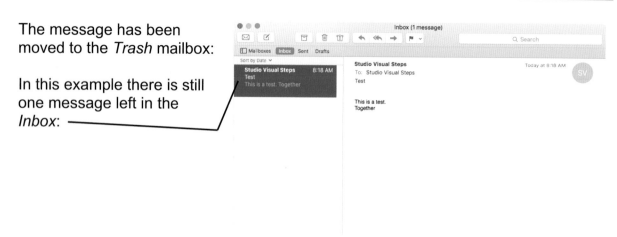

You can view the contents of the *Trash* mailbox like this:

☞ **Click** **Mailboxes**

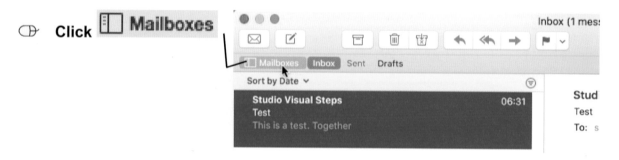

You will see an extra pane in the *Mail* window, displaying various mailboxes:

You will see the *Inbox*, *Sent* and *Trash* mailboxes: ──

☞ **Click** 🗑 **Trash**

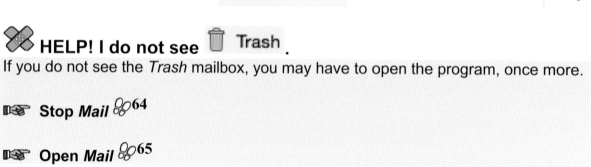

HELP! I do not see 🗑 **Trash** .

If you do not see the *Trash* mailbox, you may have to open the program, once more.

☞ **Stop** *Mail* ᵍᵍ64

☞ **Open** *Mail* ᵍᵍ65

The deleted message has been moved to the *Trash* mailbox:

You can hide the mailboxes like this:

 Click [Mailboxes]

💡 Tip
Trash mailbox is emptied automatically
By default, the messages in the *Trash* mailbox will be removed automatically after one month. In the *Tips* at the end of this chapter you can read how to adjust this setting.

This is how you permanently delete all the messages in the *Trash* mailbox:

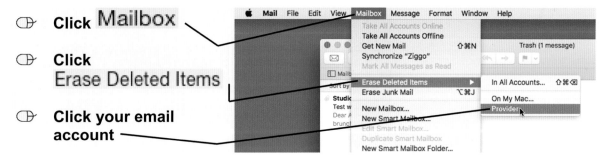

☞ **Click** Mailbox

☞ **Click** Erase Deleted Items

☞ **Click your email account**

You will see a warning message. If you really want to delete all the messages in the *Trash* mailbox for good:

☞ **Click** Erase

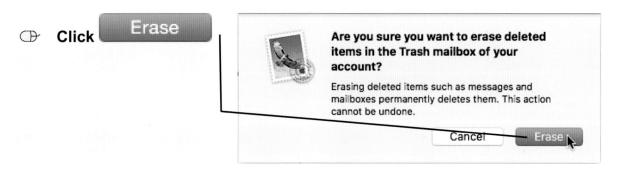

Now the *Trash* mailbox is empty.

5.8 Stop Mail

Now you can close the *Mail* window:

☞ **Close the *Mail* window** ⏱12

Mail will still remain active. You can tell this by the dot 🔲 below the 🔲 icon.
Every five minutes, the program will continue to check for new messages.

If you want to stop *Mail* altogether:

👆 **Click Mail**

👆 **Click Quit Mail**

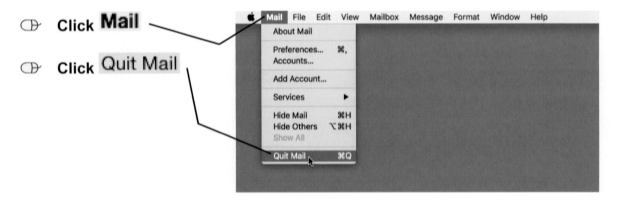

You have learned how to send and receive email messages. In the following
exercises you can practice these actions once more.

5.9 Exercises

The following exercises will help you master what you have just learned. Have you forgotten how to do something? Use the number beside the footsteps 𝒫1 to look it up in the appendix *How Do I Do That Again?* at the end of the book.

Exercise: Send an Email with an Attachment

In this exercise you will be sending an email message and attaching the document named *letter* to the message. In *Chapter 3 Working with Folders and Files in Finder* you created this document and stored it in the *letters* folder. If you have not done this, you can select a different text file as an attachment.

☞ Open *Mail*. 𝒫65

☞ Open a new email message. 𝒫59

☞ Add your own email address with the address panel. 𝒫66

☞ Enter the following subject for this message: `Email with attachment`. 𝒫60

☞ Enter this text: 𝒫61
```
Hereby I send you the text file.
Kind regards,
(Your name)
```

☞ Add the text file named *letter* from the *letters* folder as an attachment. 𝒫67

☞ Insert two blank lines between your name and the attachment. 𝒫68

☞ Send the email message. 𝒫62

Exercise: Receive and View an Email with an Attachment

☞ Check for new messages. &&**63**

☞ If necessary, open the *Inbox*. &&**69**

☞ Open the message with the attachment. &&**70**

☞ View the attachment. &&**71**

☞ Close the window with the attachment. &&**12**

☞ Save the attachment in the *Documents* folder with the name:
  `letter as an attachment` &&**72**

Exercise: Delete an Email

☞ Move the email message to the *Trash* mailbox. &&**73**

☞ View the contents of the *Trash* mailbox. &&**74**

☞ Delete all the messages in the *Trash* mailbox. &&**75**

Exercise: Stop Mail

☞ Close the *Mail* window. &&**12**

☞ Quit *Mail*. &&**64**

5.10 Background Information

Dictionary

Account	A combination of a user name and a password that gives access to a particular private service. A subscription with an Internet Service Provider (ISP) is also called an account.
Address panel	A window in *Mail* where you can select an email address for the email message you want to send.
AOL	Short for *America Online*, a well-known American Internet provider.
Archive	A mailbox in *Mail* you can use to store messages that you have read, but want to keep handy until you move or delete them.
Attachment	Documents, images and other files that are sent with an email message. A message that contains an attachment can be easily recognized by the paperclip icon.
Contacts	An *MacOS* program that lets you save, view and change the data of your contacts.
Email	Short for *electronic mail*. These are messages sent through the Internet.
Email account	The server name, user name, password and the email address that are used by *Mail* to connect to an email service.
Gmail	Free email service developed by *Google,* the creator of the well-known search engine.
Hotmail	Free email service from *Microsoft*.
IMAP	IMAP stands for *Internet Message Access Protocol*. This means that you manage your email messages on the mail server. The messages you have read will remain stored on the mail server, until you delete them. IMAP is useful when you manage your email messages on multiple computers. Your mailbox will look the same on each computer or device. If you create new folders to organize your messages, these same folders will be visible on each computer. If you want to use IMAP, you will need to set up your email account as an IMAP account on each individual computer or device.

- Continue on the next page -

Inbox	A mailbox in *Mail* in which you can view received messages.
Internet Service Provider	A company that provides access to the Internet, usually for a fee. The usual way of connecting to an Internet Service Provider (also just called provider or ISP) is through a broadband connection, such as a fixed cable connection or DSL. Many Internet providers offer additional services, such as email accounts, spam filters and space to host a website.
Mail	A program in *MacOS* that lets you send and receive email messages.
Mailbox	A folder in *Mail*. *Mail* contains default mailboxes called *Inbox*, *Sent* and *Trash*.
POP	POP stands for *Post Office Protocol*, which is the traditional method for managing email messages. When you retrieve your email, the messages are usually immediately deleted from the server. But the default setting for POP accounts in *Mail* is for saving a copy on the server after the message has been retrieved, for one week. This means you have enough time to retrieve this message on your computer or on a different device.
Provider	See Internet Service Provider.
Sent	A mailbox in *Mail* where the messages you sent are stored.
System Preferences	In the *System Preferences* window you can view and change your computer's settings. The sections in the window are divided into categories, such as the Dock, Sound, Mouse and General.
Trash	A mailbox in *Mail*, where the deleted messages are stored. A message is only permanently deleted after you have deleted it from the *Trash* mailbox. By default, the messages in the *Trash* mailbox from *Mail* are deleted after one month.
Yahoo!	A search engine that also offers free email services.

Source: Apple Dictionary, Wikipedia

5.11 Tips

 Tip
Set up a Hotmail, Live, Outlook or Gmail account in Mail
If you have an email account that ends with *hotmail.com*, *live.com*, *outlook.com* or *gmail.com*, you can also set up this account in *Mail*:

☞ **Open *System Preferences*** ℅⁷⁶

🖰 **Click** Internet Accounts

🖰 **Drag the scroll bar down**

🖰 **Click** Add Other Account...

🖰 **Click** @ **Mail account**

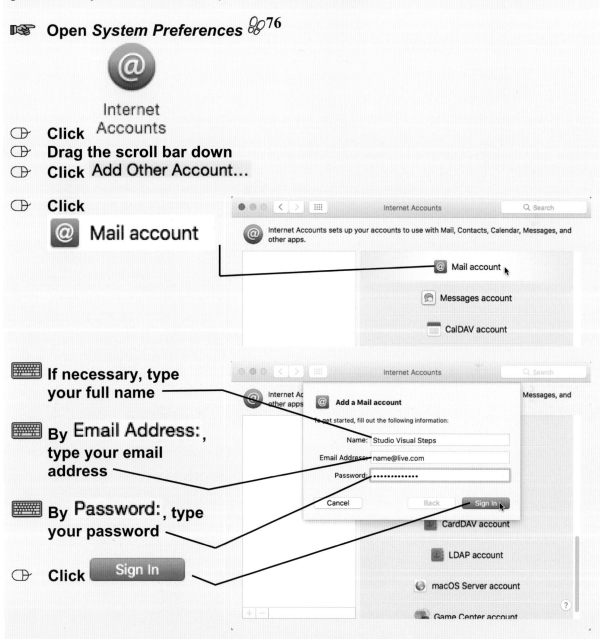

⌨ **If necessary, type your full name**

⌨ **By** Email Address:, **type your email address**

⌨ **By** Password:, **type your password**

🖰 **Click** Sign In

The account settings will be found and the account will be added.

Tip

Disable Autocorrection
The autocorrection function in *MacOS* may lead to unwanted corrections. The dictionary may not recognize the words you type, but will suggest a correction nevertheless. This may result in some strange corrections, which you might accept without noticing, when you type a period, a comma or a blank space. If you would like to disable the autocorrection function, proceed as follows:

☞ **Open** *System Preferences* 🦶76

☞ **Click** Keyboard

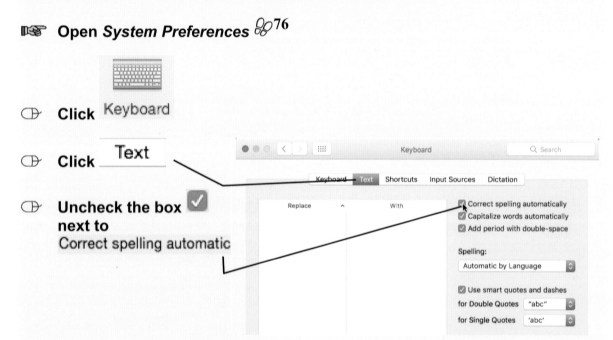

☞ **Click** Text

☞ **Uncheck the box** ✅ **next to**
Correct spelling automatic

Now any text you write will no longer be corrected while you are typing.

 Tip

Add text to the Mail buttons
Do you have trouble remembering what the buttons on the *Mail* toolbar can do? By using the Control key, you can easily add text to these buttons:

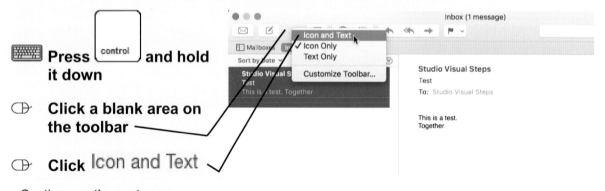

⌨ **Press** control **and hold it down**

☞ **Click a blank area on the toolbar**

☞ **Click** Icon and Text

- Continue on the next page -

Now a descriptive text will
appear below the buttons:

Tip
Open message in separate window
Sometimes, the message is easier to read if you open it in a separate window. This
is how you do that:

☞ **Double-click the
message**

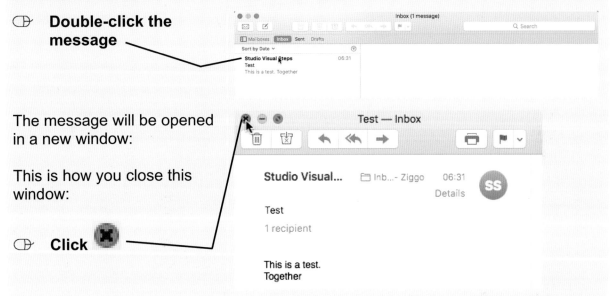

The message will be opened
in a new window:

This is how you close this
window:

☞ **Click** ✖

In the toolbar above the message you will see some of the same buttons as in the
main window of the *Mail* program. But you have not seen the 🖨 button before.
This button can be used to print a message.

Tip
Use Contacts
In this chapter you have added an email address to *Contacts*. You can also add
home address information, phone numbers, and other information as well. You can
open *Contacts* from the *Dock*:

☞ **Click**

- Continue on the next page -

The address book is opened. It looks like this:

☞ **Click your name**

You will see your email address:

You can add extra information:

☞ **Click** Edit

You can add a home phone number:

☞ **Click** mobile ⇕

☞ **Click** home

☞ **By** home ⇕ **, click** Phone

⌨ **Type the phone number**

⌨ **Press** enter / return

In the same way you can enter other data. After you have finished entering data:

☞ **Click** Done

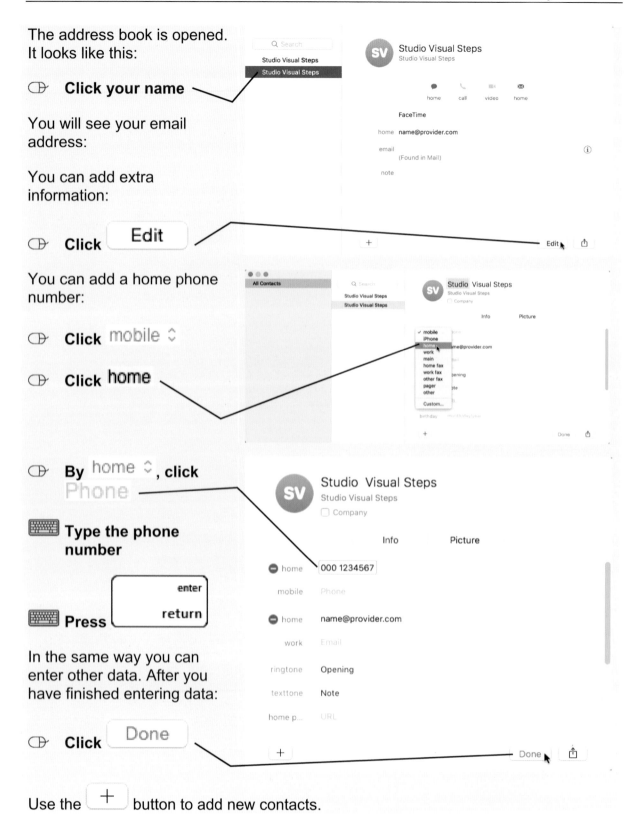

Use the ⊕ button to add new contacts.

💡 Tip

Save email messages on the server or not?

For POP email accounts, you can set your own preferences for saving a copy of the incoming messages on the mail server. If a copy is saved, you can also retrieve the message on your desktop computer or iPad, after you have received the message on your laptop, for example. This is how you can change the *Mail* settings:

☞ Click **Mail**

☞ Click **Preferences...**

☞ Click **Accounts**

☞ Click **Advanced**

In this example the option **Remove copy from server after retrieving a message:** has not been selected: You may see a different setting. This depends on the type of account you are using.

This is how you can change the period for saving the messages on the mail server:

☞ If necessary, check the box ✔ next to **Remove copy from serv**

☞ Click 🔼

☞ Click the desired option

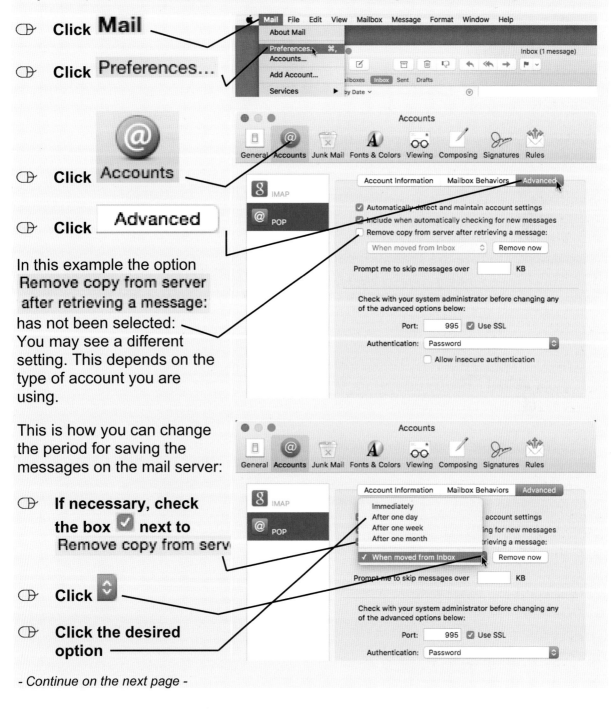

- Continue on the next page -

If you do not want to automatically delete the messages from the mail server:

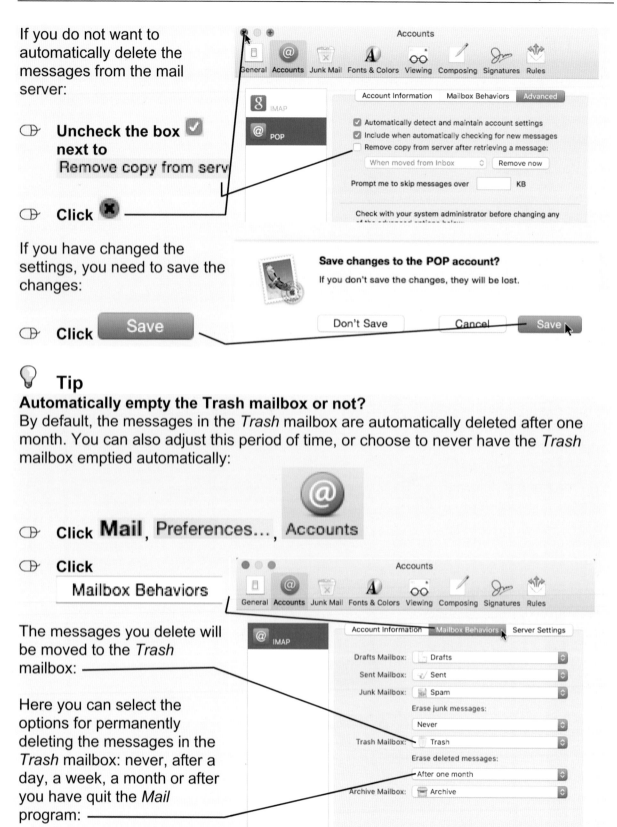

☞ **Uncheck the box** ✅ **next to** ☐ Remove copy from serv

☞ **Click** ✖ ─

If you have changed the settings, you need to save the changes:

☞ **Click** Save

Save changes to the POP account?
If you don't save the changes, they will be lost.

Don't Save   Cancel   Save

💡 **Tip**
Automatically empty the Trash mailbox or not?
By default, the messages in the *Trash* mailbox are automatically deleted after one month. You can also adjust this period of time, or choose to never have the *Trash* mailbox emptied automatically:

☞ **Click** **Mail**, Preferences..., Accounts

☞ **Click** Mailbox Behaviors

The messages you delete will be moved to the *Trash* mailbox: ─

Here you can select the options for permanently deleting the messages in the *Trash* mailbox: never, after a day, a week, a month or after you have quit the *Mail* program: ─

Tip

Conversations
Mail will automatically group the messages from a thread with a particular contact by its particular subject. This makes your mailbox easy to manage. A group of messages is called a *conversation*.

In this example, the conversation consists of 3 » messages: ——————

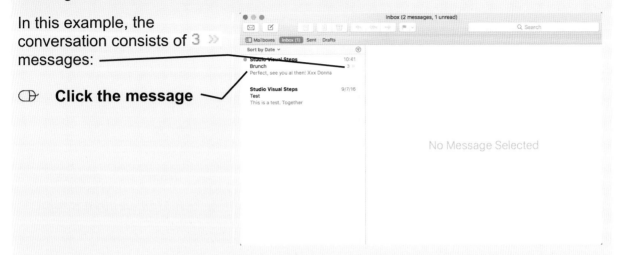

☞ **Click the message** —————

In a conversation, only the received messages will be counted. The messages sent by you will not be counted. In this example, the contact has sent two email messages about the same subject.

The messages are displayed one below the other. The most recent message is the one down below: ——————

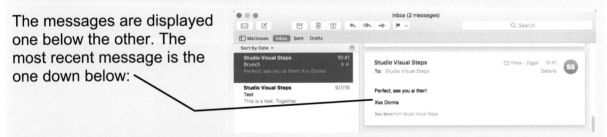

A huge advantage of these conversations is, that *Mail* will hide repeated occurrences of the same text in messages, such as email signatures and original emails that are copied in a reply. As a result, you will only see the parts of the conversation that are important to you.

If you would like to see the entire message after all:

☞ **Click**
       See More from Studio Visual

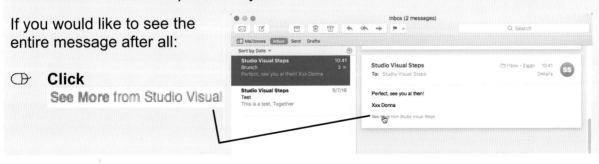

Tip

Notifications
You may have noticed that
when you receive an email
and the *Mail* window is
closed, a notification banner
appears in the top right-hand
corner of your screen:

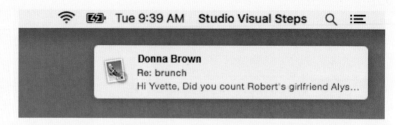

When you place the mouse
pointer on the banner, two
options appear:

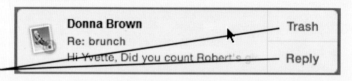

With [Reply], you can start typing a reply in *Mail*. With [Trash], you can
delete the message right away. When you click the banner, the *Mail* window opens
and you see the message.

If you do not click the banner, it disappears automatically after a couple of seconds.
But you can still view all your notifications in the *Notification Center* like this:

☞ **Click** ☰

You see various sections of
the *Notification Center* like
the weather and the stocks.
When you use the *MacOS*
calendar, you will see the
scheduled events for today
and tomorrow here:

☞ **Click** **Notifications**

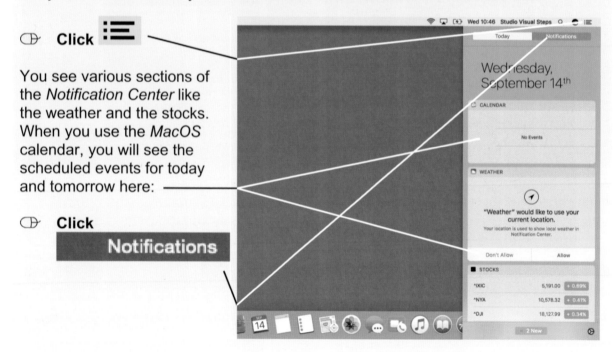

- Continue on the next page -

If you see a notification, you can open the message in the accompanying program by clicking the notification.

To close all notifications for a program, you click .

A notification in the *Notification Center* disappears when you click it and the associated program opens. When you open a message you have been notified about directly in *Mail*, the notification for that message also disappears from the *Notification Center*.

You can receive notifications for many programs in the *Notification Center*. You can view the list like this:

☞ **Open *System Preferences*** ⑧⑧76

⊕ **Click** Notifications

You see the list of programs that use the *Notification Center*:

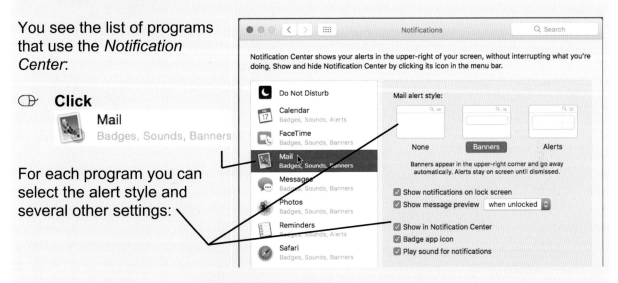

⊕ **Click**

    Mail
    Badges, Sounds, Banners

For each program you can select the alert style and several other settings:

The number shown on the **Badge app icon** indicates the number of new

messages  .

☞ **Close the window** ⑧⑧12

Tip

Search the text of the email messages
If you search with *Spotlight*, the program will also search the text of the email

messages in your mailboxes. You can open *Spotlight* by clicking in the top right corner of the menu bar.

In this example we have searched for the name 'Alyssa': —————————

Three emails have been found: ——————————

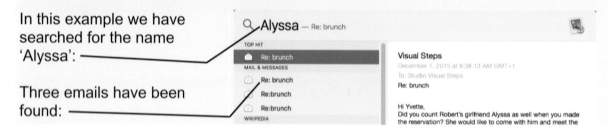

 Tip

Archiving
In the *Archive* mailbox you can store messages that you have already read, but want to keep handy until you move or delete them. You can archive a message or conversation like this:

☞ **Click the message**

☞ **Click**

The message (or the conversation) disappears from the *Inbox*. When this is the first message that was archived, the *Archive* mailbox will be created in the mailbox list:

☞ **Click** ⊞ **Mailboxes**

☞ **Click** ⊟ **Archive**

The message will stay in the *Archive* mailbox until you move or delete it.

Please note: you may not see this mailbox. This depends on the type of account you use.

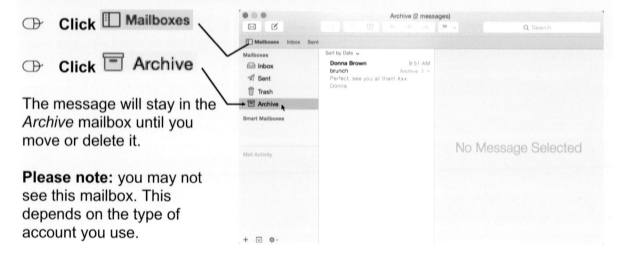

6. Photos, Videos and Music

Your Mac has a multitude of built-in programs for handling all of your photo, video and music needs. This chapter covers the basic functionality of *Image Capture*, *Preview, iTunes, QuickTime Player* and *DVD Player*.

The *Image Capture* program lets you transfer (import) photos from your digital camera, iPhone, iPad or iPod touch to your Mac. You can view the imported photos in the *Preview* program. The *Preview* program also has various options for editing photos, such as rotating or cropping a photo and adjusting exposure and color.

The *iTunes* program is a very extensive music player for your Mac. You can use it to import a CD, play music and purchase new music.
You can use the *QuickTime Player* program to play a video file and the *DVD Player* program to play a DVD. This chapter also shows you how to navigate the menu on a DVD and how to play the DVD.

In this chapter you will learn how to:

- import photos with *Image Capture*;
- view and edit photos with *Preview*;
- import a CD and play music with *iTunes*;
- play a video file with *QuickTime Player* and play a DVD with *DVD Player*.

 Please note:

If you want to follow the steps shown in the examples in *section 6.1 Importing Photos with Image Capture* and *6.2 Your Photos in Finder*, you will need to have a digital camera, iPhone, iPad or iPod touch with a few photos stored on the device. If you do not own these items, you can just read through the sections and continue later with the steps in *section 6.3 Viewing Photos in Preview*.

 Please note:

The MacBook Air, the Mac mini and the latest models of the iMac, MacBook and MacBook Pro are not equipped with a CD/DVD player. If necessary, you can connect an external player or burner or just read through the sections about playing a CD or DVD.

 Please note:

To work with the section of this chapter that handles *iTunes* and *DVD Player* you will need to have a music CD and a movie or TV series on DVD. If you do not have these items, you can just read through the section.

6.1 Importing Photos with Image Capture

When you *import* a file, it means you will be transferring it from some other device to your Mac. First you need to open *Image Capture*:

☞ **Open** *Launchpad* $\mathscr{G}^2$

☞ **Open** *Image Capture*  $\mathscr{G}^{77}$

You see the *Image Capture* window:

If you want to import the photos from your digital camera, iPhone, iPad or iPod touch, you will need to connect the device to your Mac. For connecting the device you can use a USB cable, for example:

☞ **Connect the digital camera with the cable included in the camera packaging**

☞ **Insert the other end of the cable into the USB port of your Mac**

☞ **Turn the camera on**

With your iPhone, iPad or iPod touch you can use the Lightning-to-USB-cable included in the package:

 Connect the small end of the Lightning-to-USB-cable to your iPhone, iPad or iPod touch

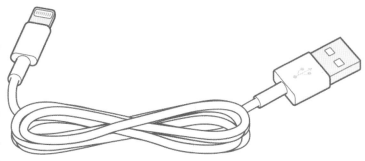

 Connect the opposite end to one of the USB ports on your Mac

Source: iPad, iPhone and iPod touch User Guides

💡 **Tip**
USB ports
You can refer to *section 3.12 Copying to a USB Stick* for more information about the location of the USB ports on your Mac.

If your digital camera is equipped with an SD memory card, you can insert the SD card directly into the SD card reader.

The SD card reader is located on the back of the monitor:

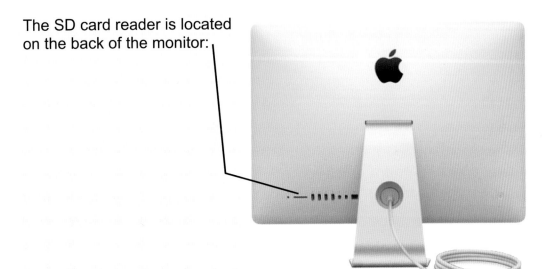

Or it is located on the right-hand side:

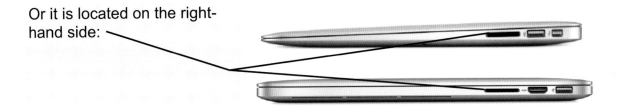

On the Mac mini or Mac Pro, the SD card reader is located on the back:

☞ **Carefully insert the SD card into the slot with the printed side pointing upwards**

⊕ **Click your camera, for example 🔘 D7000**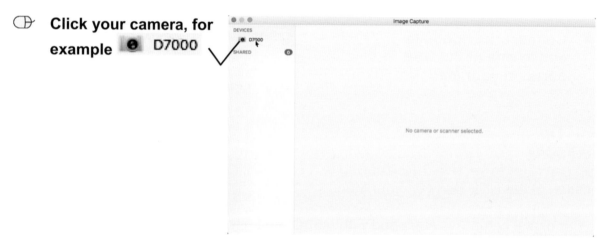

✕ HELP! There are other open programs.

When you connect your camera to your computer, another program may open, for instance, an application that came with your camera.

When you connect your iPhone or iPad, the *iTunes* program may open as well.

If that is the case, you can simply close these programs:

☞ **If necessary, quit the program** 🔗⁷⁸

You see the photos that are on your device. By every photo you see information about the file. You can display more photos in the window like this:

Click

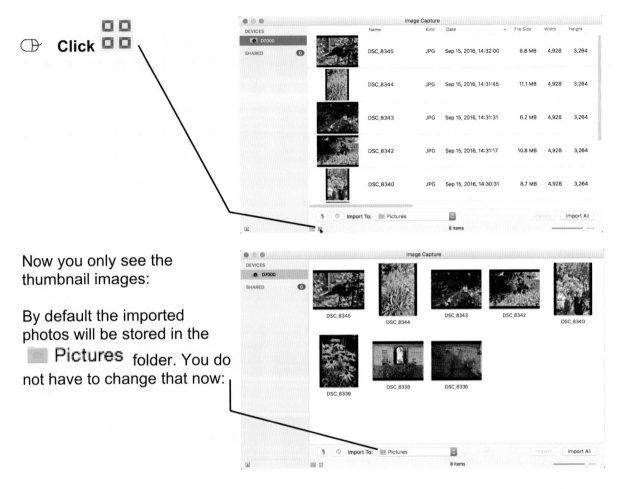

Now you only see the thumbnail images:

By default the imported photos will be stored in the Pictures folder. You do not have to change that now:

You can import all the photo's at once, or import a selection of the photos on the device:

If you want to import all the photos:

Click **Import All**

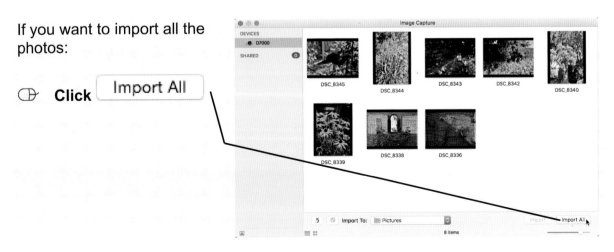

If you do not want to import all the photos, you can select a number of them with the Command key:

Press ⌘ command and hold it down

Click the desired photos

Release ⌘ command

Click Import

The photos will be imported:

Once the import is complete, a green check mark ✓ will appear on the photos that have been imported:

These check marks remain visible, even if you disconnect and reconnect the device.

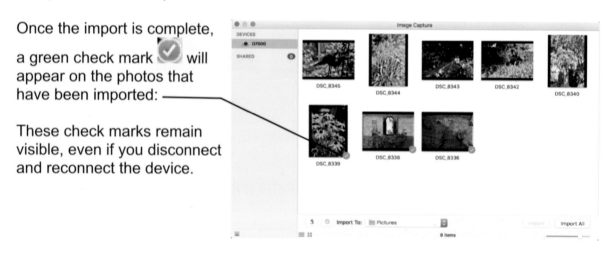

You can stop the program now:

☞ Quit *Image Capture* ℘⁷⁸

☞ Disconnect your device from the USB port of your Mac

Or:

☞ Remove the SD card

☺ Tip

Start Image Capture or another program automatically
In this section you have opened *Image Capture* before you connected your device. The default setting in *MacOS* is that *Image Capture* starts automatically when you connect a (device with a) digital camera. If you want you can adjust this setting as follows:

In the bottom left corner

⊕ **Click** 🖼️

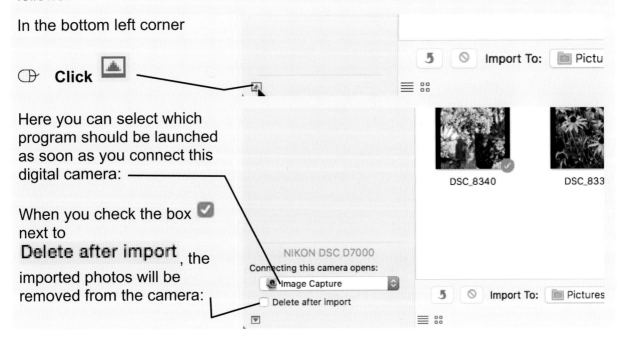

Here you can select which program should be launched as soon as you connect this digital camera:

When you check the box ☑️ next to

Delete after import , the imported photos will be removed from the camera:

6.2 Your Photos in Finder

You will take a look at the Pictures folder in Finder. First, you will add this folder to the folder list:

☞ **Open *Finder*** ✎²⁶

It is very easy to add a folder:

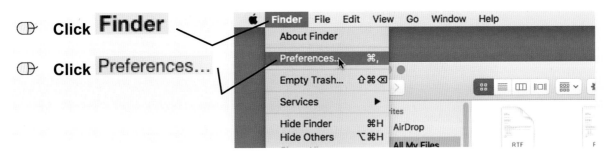

⊕ **Click Finder**

⊕ **Click Preferences…**

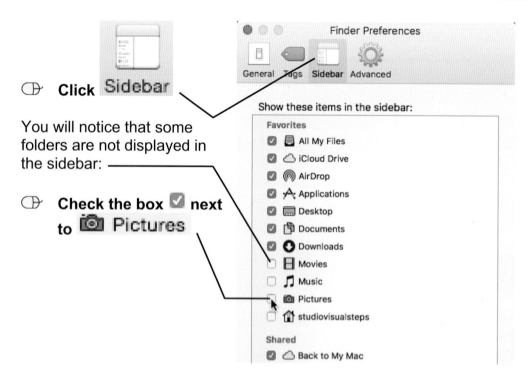

Click Sidebar

You will notice that some folders are not displayed in the sidebar: ────────

Check the box ☑ next to 📷 Pictures

☞ **Close the *Finder Preferences* window** ✌12

The folder has been added to the sidebar:

Click 📷 Pictures

You will see the photos:

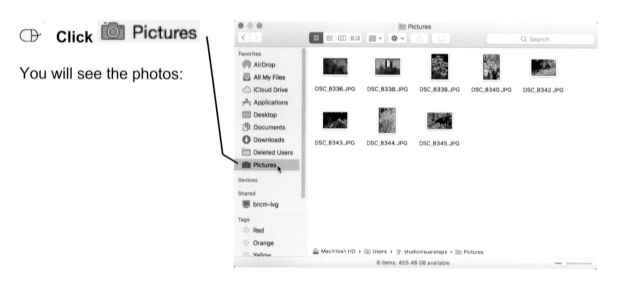

6.3 Viewing Photos in Preview

 Please note:
From this point on you can use the practice files that come with this chapter to follow the examples. That way what you see on your screen will be the same as the screenshots in this book. You can download these practice files from the website accompanying this book and import them into *Finder*. You can read how to do that in *Appendix C Downloading the Practice Files*.

☞ **Follow the steps in *Appendix C Downloading the Practice Files***

☞ **If necessary, open *Finder*** ⬚⬚26

Photos are automatically opened in the *Preview* application:

🖰 **If necessary, click**
    📷 **Pictures** ⎯⎯⎯

You see the practice photos:

🖰 **If necessary, click**
    ⬚⬚
    ⬚⬚ ⎯⎯⎯

🖰 **Double-click**

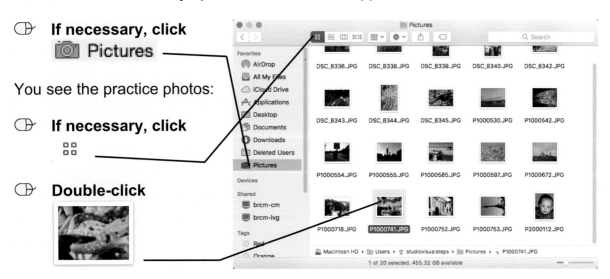

You will see the photo in the *Preview* window:

HELP! The photo opens in another program.

If another program has opened, it means that this program has been set as the standard program to open photos on your Mac. You can still open the photo in *Preview* by doing the following:

☞ **Quit the program** 👣78

In *Finder*:

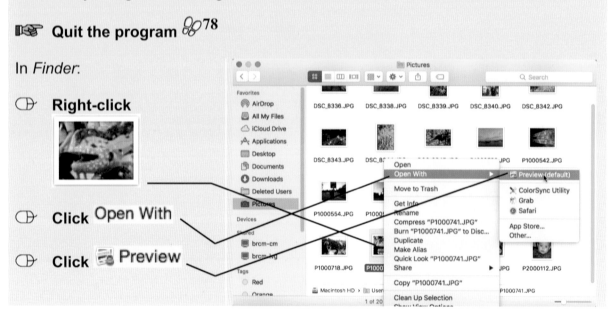

☞ **Right-click**

☞ **Click** Open With

☞ **Click** 📷 Preview

You can zoom in on the photo like this:

⊕ **Click** 🔍⊕ **twice**

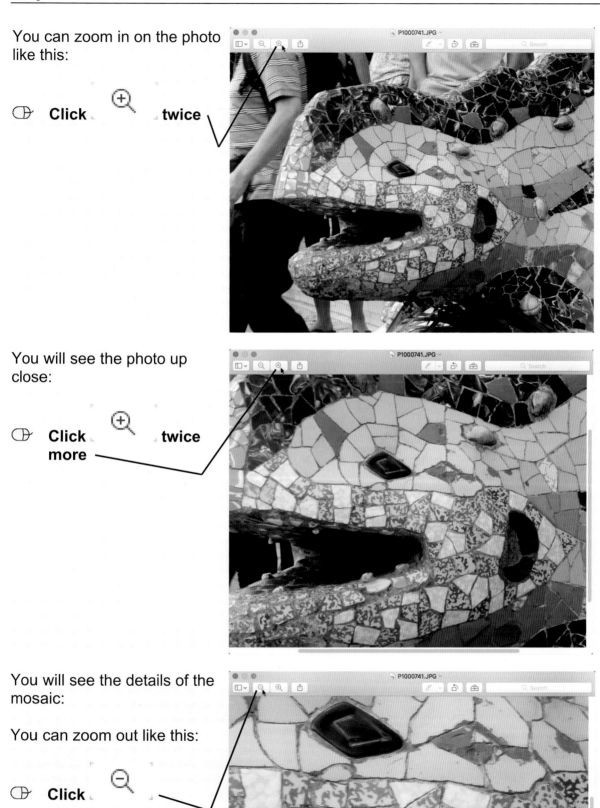

You will see the photo up close:

⊕ **Click** 🔍⊕ **twice more**

You will see the details of the mosaic:

You can zoom out like this:

⊕ **Click** 🔍⊖

Tip

Other ways to zoom

You can also zoom in and out in a similar way as you do in *Safari*:

⊕   **Tap the Magic Mouse twice in rapid succession**

Or:

☞   **Tap the (Magic) trackpad twice in rapid succession**

To zoom in with a keyboard combination:

To zoom out:

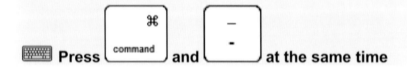

To fit the photo in the window:

⊕   **Click** View

⊕   **Click** Zoom to Fit

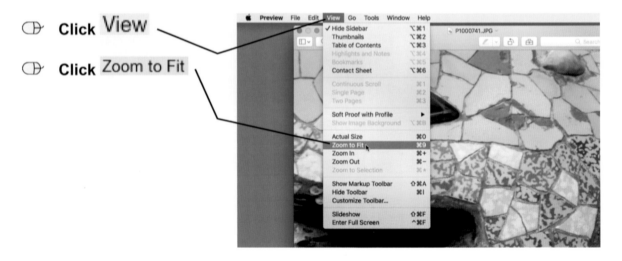

You will see the entire photo
once more:

It is also possible to use a magnifying glass to take a closer look at the details of the
photo. That can be done as follows:

☞ **Click** Tools

☞ **Click**
Show Magnifier

The pointer will change into a magnifying glass.

☞ **Move the magnifier
over the photo**

When you no longer need the
magnifier:

⌨ **Press** ⎋ ESC

The magnifier will disappear.

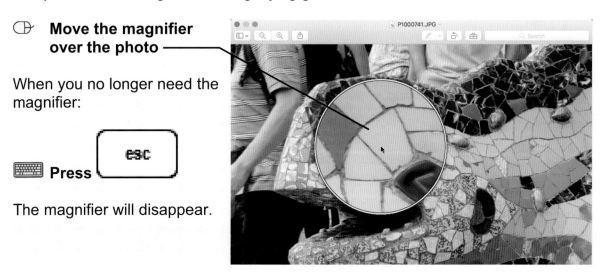

You can also view a photo in full screen mode:

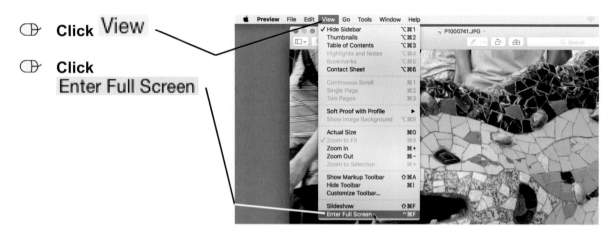

⊕ **Click** View

⊕ **Click**
    Enter Full Screen

Depending on the size of your
screen, the picture will be
displayed full screen, with or
without black edges:

To close the full screen view:

 **Press** esc

☞ **Close the** *Preview* **window** 🐾 12

6.4 Photo Editing

Preview offers a number of options for editing and enhancing photos. For example,
you can:
- rotate photos;
- correct photos automatically;
- adjust the exposure;
- crop photos;
- adjust the color;
- use the sepia effect.

You will try these options with the practice files.

6.5 Rotating a Photo

Another common problem that happens to pictures taken with a digital camera is that they are not displayed in the correct orientation and need to be rotated. This is easily done in *Preview*. You can practice rotating a photo with the photo of the Sagrada Familia in Barcelona:

☞ **Double-click**

The photo will be opened in *Preview*:

☞ **Click**

The photo will be rotated to the left, now the image is upside down:

☞ **Click** **twice more**

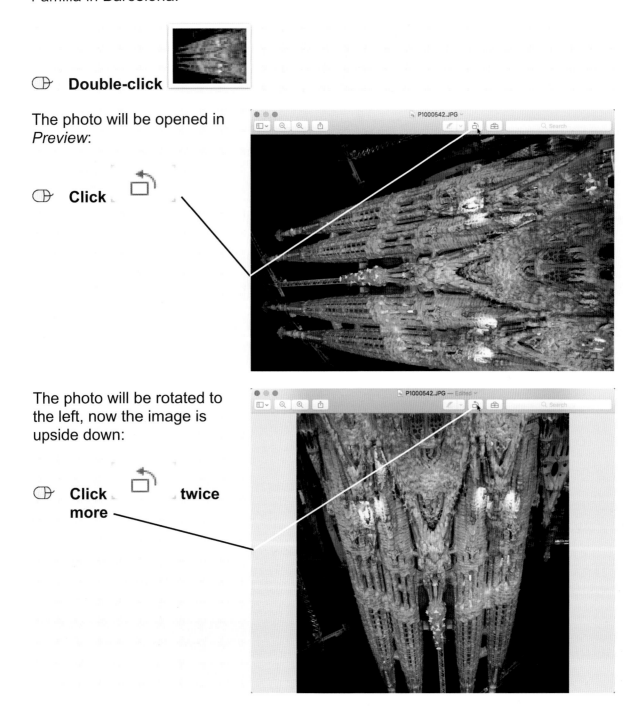

Now the photo is in the
correct position:

☞ **Close the *Preview* window** ⚆⚆[12]

6.6 Automatic Enhancement of Photos

Sometimes, your pictures turn out to be too dark or too light. The practice files
contain a photo that was taken on a dark day.

⊕ **Double-click**

The photo is dark and the colors are quite grayer. *Preview* contains tools to fix this
problem. First you open the *Markup Toolbar*:

⊕ **Click**

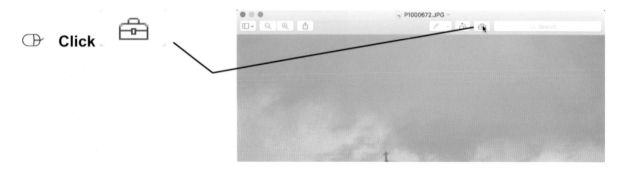

You select the tool to adjust the color of a photo. This tool also contains options to adjust the exposure and the *Auto Levels* function. The Auto Levels function gives you the option of applying a quick, automatic fix to an unsatisfactory photo:

☞ **Click**

To apply an automatic fix:

☞ **Click**
Auto Levels

This function analyzes the *histogram* that you see above the button. A histogram is a graph that shows the distribution of light and dark in a picture. Based on this analysis, a correction is made.

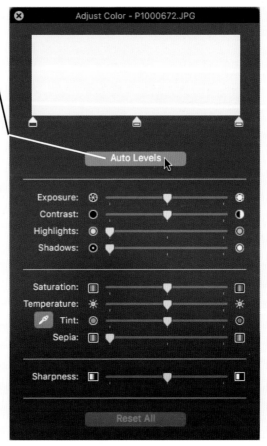

You see the result right away:

The photo has become brighter:

You can close the *Adjust Color* window:

 **Click** ⊗

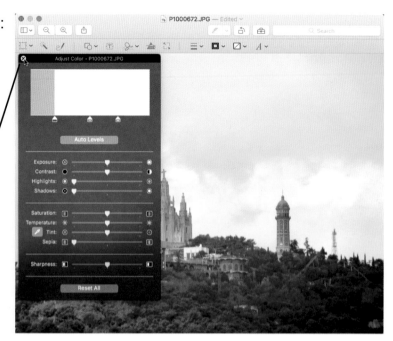

Automatic enhancement does not always produce the desired result right away. You may need to enhance the photo in other ways. In the next section you can read how to manually adjust the exposure of a photo.

☞ **Close the** *Preview* **window** ✂¹²

6.7 Adjusting the Exposure

You can open another photo where the exposure is not very good:

 **Double-click**

This photo probably should have been taken with the camera's flash. The foreground is too dark, and the sky is too light. You can try adjusting the light with the Auto Levels function:

Click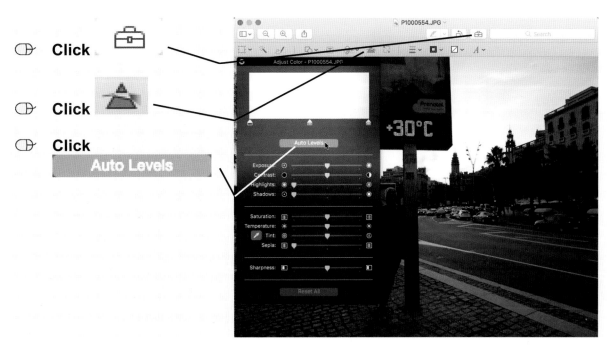

Click

Click

You will see that this adjustment does not have a lot of effect:

To undo this change:

Click

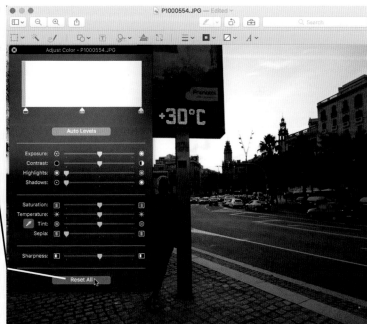

The *Adjust Color* window contains several other tools to adjust the exposure of a photo. First, you can make the shadows lighter:

☞ **By** `Shadows:` **, drag the slider ⬜ to the middle**

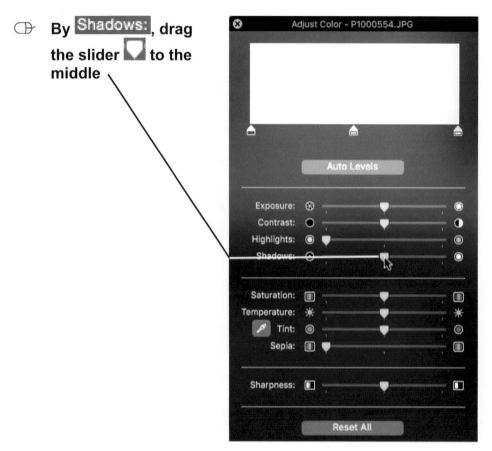

The dark areas of the photo have become lighter:

Now you can make the light areas darker:

⊕ **By** Highlights:**, drag the slider ▽ to the right**

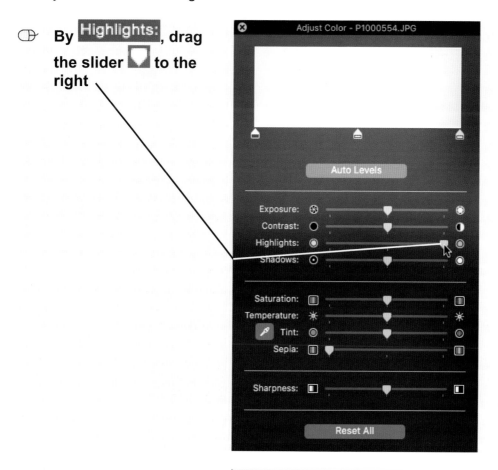

The sky is less bright and you see some more detail in the clouds:

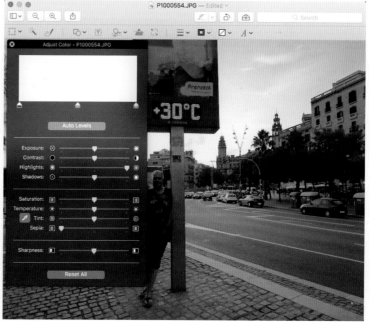

Now you make the entire photo a bit lighter:

☞   **By** Exposure:**, drag**
     the slider  **a little bit**
     to the right

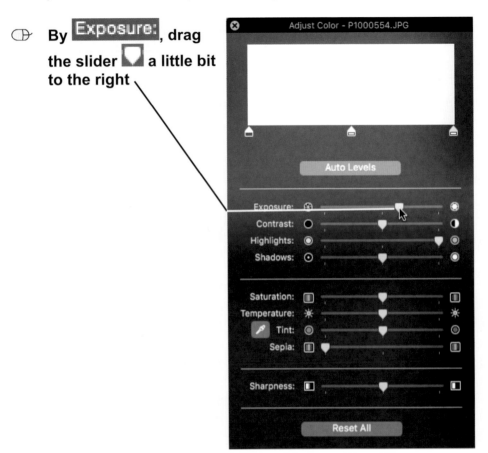

The exposure of the photo is
more balanced now. It will
never be a very good picture,
but you will see more clearly
what is in the picture:

You can close the *Adjust
Color* window:

☞   **Click** ❌

6.8 Cropping a Photo

Sometimes, you see items that you do not want to display in a picture. By cropping the image, you can decide which part of the photo you want to keep. If you crop the photo shown here for example, you can remove the large digital temperature display:

The Rectangular Selection

tool  is selected by default:

By dragging a frame on top of the photo, you can select the part of the photo you want to crop:

☞ **Position the pointer on the photo**

☞ **Hold the mouse button/trackpad down**

☞ **Drag to the bottom right**

As soon as the frame is big enough:

☞ **Release the mouse button/trackpad**

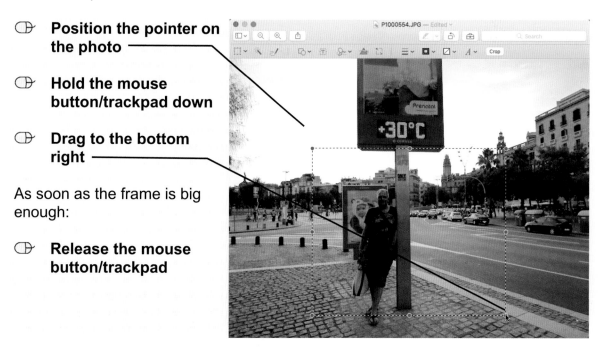

Now you can move the frame:

- ☞ **Position the pointer inside the frame** ——
- ☞ **Hold the mouse button/trackpad down**
- ☞ **Drag the frame to the right and down**

When the frame is in the correct position:

- ☞ **Release the mouse button/trackpad**

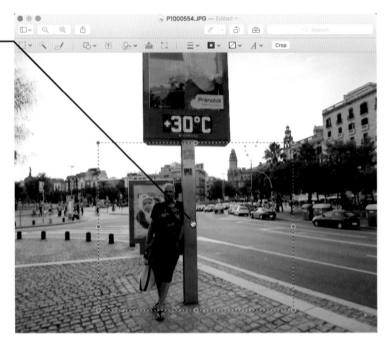

Now you can finish the cropping process:

- ☞ **Click** `Crop`

Here you see the result:

6.9 Revert to the Original Photo

If you are not satisfied with the result of an edit you have made, you can restore the original photo. In *Preview*, different versions of an edited file are saved automatically, just like in *TextEdit*. To view the previous versions of the photo:

☞ **Click** File

☞ **Click** Revert To

☞ **Click** Browse All Versions...

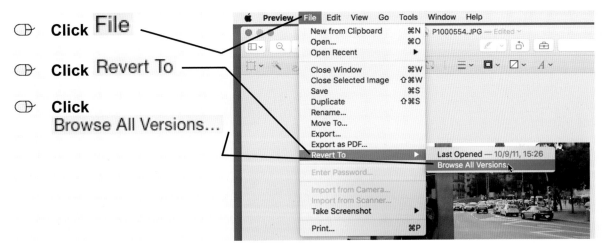

Here you see the photo in its current state:

Here you see a stack of different versions of this photo:

Below the selected version you see the date and time of when it was saved:

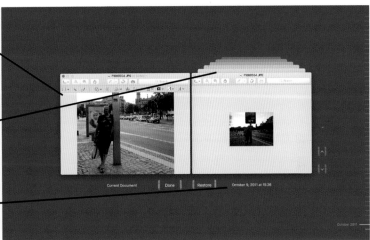

You can scroll through the different versions using the

buttons [^] and [v] :

You can also view the various versions by using the timeline:

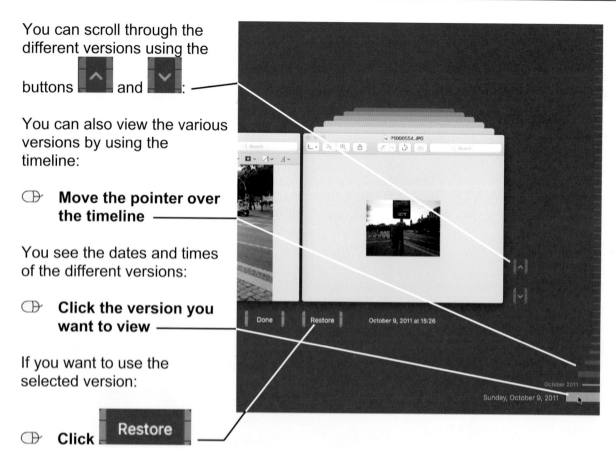

☞ **Move the pointer over the timeline** ——

You see the dates and times of the different versions:

☞ **Click the version you want to view** ——

If you want to use the selected version:

☞ **Click** Restore ——

You will see the original, dark, un-cropped photo once more.

☞ **Close the *Preview* window** ⏀¹²

6.10 Adjusting the Colors

In *Preview* you can also adjust the colors of a photo.

☞ **Double-click** [thumbnail]

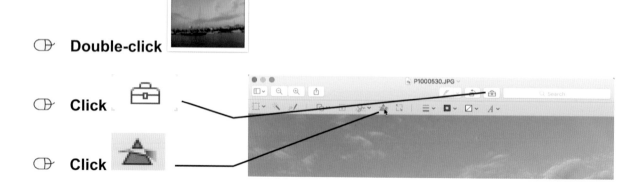

☞ **Click** 🧰

☞ **Click** 🔺

Before you adjust the colors of a photo, it is a good idea to correct the exposure first. This photo is a bit dark:

Click

You will see the effect, the photo has become a lot brighter:

The photo of the harbor was taken at sunset. This is why the buildings have an orange glow. If you want, you can correct this by adjusting the color temperature. The *Adjust Color* window contains a slider to adjust the color temperature of the photo. The photo contains a lot of red/orange hues (warm) and could become a bit bluer (cooler):

By Temperature:, **drag the slider to the left**

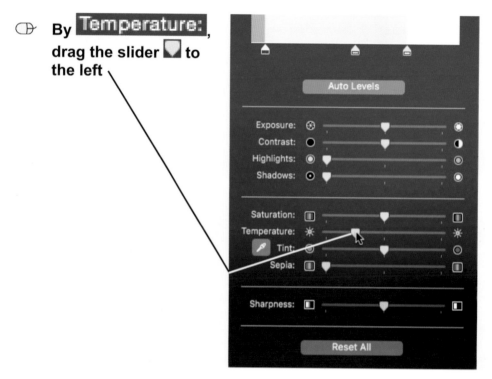

You will see the water become bluer and the houses will become less orange:

Now the sky has a pink/purple hue:

You can remove the pink hue by adding some green:

⊕ **Drag the slider** ▽ **by**
`Tint:` a little bit to
the left

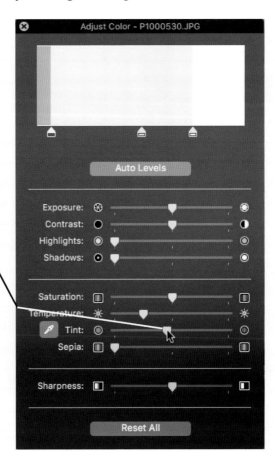

The colors look more natural
now:

You can also radically change a photo and turn it into something old-fashioned looking, if you want:

☞ **By Sepia:, drag the slider to the right**

The photo will take on a yellow/brownish hue:

You can remove the pink hue by adding some green:

🖱️ **Drag the slider ⬜ by `Tint:` a little bit to the left**

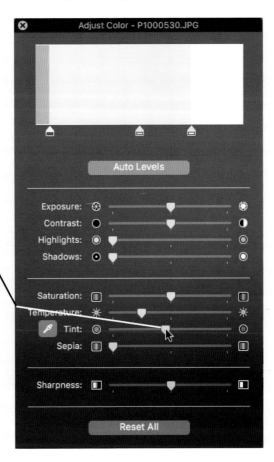

The colors look more natural now:

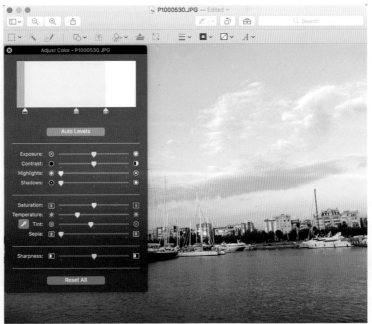

You can also radically change a photo and turn it into something old-fashioned looking, if you want:

➪ **By** `Sepia:` **, drag the slider ▼ to the right**

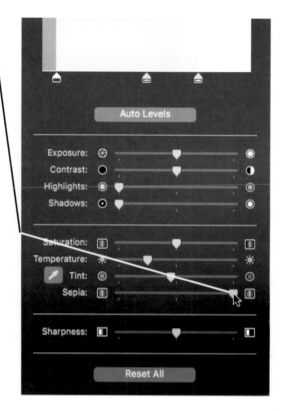

The photo will take on a yellow/brownish hue:

If you want to make the photo look even older, you can reduce the sharpness:

By  **Sharpness:** ,
drag the slider ⬇ to
the left

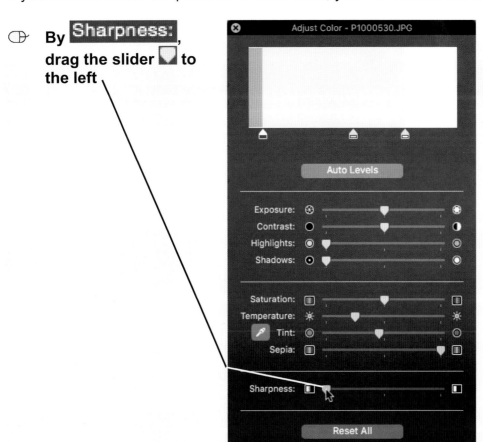

The photo looks blurry:

You can close the *Adjust Color* window:

Click ❌

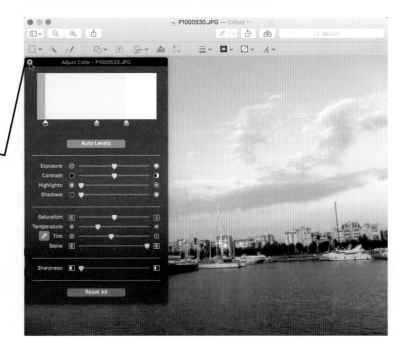

You have been introduced to a few of the options available for editing photos in *Preview*. You can use the skills you have acquired to start editing your own photos.

Now you can quit *Preview*:

☞ **Quit *Preview*** ⬈78

You can also close the *Finder* window:

☞ **Close the *Finder* window** ⬈12

6.11 Opening iTunes

iTunes is a media management program that lets you sort, play and add to your music collection. You can import music from a CD, edit the information about your music files and create playlists. You can use *iTunes* to burn MP3 CDs and DVDs. In the following sections you will be transferring music (importing) from a CD to the Mac. This means you will have a few music files stored on your computer and you will be able to listen to them right from your computer.

⊕ **Click**

If you are using *iTunes* for the first time, you will need to agree to the terms of the software licensing agreement:

⊕ **If necessary, click**
Agree

You will see the *iTunes* window:

⊕ **Click**

iTunes offers to take you to the *iTunes Store*, or scan your hard drive for media (music and videos):

You do not have to do either of these right now.

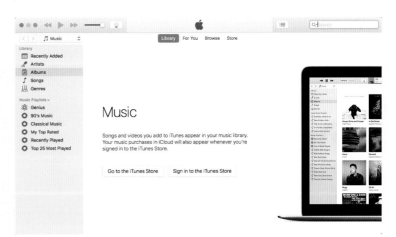

6.12 Importing a CD

In *iTunes* you can copy the tracks from a music CD and convert them to files that can be used by the computer. In *iTunes* this is called importing a CD. In other music programs it is called 'ripping'.

 Please note:

The Mac mini and the MacBook Air and the latest versions of the iMac and MacBook Pro are not equipped with a built-in CD/DVD player. You can connect an external CD/DVD player, or just read through the following sections if you like. If you don't have a built-in CD/DVD player you can also buy music in the *iTunes Store*. You will find more information about this in the *Bonus Chapter Downloading Apps and Music*. You can find more information about the bonus chapter in *Appendix B Opening Bonus Chapters*.

On the older iMac, the
CD/DVD player is located on
the right side of the screen:

☞ **Carefully insert the CD
into the slot, with the
printed side towards
you**

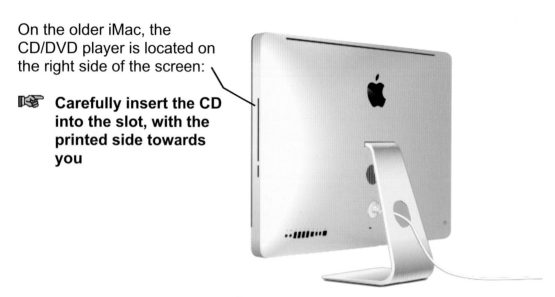

Source: iMac User Guide

On the older version of the
MacBook Pro, the CD/DVD
player can be found on the
right side of the keyboard:

☞ **Carefully insert the CD
into the slot, with the
printed side up**

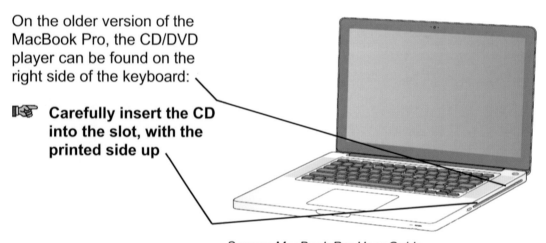

Source: MacBook Pro User Guide

If your computer is connected to the Internet, *iTunes* will search for information about
the CD. In this example multiple matches are found:

🖰 **Click the title that
matches the CD you
inserted**

🖰 **Click** **OK**

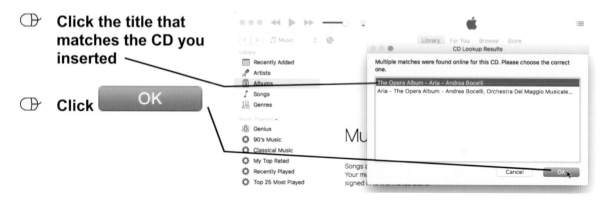

The titles of the songs on the CD (also called tracks), will automatically appear on the screen:

Here you see the title and length of the CD:

Here you see all the titles of the tracks on the CD:

A small popup window appears and *iTunes* asks if you want to import the CD:

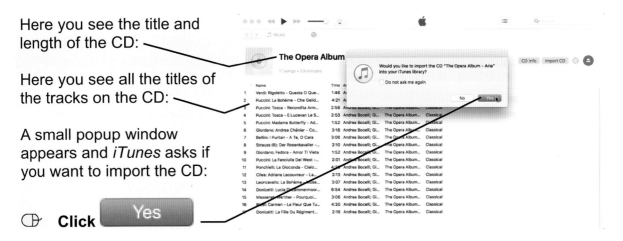

 Click Yes

You can view the progress of the importing process in the *iTunes* window:

Next to the track that is currently being imported, you will see the 🔄 symbol in the list:

By default, all tracks have been checked ✓ and will be imported:

In the information pane you can see which track is being imported and the status of the operation:

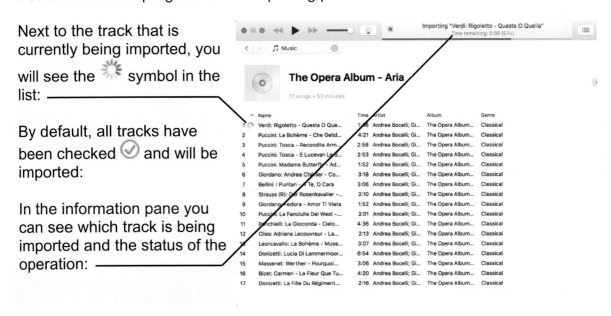

The tracks are imported one by one.

🪝 Please note:

It may take a little while to import all the tracks.

Once the CD has been imported, you will hear a sound signal.

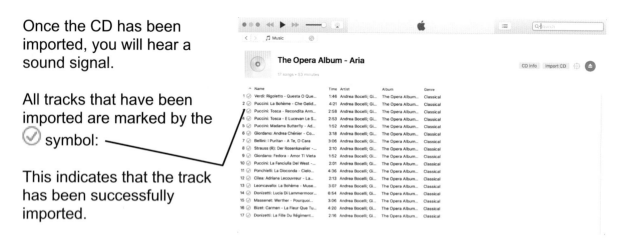

All tracks that have been imported are marked by the ⊘ symbol: ⎯⎯⎯

This indicates that the track has been successfully imported.

Now you can remove the CD/DVD from the CD/DVD drive. You do that like this:

⊕ **Click** ⏏ ⎯⎯⎯⎯⎯⎯⎯⎯⎯

On your own computer, you will see a different CD title.

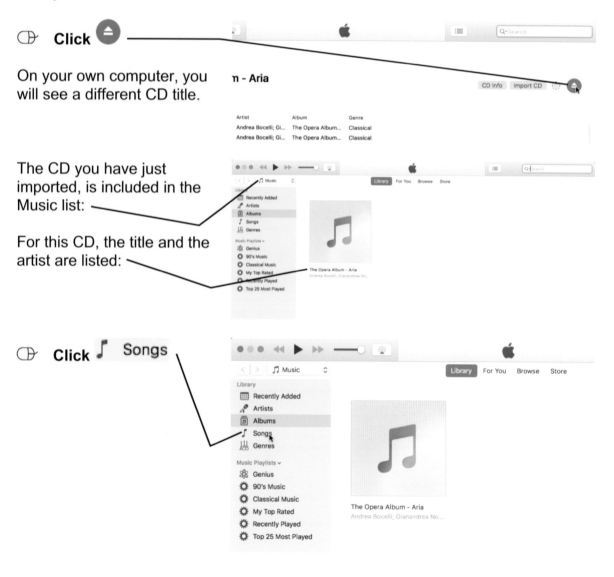

The CD you have just imported, is included in the Music list: ⎯⎯⎯

For this CD, the title and the artist are listed: ⎯⎯⎯

⊕ **Click** ♪ **Songs**

You will see the songs that
you have just imported:

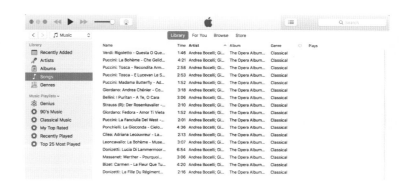

6.13 Playing Music

You can easily play music in *iTunes*. For example, you can play the music you just
imported in the previous step.

You can practice playing music by playing the first track of the imported CD:

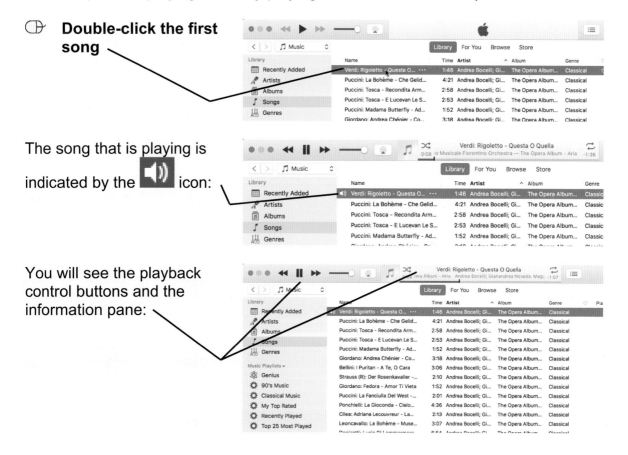

Double-click the first
song

The song that is playing is
indicated by the 🔊 icon:

You will see the playback
control buttons and the
information pane:

You can pause play by

clicking ▮▮ :

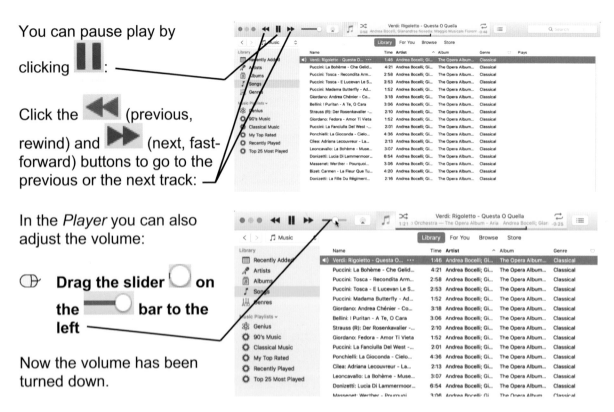

Click the ◀◀ (previous,

rewind) and ▶▶ (next, fast-
forward) buttons to go to the
previous or the next track:

In the *Player* you can also
adjust the volume:

👆 **Drag the slider ⬜ on**
the ▬⬜ bar to the
left

Now the volume has been
turned down.

One of the *iTunes* functions that you may already be familiar with (from your regular
CD player), is the option that lets you randomly play tracks. This option is also called
shuffle. Here is how you use the shuffle option in *iTunes*:

In the top right of the
information pane:

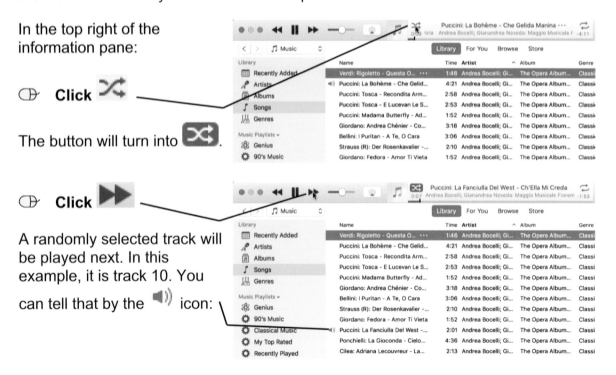

👆 **Click** ✕

The button will turn into ⊠ .

👆 **Click** ▶▶

A randomly selected track will
be played next. In this
example, it is track 10. You
can tell that by the 🔊 icon:

To turn off shuffle play:

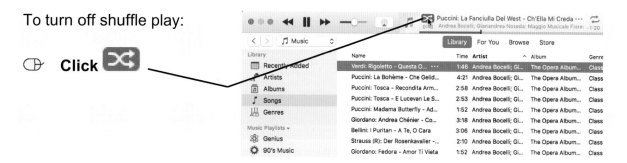

⊕ **Click** 🔀

There is another button that lets you repeat the same CD or track over and over again. This button will appear in the information pane when you activate the option:

⊕ **Click** Controls

⊕ **Click** Repeat

⊕ **Click** All

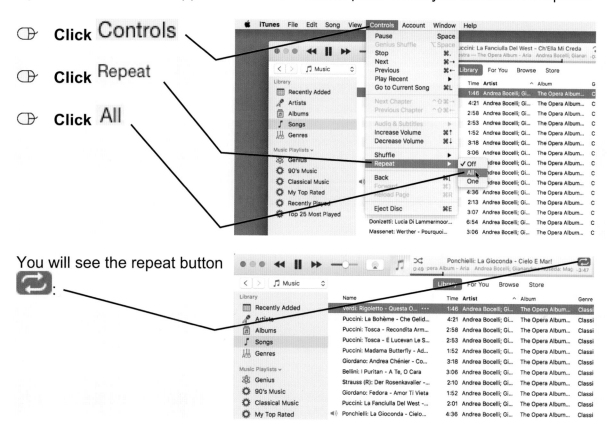

You will see the repeat button

🔁:

When the CD has finished, it will be played again.

You can also repeat a single track:

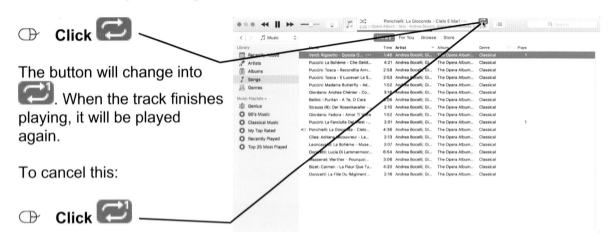

Click [repeat icon]

The button will change into [repeat one icon]. When the track finishes playing, it will be played again.

To cancel this:

Click [repeat one icon]

The button will change into [repeat icon]. This button disappears when the next song starts.

While you are playing music with *iTunes*, you can use your computer for other activities. Here is how to turn the *iTunes* window into a *mini player*:

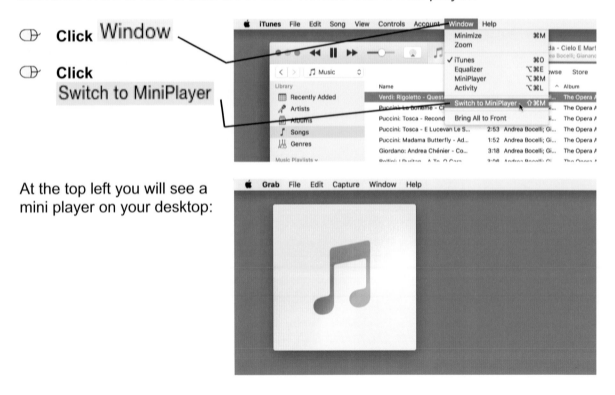

Click Window

Click Switch to MiniPlayer

At the top left you will see a mini player on your desktop:

⊕ **Slide the mouse pointer over the mini player**

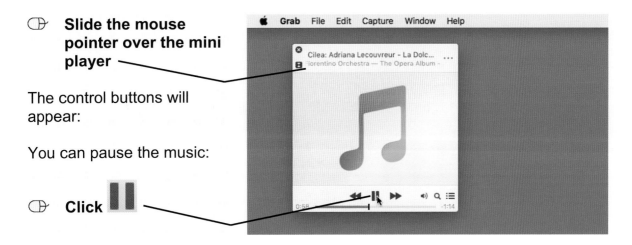

The control buttons will appear:

You can pause the music:

⊕ **Click** ▌▌

To return to the full screen view of the *iTunes* window:

⊕ **Click** Window

⊕ **Click** Switch from MiniPlayer

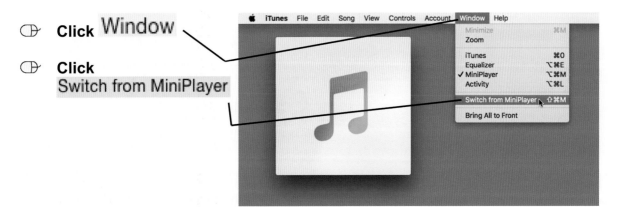

☞ **Close the *iTunes* window** 🦶12

Now you can close (quit) the program:

⊕ **Click** iTunes

⊕ **Click** Quit iTunes

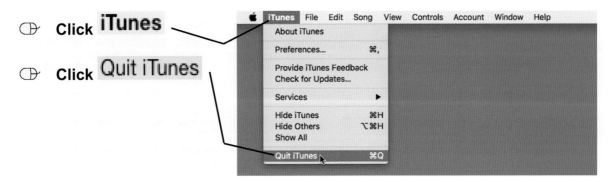

6.14 Playing a Video File

In this example we will be using the video file from the practice files. If you followed the steps in *Appendix C Downloading the Practice Files* you will have copied this folder to the *Pictures* folder on your Mac. Here is how you play a video file:

☞ **Open** *Finder* 👣²⁶

👆 **Click**  **Pictures**

👆 **If necessary, drag the scroll bar down**

👆 **Double-click**

Video file Mac.mov

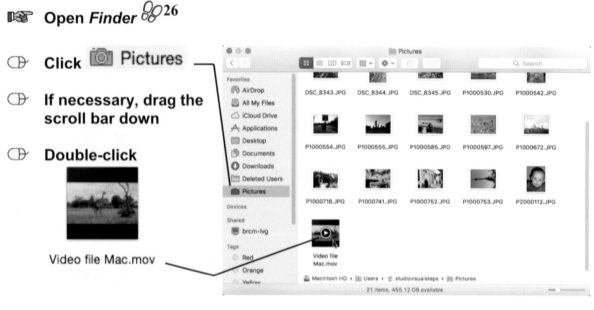

The video will be opened in the *QuickTime Player* program:

You can play the video:

👆 **Slide the mouse pointer over the window**

👆 **Click** ▶

You can adjust the volume with the slider : —————————

Here are the buttons to rewind or fast forward : —————————

You can display the video in full screen mode:

👆 **Click** ———

The video is displayed full screen:

Use the Esc key to return to the previous view:

⌨ **Press** | esc |

Now the video is displayed in a smaller window.

👉 **Close the window with the video file** 👣[12]

👉 **Quit** *Quick Time Player* 👣[78]

👉 **Close** *Finder* 👣[12]

In the next section you will learn how to play a DVD with *DVD Player*.

6.15 Playing a DVD

It is easy to play a DVD with the *DVD Player* program that comes with *MacOS*.

 Please note:

The Mac mini and the MacBook Air and the latest versions of the iMac and MacBook Pro are not equipped with a built-in CD/DVD player. You can connect an external CD/DVD player, or just read through the following sections if you like.

 Please note:

To carry out the actions in the following steps you will need to have a DVD, for example, a DVD with a movie or a TV series. If you do not have a DVD, you can just read through this section.

When a DVD is inserted into the CD/DVD station, the *DVD Player* program opens and starts playing the DVD automatically. This is the default setting in *MacOS*:

☞ **Insert a DVD into your computer's CD/DVD station**

The *DVD Player* program will open at once. If the program is opening for the very first time, you may see a window where you need to select the correct region code for your DVD player. For the USA and Canada it is region 1, for Europe it is region 2 and for Australia it is region 4.

☞ **If necessary, follow the onscreen instructions**

Now the *DVD Player* program will be started and you will see the opening scenes of the DVD. Almost every DVD has a built-in menu where you can select the languages for the subtitles, among other playback options. You can also use this menu to select a specific part of the DVD to view.

The DVD that is used in this example automatically displays the main menu, right after the copyright messages:

To play the movie:

 Click

 Please note:

The structure of the main menu can differ with each DVD. You may need to scroll through various menu options on your own DVD, before you reach the main menu or the subtitles settings.

The movie or TV episode begins in full screen mode:

While you are playing the video full screen, you will see a command bar at the bottom of the screen every time you move the pointer:

These are the functions for the various buttons:

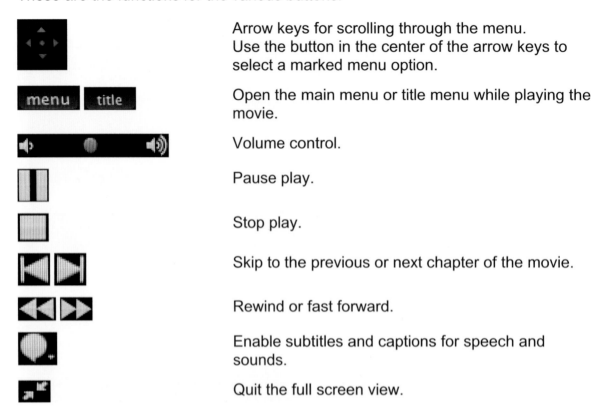

Arrow keys for scrolling through the menu.
Use the button in the center of the arrow keys to select a marked menu option.

Open the main menu or title menu while playing the movie.

Volume control.

Pause play.

Stop play.

Skip to the previous or next chapter of the movie.

Rewind or fast forward.

Enable subtitles and captions for speech and sounds.

Quit the full screen view.

Now you can close the full screen view:

 **Click**

 Tip
Another method for quitting the full screen view
You can also close the full screen view with a single action by pressing the Esc key.

 **Press** [esc]

When the *DVD Player* window is minimized, you will see the control panel of the *DVD Player* with similar buttons. To stop the DVD from playing altogether:

Click

HELP! I cannot see the control panel.

If the control panel is hidden, you can open it from the *Dock*:

⊕ **Click**

Now you can eject the DVD and close *DVD Player*.

⊕ **Click** eject

☞ **Quit** *DVD Player* 👣78

In this chapter you have learned how to work with several of the Mac's built-in programs: *Image Capture*, *Preview*, *iTunes*, *Quick Time Player* and the *DVD Player*. In the next chapter you will learn how to modify the settings of your computer to better suit your needs and requirements.

6.16 Exercises

The following exercises will help you master what you have just learned. Have you forgotten how to do something? Use the number beside the footsteps $\mathscr{Y}$[1] to look it up in the appendix *How Do I Do That Again?* at the end of the book.

Exercise: Photo Editing

In this exercise you will repeat the actions necessary to edit a photo in *Preview*.

☞ Open *Finder*. $\mathscr{Y}$[26]

☞ Open the *Pictures* folder. $\mathscr{Y}$[80]

☞ Open the photo. $\mathscr{Y}$[79]

☞ Rotate the photo, until it is upright. $\mathscr{Y}$[81]

☞ Revert to the original photo. $\mathscr{Y}$[82]

☞ Close the *Preview* window. $\mathscr{Y}$[12]

☞ Open the photo. $\mathscr{Y}$[79]

☞ Display the *Markup Toolbar*. $\mathscr{Y}$[83]

☞ Crop the photo so that it contains just the house. $\mathscr{Y}$[84]

☞ Open the *Adjust Color* window. $\mathscr{Y}$[85]

☞ Change the photo color to sepia. $\mathscr{Y}$[86]

☞ Revert to the original photo. $\mathscr{Y}$[82]

☞ Quit *Preview*. $\mathscr{Y}$[78]

☞ Close *Finder*. $\mathscr{Y}$[12]

Exercise: Import a CD in iTunes

In this exercise you will repeat the process of importing a CD into *iTunes*.

☞ Open *iTunes*. &*87*

☞ Insert a CD into the CD/DVD station.

☞ Import the music. &*88*

☞ Remove the CD/DVD from the CD/DVD station. &*89*

Exercise: Play Music

In this exercise you repeat the actions needed to play music.

☞ Play the music in *iTunes*. &*90*

☞ Play the songs in shuffle mode. &*91*

☞ Switch to the mini player. &*92*

☞ Return to the *iTunes* window. &*93*

☞ Close the *iTunes* window. &*12*

☞ Quit *iTunes*. &*78*

Exercise: View a DVD

In this exercise you are going to repeat the actions needed to use the *DVD Player*.

☞ Insert a DVD into the CD/DVD station.

☞ Play the DVD in *DVD Player*. &*94*

☞ Close the full screen view. &*95*

☞ Quit *DVD Player*. &*78*

6.17 Background Information

Dictionary

Crop	Removing certain parts of a picture to focus attention on a particular area.
DVD Player	A program with which you can play DVDs.
Image Capture	An *Apple* program that lets you transfer photos from digital cameras, scanners or other devices to your computer through a network or cable connected to your computer.
Import	Transferring digital photos from a digital camera or other device to your computer. Also refers to the transferring of music files from a CD, for example, to the Mac.
iTunes	A program that lets you play CDs, import music from CDs or purchase music in the *iTunes Store*. The media files can be arranged by album, artist, playlist and more. Playlists can be burned to a disc, or transferred to an iPad, iPhone, iPod or other media player.
iTunes Store	An online store linked to *iTunes*. Here you can listen to audio fragments for free and download songs or albums for a fee. In the *iTunes Store* you can buy not only music, but games, movies, TV series, ringtones and more.
Preview	A program that lets you view PDF files, images, text documents, and many other types of files on your Mac.
QuickTime Player	The multimedia playback application included with *MacOS* that can play audio, MP3 music files, movies as well as many other file types. There is also a version for *Windows*.
Rotate	Turn an image sideways to the left or right, usually a quarter turn.
SD card	Short for *Secure Digital* card. A memory card about the size of a stamp, used by digital cameras and smartphones to store data.

- Continue on the next page -

Sepia	A yellow/brown shade often seen in old photographs.
Shuffle	Play tracks on a CD or in a playlist in random order.
Slideshow	Successive display of a group of pictures on a full screen.
Template	A document containing standard data that can be used as a basis for a new document. For instance, *Mail* offers various templates for creating email messages with sample texts, background images and space for your own photos.

Source: Apple Dictionary, Wikipedia

6.18 Tips

 Tip
Slideshow
In *Preview* you can also display your photos in a slideshow. You can choose from various animated themes, each with its own soundtrack. First you need to open multiple pictures in *Preview*:

☞ **Open** *Finder* 👣²⁶

⊕ **Click** 📷 **Pictures**

⊕ **Click** ≡

⊕ **Click the first photo**

⊕ **Press** [Shift] **and hold it down**

⊕ **Click the last photo**

⊕ **Release** [Shift]

Now you open the selected photos in *Preview*:

⊕ **Right-click on the selected photos**

⊕ **Click** Open With

⊕ **Click** 🖼 Preview

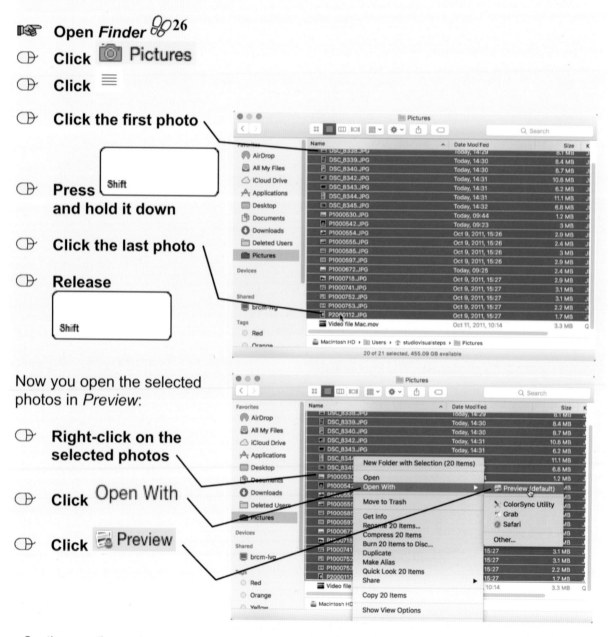

- Continue on the next page -

You will see the first photo:

On the left you see a sidebar that contains thumbnails of all the photos that are open:

This is how you start the slideshow:

⊕ **Click** View

⊕ **Click** Slideshow

The slideshow begins. The photos will be displayed one by one:

To stop the slideshow:

⊕ **Click** ⊗

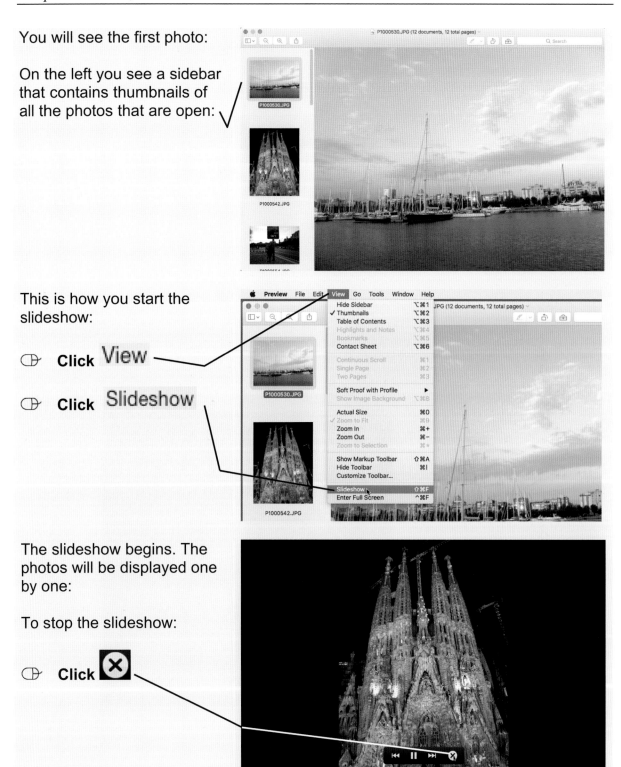

💡 Tip

Removing a color cast
Preview contains a handy tool to quickly remove a color cast from a photo:

 Open *Finder* ⏻⏻²⁶

Click 📷 Pictures

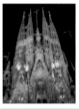

Double-click

Click 🧰

Click ⛰️

This photo of the Sagrada Familia cathedral in Barcelona was taken at night. Although the cathedral was lit by various spotlights, the picture is still quite dark and has a yellowish hue:

You can adjust the exposure:

Click
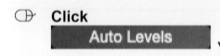

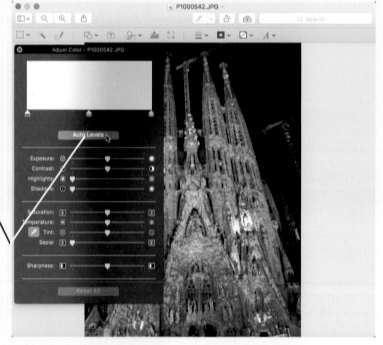

- Continue on the next page -

The photo has become a bit brighter:

⬥ By 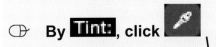, click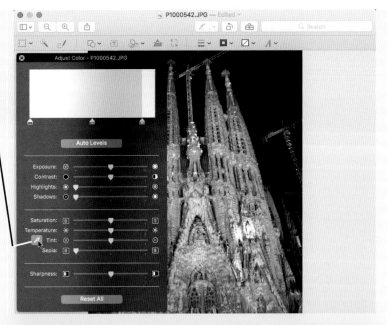

The pointer has changed into a pipette 🖋. Use this pipette to click a part of the photo that is supposed to be white or gray, in this case one of the doves on the middle tower:

⬥ **Click a dove**

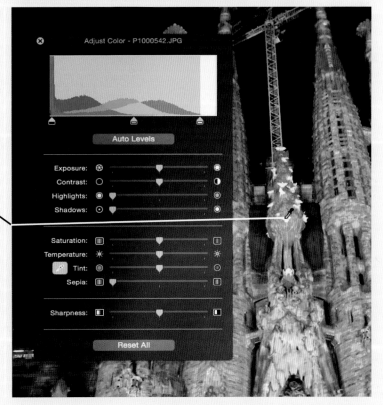

- Continue on the next page -

The yellow hue has mostly disappeared:

💡 Tip

Use templates with photos
In *Mail* you can easily send an email message with an attractive background and a photo, by using *templates*:

☞ **Open *Mail*** 🐾65

☞ **Open a new email message** 🐾59

Open the templates pane:

👆 **Click**

- Continue on the next page -

You will see all sorts of templates for emails, suitable for various occasions:

⊕ **Click**

⊕ **Click a template**

You can replace the text in the template by your own message. By adding your own photos, you can personalize your message and create an authentic, surprising and original email. You can replace the photos in the template by dragging your own photos from *Finder*.

☞ **Open** *Finder* 🐾²⁶

⊕ **Click** 📷 **Pictures**

⊕ **Position the pointer on a photo** ────────

⊕ **Hold the mouse button/trackpad down**

⊕ **Drag the photo to one of the photos in the template** ──────

⊕ **Release the mouse button/trackpad**

Now the photo has been pasted into the template: ────

You can use this same method to replace all the photos.

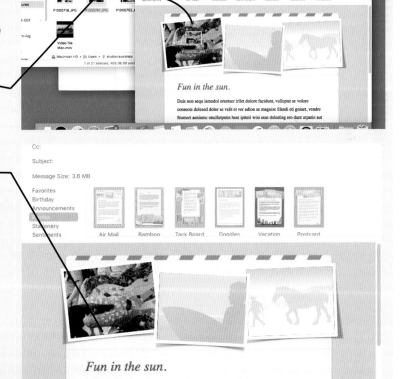

💡 Tip

Sending photos as attachments
Instead of using the template, you can also send an email with photos as an attachment:

☞ **Open** *Mail* 😙⁶⁵

☞ **Open a new email message** 😙⁵⁹

☞ **Add a photo as an attachment** 😙⁶⁷

You can also add multiple photos by holding ⌘ command down while selecting photos.

When you send a message with photos as attachments, bear in mind that there is a maximum message size. You might not be able to send many photo files at once, or very large photo files. Also take into account that the recipient's mailbox may become full as a result of your email. If the size limit has been exceeded you will receive an error message.

Hotmail has a 10 MB maximum email size limit for emails sent or received. For *Gmail*, *Yahoo Mail* and *AOL* the size limit is 25 MB.

Before you send an email with photos attached, you can check the size of the attached files:

In this example the message size is 3.1 MB with three photos attached:

The photos have been attached in their Actual Size:

- Continue on the next page -

You can reduce the size of the photos like this:

☞ **Click** Actual Size ↕ , Small

Now the message size has been reduced to 45 KB:

This means you can attach a lot more photos before you reach the maximum email size limit.

💡 **Tip**

Pick the next song

When you already know what song you want to hear next, you can put it in a queue:

☞ **Place the mouse pointer on the song you want to hear next**

☞ **Right-click the song**

☞ **Click Play Next**

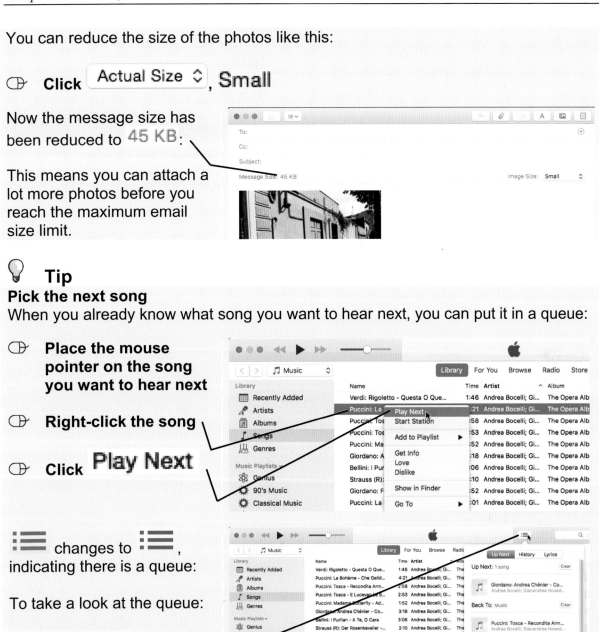

≣ changes to ≣, indicating there is a queue:

To take a look at the queue:

☞ **Click** ≣

Notes

Write your notes down here.

7. Customizing Settings to Suit Your Needs

There are many components on your computer for which you can adjust the settings yourself to suit your own needs and preferences. Changing the settings on your computer is worth the trouble. It can make difficult operations a bit easier and in the long term, it can also prevent harmful side-effects such as R.S.I. from occurring. For instance, you can adjust the mouse in such a way that you can more easily work with it. This will prevent you from overburdening your wrist.

In this chapter you will read about a number of features on your computer that you can easily customize. We will pay special attention to the items that can be important for your motor skills, your eyesight and your sense of hearing.
You can freely experiment with these settings to discover whether the new settings are an improvement or not. Just give it a try. All the settings you have changed can easily be reset to their original status.

In this chapter you will learn how to:

- adjust the settings for the mouse and/or trackpad;
- change the wallpaper for your desktop;
- adjust the size of the icons;
- adjust the *Finder* window;
- change the sound settings;
- using Split View.

7.1 Adjusting the Mouse and the Trackpad

To make it easier to use the mouse or the trackpad, you can adjust some of the settings. To change settings, you first need to open the *System Preferences* window from the *Dock*:

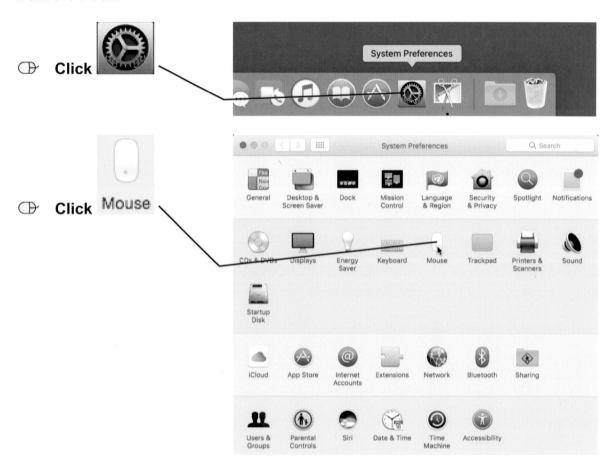

☞ **Click** [System Preferences icon]

☞ **Click Mouse**

One of the settings you can change is the speed of the mouse. The mouse speed determines the relationship between the movement of the mouse across a work surface or mouse pad and the movement of the pointer on the screen.

- If the pointer has been set to *fast*, a very tiny movement of the mouse will suffice to move the pointer on the screen a long way.
- If the pointer has been set to *slow*, a larger movement of the mouse is required to move the pointer on the screen over just a small distance.

For most people, the best setting for the mouse speed is when they move the mouse over an area the size of a CD case, the mouse on the screen moves from one corner of the screen to the other.

By **Tracking** you can drag the slider to the left (slow) or to the right (fast):

⊕ **Drag the slider** towards **Slow** or **Fast**

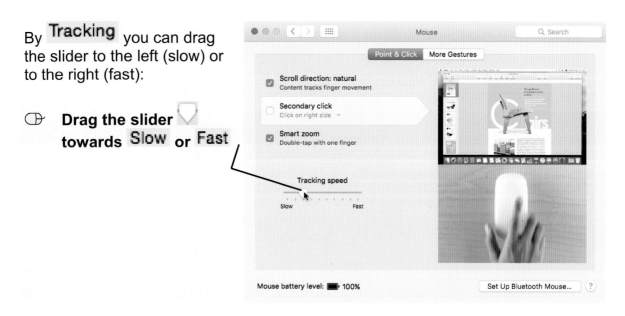

You can test the speed by moving the mouse across the surface of your desk. After you have set the preferred speed, you will return to the *System Preferences* overview:

⊕ **Click** ▦

You can adjust the same settings for a trackpad. Here is how you do that:

⊕ **Click** Trackpad

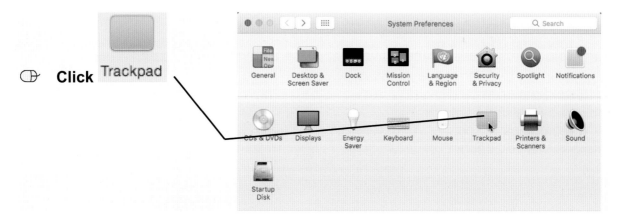

☞ **Drag the slider**
   towards Slow **or** Fast

To return to the *System
Preferences*:

☞ **Click** ▦

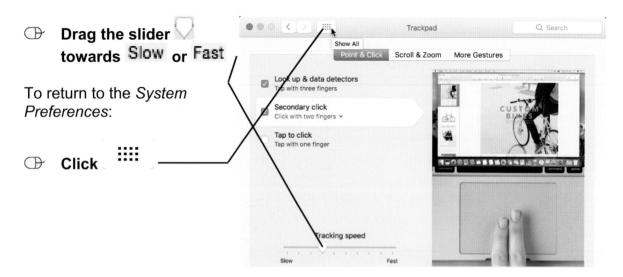

You can change even more settings, such as the size of the pointer and the scroll speed. You can do this in the *Accessibility* window:

☞ **Click** Accessibility

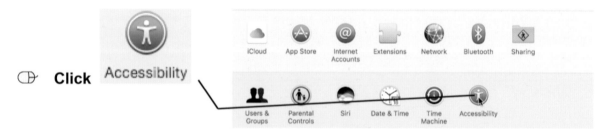

The pointer will be easier to see if you make it bigger. Here is how to adjust the size:

☞ **Click** 🖥 Display

By Cursor size: :

☞ **Drag the slider**
   towards Normal **or**
   Large

In this example we have chosen a very large pointer, so you can clearly see the effect in this screenshot:

But of course you can select the size that works best for you.

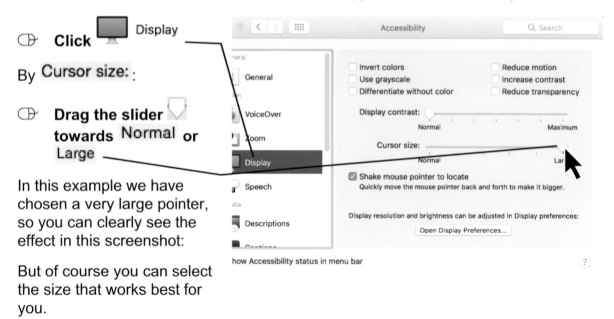

You can also change the double-click interval (the double-click speed) and the scroll speed. If you do not double-click fast enough, the computer will not recognize the two clicks as a double-click. Perhaps a different setting will make it easier for you to use the double-click. The scroll speed determines how fast you can scroll.

- Set the double-click interval to *slower* if double-clicking is difficult for you.
- Set the double-click interval to *faster* if you want to be able to double-click faster (as an experienced user).

To adjust the double-click speed:

☞ **Scroll downwards on the left-side of the window** ✂️**44**

⬚ **Click**
Mouse & Trackpad

⬚ **Drag the slider** ▽ **towards Slow or Fast**

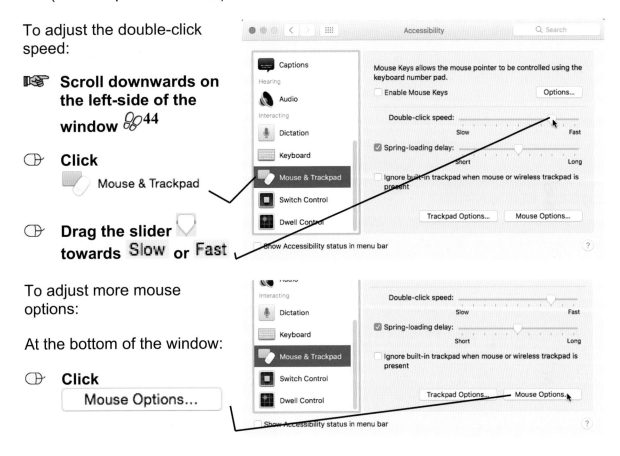

To adjust more mouse options:

At the bottom of the window:

⬚ **Click**
Mouse Options...

This is how you change the settings:

By **Scrolling speed:** .

⬚ **Drag the slider** ▽ **towards Slow or Fast**

⬚ **Click OK**

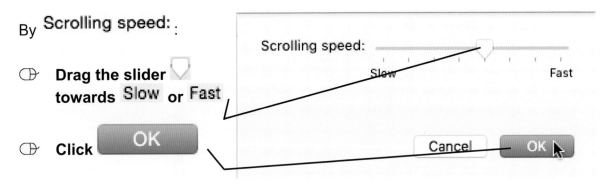

For the trackpad, you can also adjust the scroll speed:

You will see the *Accessibility* window once more:

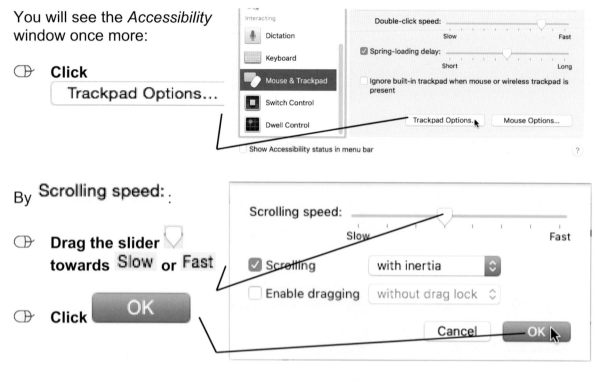

☞ **Click**

    Trackpad Options...

By **Scrolling speed:** .

☞ **Drag the slider** ▽
   towards Slow **or** Fast

☞ **Click** OK

📖☞ **Show the *System Preferences* overview** ✂96

7.2 Changing the Desktop Wallpaper

A lot of people prefer working with a calm background on their computer desktop. But perhaps you think your wallpaper is a bit boring and you would rather have a livelier background. It is very simple to select a different background:

☞ **Click** Desktop & Screen Saver

⊕ **Click**

    Desktop Pictures

👉 **Scroll downwards on the right-side of the window** 𝒢𝒢⁴⁴

In this example, we have selected the picture of the lion:

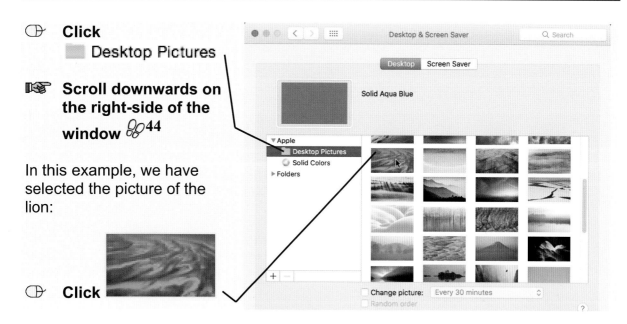

⊕ **Click**

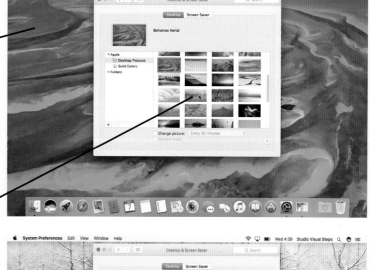

Now you will see the image as your desktop wallpaper:

Take a look at another wallpaper:

👉 **Scroll upwards on the right-side of the window** 𝒢𝒢⁴⁵

⊕ **Click**

The new wallpaper will be displayed at once:

If you are not satisfied with any of the standard wallpapers, you can use one of your own photos as a wallpaper. Here is how to do that:

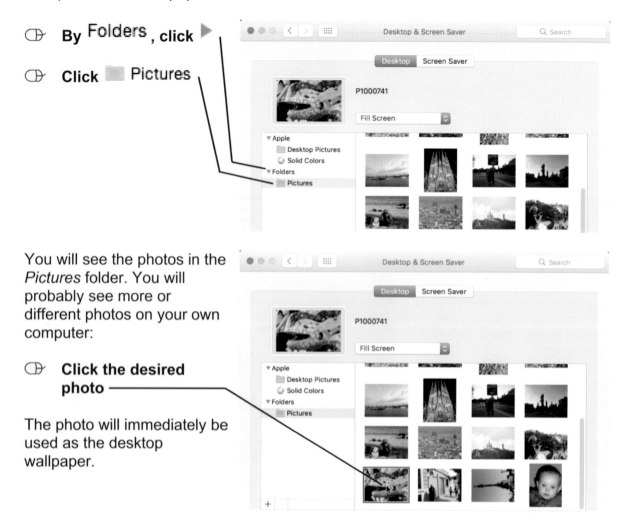

By Folders, click ▶

Click █ Pictures

You will see the photos in the *Pictures* folder. You will probably see more or different photos on your own computer:

Click the desired photo

The photo will immediately be used as the desktop wallpaper.

With the Change picture: option you can set your desktop wallpaper to change automatically after a set period of time. Here is how to set this option:

☞ **Check the box** ✓ **next to** Change picture:

You can select the time period for the wallpaper images to change:

☞ **By** Every 30 minutes, **click** ⇕

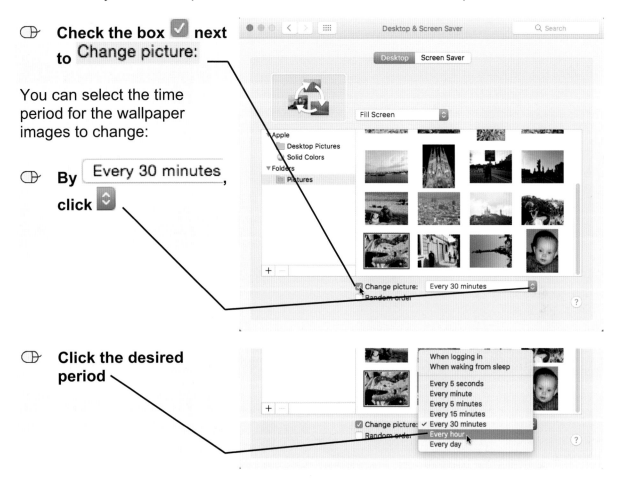

☞ **Click the desired period**

7.3 The Screen saver

If you do not use your computer for a while, you can set a screen saver. In the past, a screen saver prevented your screen from 'burning-in' when the exact same frozen image is displayed on your screen for longer periods of time. The improvement of the screens since 1990 has reduced the need to protect the screen this way. LCD screens have made burning-in a thing of the past. Screen savers are no longer a necessity, but they are fun to watch.

First take a look at a couple of examples:

👉 **Click**

Screen Saver

👉 **Scroll downwards on the left-side of the screen** 👣44

In the preview you can see what the screen saver

Flurry   will look like:

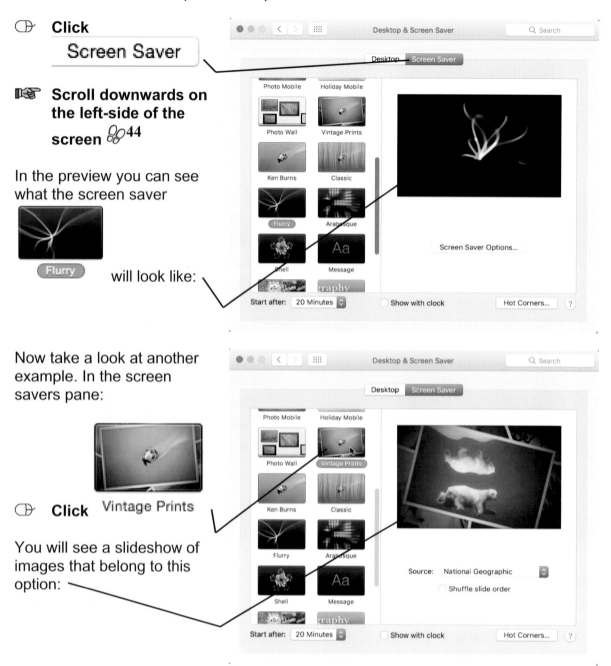

Now take a look at another example. In the screen savers pane:

👉 **Click** Vintage Prints

You will see a slideshow of images that belong to this option:

By default, the source 'National Geographic' has been chosen. But you can also select photos from a different folder:

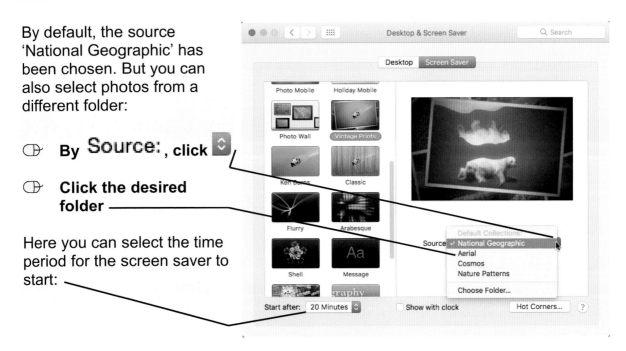

☞ **By** Source: **, click** ⬍

☞ **Click the desired folder** ─────

Here you can select the time period for the screen saver to start: ─

☞ **Show the *System Preferences* overview** ⌘⁹⁶

7.4 Adjusting the Size of the Icons

If the icons in the *Dock* are too small for your taste, you can enlarge them.

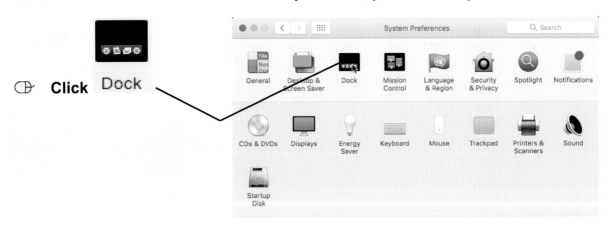

☞ **Click** Dock

By **Size:** :

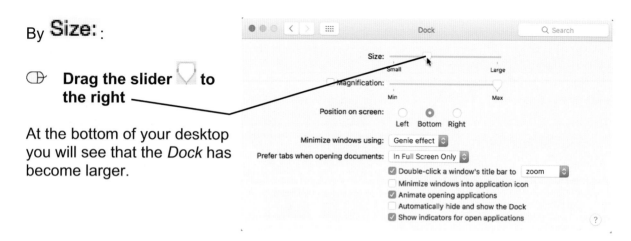

⊕ **Drag the slider** ▽ **to the right**

At the bottom of your desktop you will see that the *Dock* has become larger.

➥ **Please note:**
If the *Dock* is already taking up all of the space along the bottom of the screen, you will not be able to enlarge the *Dock* any further.

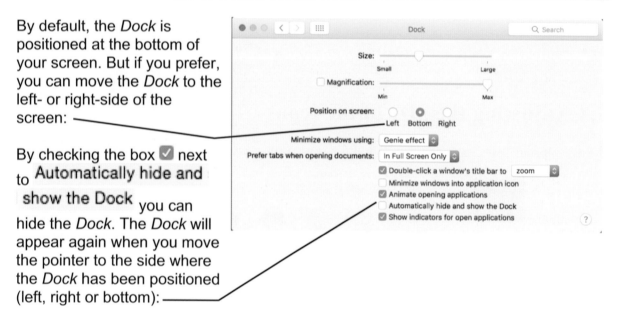

By default, the *Dock* is positioned at the bottom of your screen. But if you prefer, you can move the *Dock* to the left- or right-side of the screen:

By checking the box ☑ next to **Automatically hide and show the Dock** you can hide the *Dock*. The *Dock* will appear again when you move the pointer to the side where the *Dock* has been positioned (left, right or bottom):

☞ **Show the *System Preferences* overview** ✂ **96**

You can also enlarge the icons in the navigation pane of the *Finder* window. You can change these settings in the *General* window of the *System Preferences*:

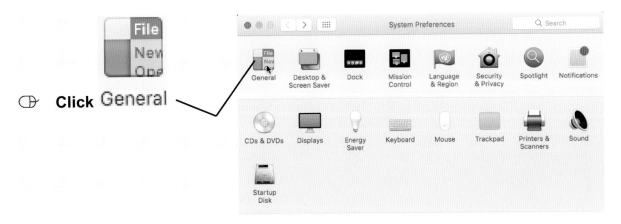

$\oplus$ **Click** General

Now the *General* window will be opened. To clearly see the effect, you need to open the *Finder* window first:

$\oplus$ **Click**

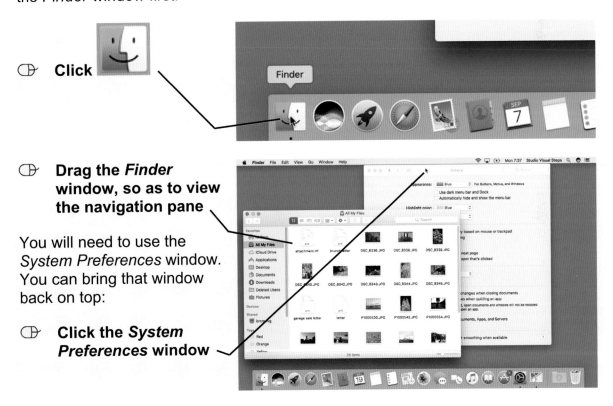

$\oplus$ **Drag the *Finder* window, so as to view the navigation pane**

You will need to use the *System Preferences* window. You can bring that window back on top:

$\oplus$ **Click the *System Preferences* window**

By Sidebar icon size:, click

Click Large

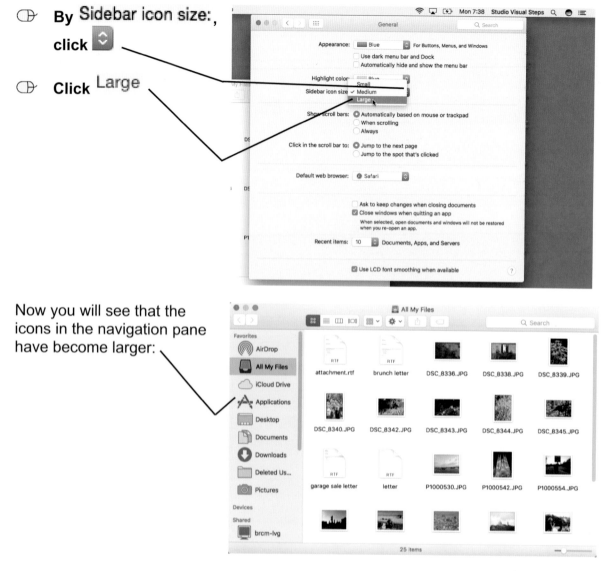

Now you will see that the icons in the navigation pane have become larger:

☞ **Close the** *System Preferences* ⑫

Now you have learned how to enlarge icons. In the next section you will learn how to adjust some additional settings in the *Finder* window.

7.5 Adjusting the Finder Window

By default, the icons in the *Finder* window are displayed as small icons. But you can change the size of the icons to suit your own preferences. The *Finder* window may still be open. If the window is closed:

☞ **If necessary, open *Finder*** 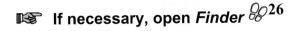**26**

⊕ **Click View**

⊕ **Click Show View Options**

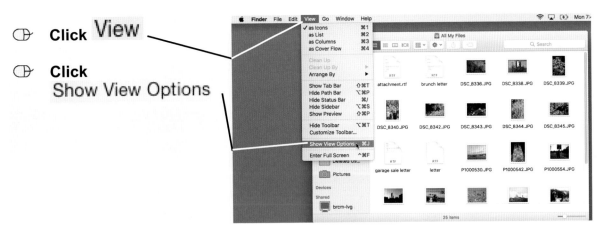

⊕ **By Icon size:, drag the slider ▽ to the right**

Right away, you can see the *Finder* icons getting larger.

You can change a couple of other settings too.

With **Grid spacing:** you can adjust the distance between the icons:

By default, the file name (label) is displayed below the icon. Here you can change the position of the text, so it will be displayed to the right of the icon:

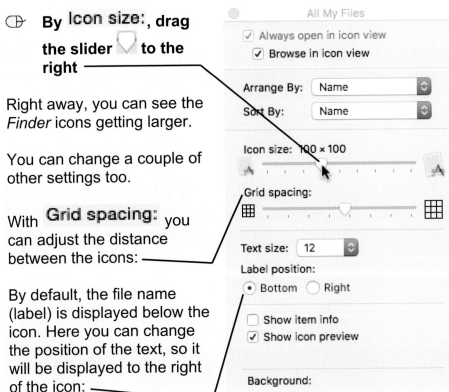

Please note:

When you make a change to the settings for the *Finder* window, those settings are only saved for the window that is currently open (in this case, the *All my files* folder).

When you open another *Finder* window, for instance the *Documents* folder, you will need to repeat the actions you just did once more. But once you have applied these changes, they will be saved whenever you close and open the window again. However, if you select a different *view* in a *Finder* window, you will see a new set of viewing options available that can be set for that view.

If you find it difficult to read the file names (labels) below the icons, you can adjust the font size. Here is how you do that:

☞ **By** Text size: **, click**

☞ **Click the desired size, for example,** 14

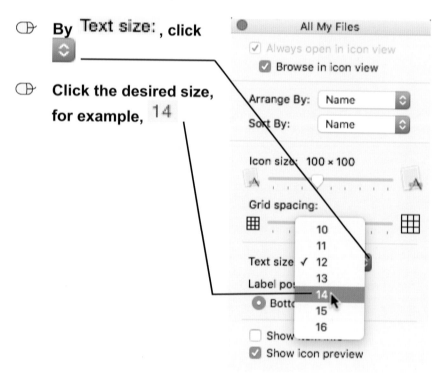

The labels will become larger:

Now you can close the window with the view options:

☞ **Click** ✖

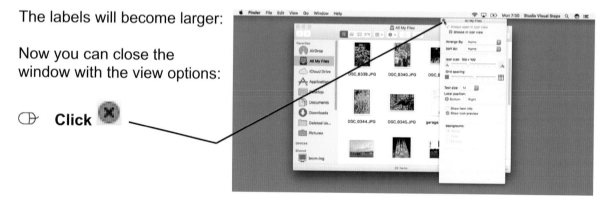

In the *Finder* buttons toolbar you will always see these icons

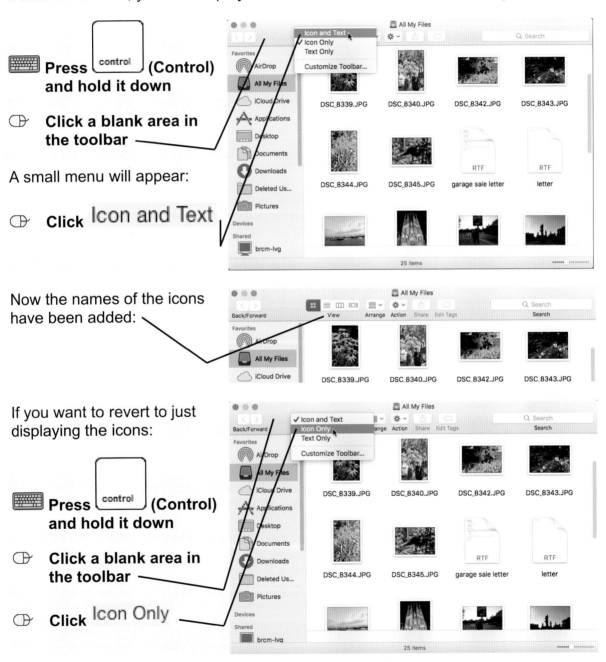

. But perhaps you do not know what they mean.

If that is the case, you can display the names of the icons. Here is how you do that:

Press control **(Control) and hold it down**

👆 **Click a blank area in the toolbar**

A small menu will appear:

👆 **Click** Icon and Text

Now the names of the icons have been added:

If you want to revert to just displaying the icons:

Press control **(Control) and hold it down**

👆 **Click a blank area in the toolbar**

👆 **Click** Icon Only

☞ **Close the *Finder* window** 👣 **12**

7.6 Sound Settings

If you use a program in which audio tracks or sounds are played, it may sometimes be necessary to adjust the volume level. You can adjust the volume level with the volume buttons on your keyboard and in the *System Preferences* window. You can recognize the volume buttons on the keyboard by the images below:

Mute the sound.

Turn the volume down.

Turn the volume up.

➥ **Please note:**
The volume buttons on your keyboard may be located in a different spot. If this is the case, look for the keys with the ◀ , ◀) , and ◀◔ symbols.

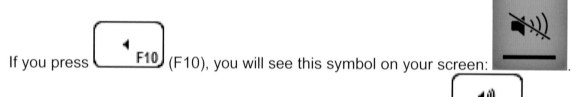

If you press (F10), you will see this symbol on your screen: .
This means the sound has been turned off (muted). If you press (F12)

next, you will see this symbol . The volume will gradually be turned up, step by step, a little at a time. Each time you turn the volume up, you will see a new white block ☐ below the symbol. These white blocks indicate the volume level.

You can also adjust the volume settings in the *System Preferences* window. Here is how to do that:

☞ **Open *System Preferences*** ℰ76

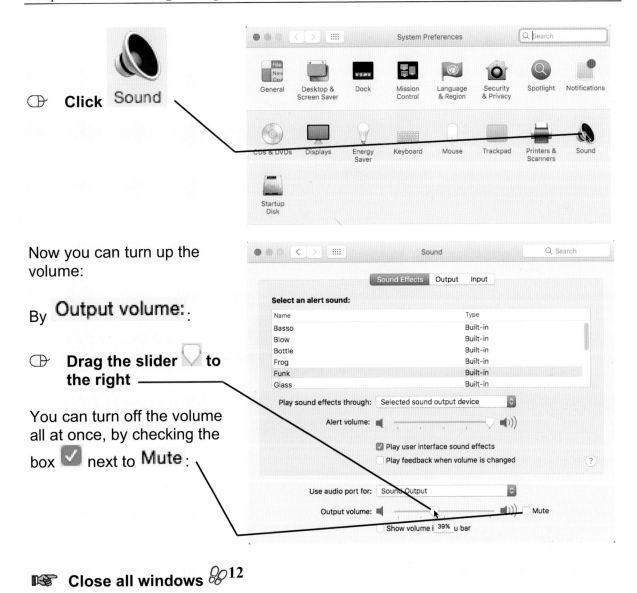

⊕ **Click** Sound

Now you can turn up the volume:

By **Output volume:**.

⊕ **Drag the slider ▽ to the right** ——

You can turn off the volume all at once, by checking the box ☑ next to **Mute**:

☞ **Close all windows** ☙¹²

7.7 Split View

Split View is a useful function that provides you with an option for simultaneously using two programs, side by side. In this section you will learn two different ways of activating Split View on your Mac. First, you open *Safari*:

☞ **Open** *Safari* ☙⁴²

In this example you see the www.yahoo.com website. It does not matter which website you use, for the purpose of this exercise.

You are going to display the *Safari* window on full screen:

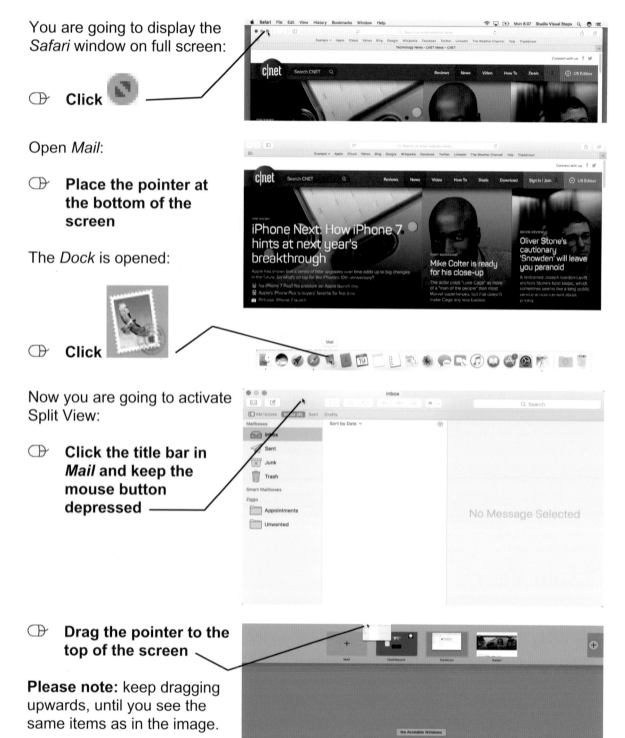

☞ **Click**

Open *Mail*:

☞ **Place the pointer at the bottom of the screen**

The *Dock* is opened:

☞ **Click**

Now you are going to activate Split View:

☞ **Click the title bar in *Mail* and keep the mouse button depressed**

☞ **Drag the pointer to the top of the screen**

Please note: keep dragging upwards, until you see the same items as in the image.

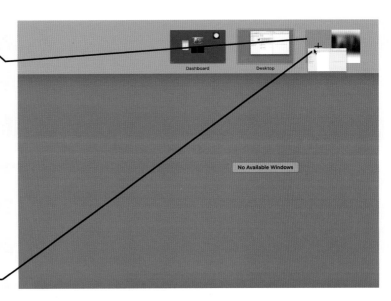

⊕ **Place the pointer on the *Safari* thumbnail**

⊕ **Release the mouse button**

The windows have been displayed in the Split View mode:

⊕ **If necessary, click the Split View mode'**

Split View has been activated. You will see both programs on your screen:

Now you can simultaneously use both programs.

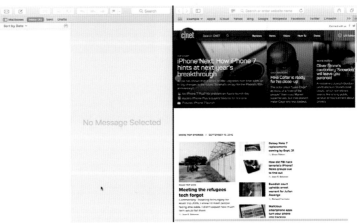

Close Split View:

⊕ **Place the pointer at the top of the screen**

The title bar appears:

⊕ **By *Mail*, click**

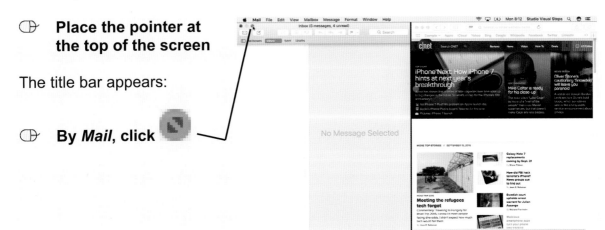

You will see the *Mail* window again as a separate window on your screen:

Display *Safari* again:

☞ **Click**

Now you are also going to restore the *Safari* window to its original size:

☞ **Click**

After you have viewed one of the two methods of activating Split View, you are going to activate this function in another way in the next couple of steps. You will need to have opened multiple programs on your desktop. The *Safari* and *Mail* programs are still open:

☞ **Click** **and keep the mouse button depressed, until you see the same screen as in the image**

☞ **Release the mouse button**

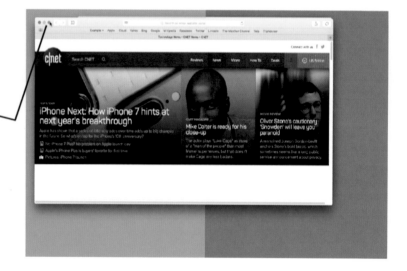

Safari is on the left-hand site of the screen:

⊕ **Click *Mail* on the right-hand side of the screen**

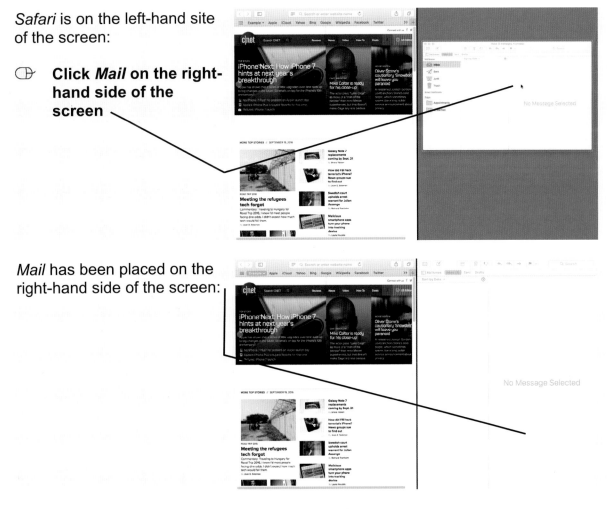

Mail has been placed on the right-hand side of the screen:

☞ **Quit all programs** ✤⁹⁸

Now you have arrived at the end of this book. You have learned how to work with the Mac. Now you can start using and enjoying this user-friendly computer!

If you want to learn more about the Mac and its programs, you can read and use the bonus chapters. On the web page **www.visualsteps.com/macossierra** you will find the following bonus chapters:

- *Bonus Chapter Basic Text Editing Operations*
  You can work through this chapter if you want to expand your basic knowledge of typing, selecting, cutting and pasting text.
- *Bonus Chapter Downloading Apps and Music*
  Apps are programs that can be used on the Mac, iPad or iPhone.

7.8 Visual Steps Website and Newsletter

By now we hope you have noticed that the Visual Steps method is an excellent method for quickly and efficiently learning more about computers, tablets, other devices and software applications. All books published by Visual Steps use this same method.
In various series, we have published a large number of books on a wide variety of topics including *Windows*, *MacOS*, the iPad, iPhone, Samsung Galaxy Tab, Kindle, photo editing and many other topics.

On the **www.visualsteps.com** website you will find a full product summary by clicking the blue *Catalog* button. For each book there is an extensive description, the full table of contents and a sample chapter (PDF file). In this way, you can quickly determine if a specific title will meet your expectations. You can order a book directly online from this website or other online book retailers. All titles are also available in bookstores in the USA, Canada, United Kingdom, Australia and New Zealand.

Furthermore, the website offers many extras, among other things:
- free computer guides and booklets (PDF files) covering all sorts of subjects;
- frequently asked questions and their answers;
- information on the free Computer Certificate that you can acquire at the certificate's website **www.ccforseniors.com**;
- a free email notification service: let's you know when a new book is published.

There is always more to learn. Visual Steps offers many other books on computer-related subjects. Each Visual Steps book has been written using the same step-by-step method with short, concise instructions and screenshots illustrating every step.

Would you like to be informed when a new Visual Steps title becomes available? Subscribe to the free Visual Steps newsletter (no strings attached) and you will receive this information in your inbox.
The Newsletter is sent approximately each month and includes information about
- the latest titles;
- supplemental information concerning titles previously released;
- new free computer booklets and guides;
When you subscribe to our Newsletter you will have direct access to the free booklets on the **www.visualsteps.com/info_downloads.php** web page.

7.9 Background Information

Dictionary

Apps	*Apps* stands for applications. These are programs you can install on your Mac, iPad or iPhone.
Desktop	The working space on a computer screen. When you open a program, it will appear on the desktop.
Desktop wallpaper	The background for a desktop, usually one of the wallpapers included in the Mac software, but it can also be a uniform color or a digital photo from your own collection.
Dock	A component in *MacOS* that is used to open (or launch) programs. By default, the *Dock* is positioned at the bottom of the screen. It contains icons for many of the programs installed on the Mac.
Hot Corners	The option *Hot Corners* can be used to connect a specific action to the four corners of your screen. For example opening *Launchpad*, or starting the screen saver. You can activate a *Hot Corner* by simply positioning the pointer in the desired corner of the screen.
Screen saver	An animated image or pattern that appears on the screen when the mouse or keyboard has been idle for a while. The Mac offers a number of different screen savers. You can choose the one you like best in *System Preferences*.
Siri	A function that lets you give verbal instructions for the Mac to execute, and lets you ask the Mac for information.
Split View	Split View makes it possible to fill your screen with two apps, without having to manually move and resize the windows.
System Preferences	In *System Preferences* you can view and change the settings for the Mac. The various sections in the window have been divided into categories, such as Dock, Sound, Mouse and General.

Source: Apple Dictionary, www.apple.com, Wikipedia

7.10 Tips

 Tip
Quickly open the Sound window
In the *Sound* window you can adjust the volume of your computer sounds. You can quickly open this window with the Alt key and the volume key:

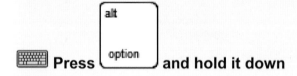
 Press 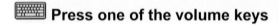 **and hold it down**

Press one of the volume keys

 Tip
Quickly maximize the Dock
In this chapter you have learned how to adjust the size of the *Dock* from the *System Preferences* window. But you can also change the settings from the *Dock* itself. For example, you can quickly enlarge the *Dock*. You can do that like this:

At the bottom right in the *Dock*:

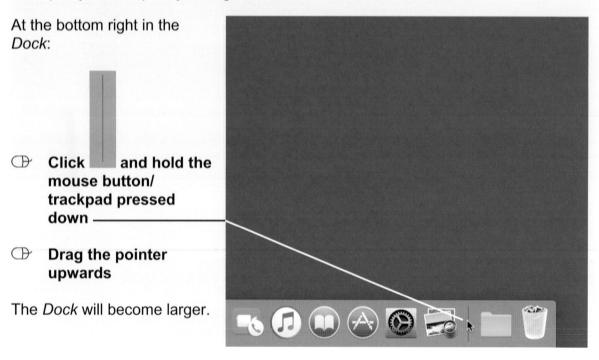

☞ **Click** and hold the mouse button/ trackpad pressed down

☞ **Drag the pointer upwards**

The *Dock* will become larger.

Tip

Quickly enlarge the icons in the Dock

You can enlarge the icons if you position the pointer on the *Dock*. This way, you will be able to see the icons better. This is how you do it with the Control key:

Press control **and hold it down**

Click

You will see a small window:

To enlarge the icons:

Click
Turn Magnification On

Position the pointer on an icon, for example

Some icons have now become larger:

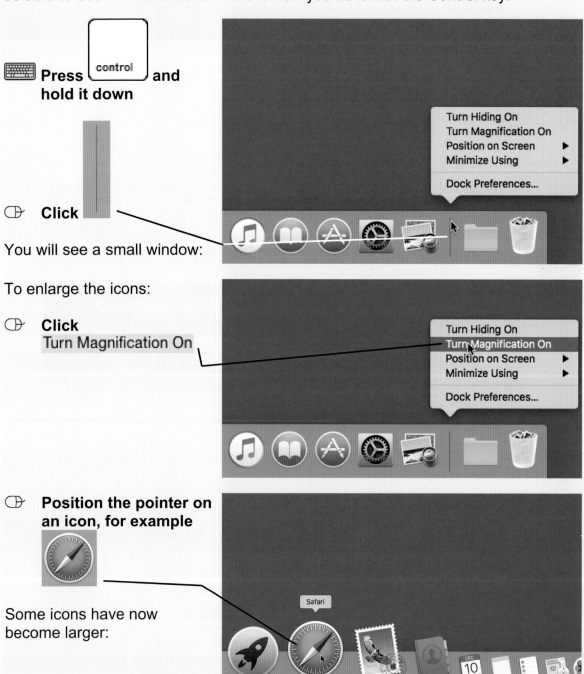

Tip

Hot Corners
The option *Hot Corners* can be used to connect a specific action to the four corners
of your screen. For example opening *Launchpad*, or starting the screen saver.

You can activate a *Hot Corner* by simply positioning the pointer in the desired corner
of the screen. To set the *Hot Corners*:

☞ **Open *System Preferences*** ᴼ⁷⁶

Desktop &
Screen Saver
⊕ **Click**

⊕ **Click**  Screen Saver

⊕ **Click**
    Hot Corners...

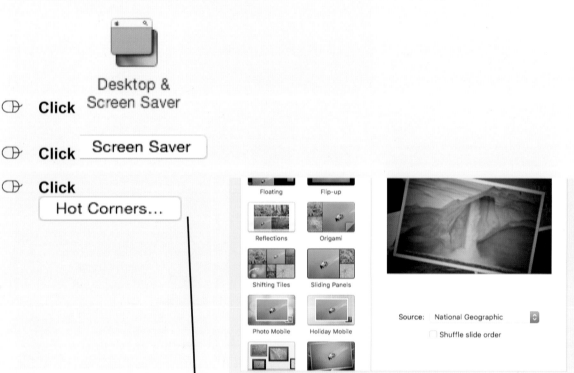

You see drop-down menus
for each corner of the screen.
In this example, there are no
functions assigned to the
corners yet.

⊕ **By the bottom left**
    corner, click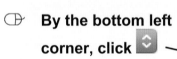

- Continue on the next page -

For each corner of the screen you can select one of these options:

Start Screen Saver
Disable Screen Saver

Mission Control
Application Windows
Desktop
Dashboard
Notification Center

Launchpad

Put Display to Sleep

✓ -

In this example you assign the function Put Display to Sleep to the bottom left corner. This way, your screen will be put to sleep when you position the pointer in the bottom left corner.

☞ **Click**
Put Display to Sleep

☞ **Click** OK

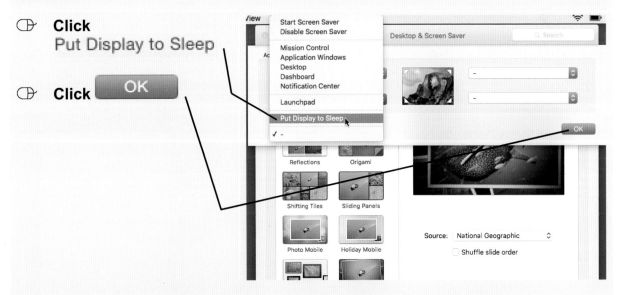

☞ **Position the pointer in the bottom left corner of your screen**

You will see that your screen goes to sleep.

☞ **Move your mouse or touch your trackpad**

Your screen will wake up again.

☞ **Close the *System Preferences* ℰ℘¹²**

Tip

Siri

The Mac has a useful function with which you can give verbal instructions to execute, and you can also use it to ask for information. You use *Siri* like this:

In the top right of the window:

 **Click**

Or on the *Dock*:

 **Click**

Please note: if you do not see this button you can put on *Siri* in the *System Preferences* window.

☞ **Speak loudly and clearly and ask: What's the weather in New York?**

You will both see and hear the answer:

You close the window by clicking ☒.

If *Siri* does not work, you may have to connect a microphone you can use to speak to your Mac.

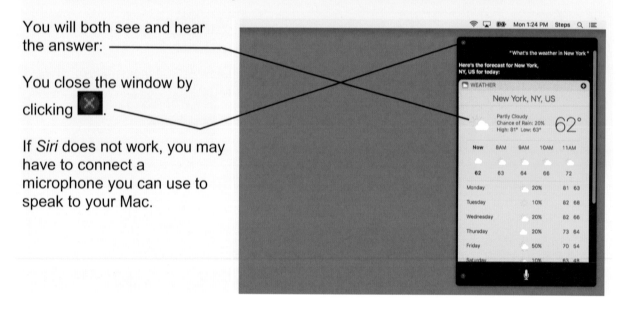

Appendix A. How Do I Do That Again?

The actions and exercises in this book are marked with footsteps: 1
In this appendix you can look up the numbers of the footsteps and read how to execute certain operations.

1 Log in
- Click the icon with your name on it
- If necessary, enter the password
- Click

2 Open *Launchpad*
On the Dock:
- Click

3 Open *Dashboard*
On the Dock:
- Click

4 Calculate with the *Calculator* widget
- Click the buttons you want to use for the sum, for example

5 Drag a widget
- Position the pointer on the widget you want to move
- Press the mouse button/ trackpad and hold it down

- Drag the widget to the desired location
- Release the mouse button/ trackpad

6 Return to the desktop
- Click

7 Switch the Mac to sleep mode
- Click
- Click **Sleep**

Or:
- Close the screen cover of your MacBook Pro or MacBook Air

8 Wake up the Mac from sleep mode
- Click the mouse

Or:
- Press a random key on the keyboard

Or:
- Briefly press the power switch

Or:
- Open the screen cover of your MacBook Pro or MacBook Air

9 Switch off the Mac
- Click

- Click **Shut Down...**

- Click

10 Open *TextEdit*
On the Dock:

- Click

- Click

- Click

11 Insert blank line
- Click the spot where you want to insert a blank line

- Press [enter / return]

12 Close window

- Click

13 Open a recently edited document through the menu bar
- Click File

- Click Open Recent

- Click the desired document

14 Minimize window

- Click

15 Open minimized window in the *Dock*

- Click

Or:

- Click

16 Maximize window

- Click

17 Restore maximized window

- Click

18 Start a bulleted list

- Click

- Click the desired type of bullet

19 Type a list
- Type the first item

- Press [enter / return]

- Type the next item

- Press [enter / return]

- Repeat this for all the items

20 Close a bulleted list

- Press [enter / return] twice

21 Save a letter in the *Documents* folder
- Click File
- Click Save...
- If necessary, click ⌄
- If necessary, click 📄 Documents
- Enter a name for the document
- Click **Save**

22 View the print preview
- Click File
- Click Print...

23 Print a letter
- Click Print...

24 Quit *TextEdit*
- Click **TextEdit**
- Click Quit TextEdit

25 Open a folder
- Double-click the folder

26 Open *Finder*
On the Dock:
- Click 🙂

27 Open the *Documents* folder
- Click 📄 Documents

28 Copy a file
- Select a file
- Click Edit
- Click Copy "brunch letter"
- Open the correct folder
- Click Edit
- Click Paste Item

29 Create new folder
- Click File
- Click New Folder
- Type the name of the folder
- Press

30 Move a file
- Click the file and hold the mouse button/trackpad down
- Drag the file to the desired folder

As soon as the folder is opened:
- Release the mouse button/trackpad

31 Change the name of a file/folder
- Click the name of the file or folder
- Click the name of the file or folder once more
- Type the new name
- Press

32 Move a file/folder to the *Trash*
- Select the file
- Click File
- Click Move to Trash

33 Open the *Trash*
On the Dock:

- Click

34 Empty the *Trash*
- Click Empty
- Click Empty Trash

35 Copy a file to USB stick
- Click the file and hold the mouse button/trackpad down
- Drag the file to the USB stick in the navigation pane

As soon as the USB stick is displayed:
- Release the mouse button/ trackpad

36 Disconnect USB stick
- By the USB stick in the navigation pane, click ⏏

37 Change the arrangement of the items to name
- Click a file
- Hold  (Command) down
- Click the other files

- Release 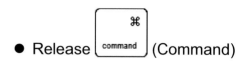 (Command)

38 Select multiple files
- Click a file
- Hold 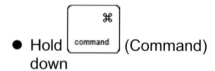 (Command) down
- Click the other files
- Release 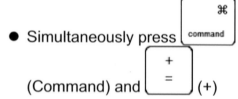 (Command)

39 Zoom in with the keyboard
- Simultaneously press  (Command) and ⌸ (+)

40 Return to previous web page
- Click ❮
- Repeat this, until you see the desired web page

41 Open a website
- Click the address bar
- Type the web address
- Press ⏎ return / enter

42 Open *Safari*
On the Dock:
- Click

43 Zoom in
With the Magic Mouse:
- Tap the Magic Mouse twice in rapid succession

With the (Magic) trackpad:
- Tap the (Magic) trackpad with two fingers, in rapid succession

With the keyboard:
- Simultaneously press 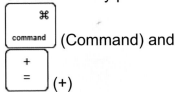 (Command) and (+)
- Repeat this until you see the web page in the desired size

44 Scroll downwards
With the Magic Mouse:
- Drag your finger upwards a bit over the Magic Mouse

With the (Magic) trackpad:
- Drag two fingers upwards over the trackpad

With the scroll wheel:
- Turn the scroll wheel away from you

45 Scroll upwards
With the Magic Mouse:
- Drag your finger downwards a bit over the Magic Mouse

With the (Magic) trackpad:
- Drag two fingers downwards over the trackpad

With the scroll wheel:
- Turn the scroll wheel towards you

46 Zoom out
With the Magic Mouse:
- Tap the Magic Mouse twice in rapid succession

With the (Magic) trackpad:
- Tap the (Magic) trackpad twice with two fingers, in rapid succession

With the keyboard:
- Simultaneously press 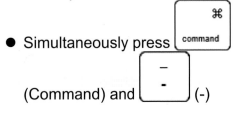 (Command) and (-)
- Repeat this until you see the web page in the desired size

47 Open a link
- Click the link

48 Open a link in a new tab
- Hold 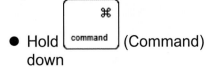 (Command) down
- Click the link
- Release

49 Go to the tab
- Click the tab

50 Close a tab
- Position the pointer on the tab
- Click ✕

51 Add a bookmark to the favorites bar

- Click ⬆️

- Click 📖 Add Bookmark

- If necessary, click ↕️

- Click 📖 Favorites

- Type the name of the bookmark

- Click **Add**

52 Add a folder to the favorites bar
On the menu bar:

- Click Bookmarks

- Click Edit Bookmarks

- If necessary, double click 📖 Favorites

- Click New Folder

- Enter a name for the folder

- Press [enter / return]

53 Move a bookmark to a folder

- Click the bookmark and hold the mouse button/trackpad down

- Drag the bookmark to the desired folder

- Release the mouse button/ trackpad

54 Delete folder

- Click the folder

- Press [←] (Backspace)

55 Close bookmarks editor
On the menu bar:

- Click Bookmarks

- Click Hide Bookmarks Editor

56 Open *Top Sites*

- Click

57 Open a website through *Top Sites*

- Click the desired website

58 Quit *Safari*

- Click **Safari**

- Click Quit Safari

59 Open a new email message

- Click ✍️

60 Add a subject

- Click the box next to Subject:

- Type the desired subject

61 Add a message

- Click the big blank area

- Type your message

62 Send an email

- Click

63 Retrieve new messages

- Click ✉

64 Quit *Mail*
- Click **Mail**

- Click Quit Mail

65 Open *Mail*

- Click

66 Add an email address

- Click ⊕

- Click your name

- Click your email address

67 Add an attachment

- Click 📎

- If necessary, click ⬍

- If necessary, double-click the desired folder

- Click the desired file

- Click Choose File

68 Insert a blank line
- Click between your name and the attachment

- Press [enter return] twice

69 Open *Inbox*
- Click Inbox

70 Open a message
- Click the message

71 View an attachment
- Place the mouse pointer on top of the line

- Click 📎 1 ⌄

- Click Quick Look

72 Save an attachment
- Place the mouse pointer on top of the line

- Click 📎 1 ⌄

- Click the name of the attachment

- Click ⬍

- Click the desired folder

- Click Save

73 Move a message to the *Trash* mailbox
- If necessary, click the message

- Click 🗑

---

74 Open the *Trash* mailbox

- Click ▦ Mailboxes

- Click 🗑 Trash

75 Delete messages from the *Trash*

- Click Mailbox

- Click Erase Deleted Items

- Click your email address

- Click [Erase]

76 Open *System Preferences*

- Click

77 Open a program in *Launchpad*

- If necessary, click [Other]

- Click the program, for

example

78 Quit program
On the menu bar:
- Click the program's name

- Click *Quit program name*

79 Open a photo
- Double-click the photo

80 Open the *Pictures* folder

- Click 📷 Pictures

81 Rotate a photo

- Click ◻↺

- Repeat this until the photo is in the correct position

82 Revert to original photo
- Click File

- Click Revert To

- Click Browse All Versions...

- Click [∧] or [∨] until you see the desired version

- Click [Restore]

83 Open the *Markup Toolbar*

- Click 🧰

84 Crop a photo
- Drag a rectangular frame over the photo

- If necessary, drag the frame

- Click Crop

85 Open the *Adjust Color* window

- Click

86 Change the color to sepia
- By Sepia:, drag the slider ▽ to the right

87 Open *iTunes*

- Click

88 Import music
If necessary, select the right title:
- Click the title that matches the CD you inserted

- Click OK

In the Import window:

- Click Yes

89 Remove CD from CD/DVD station

- Click ⏏

90 Play music
If necessary:
- Click Albums ⌄

- Click ♪ Songs

- Double-click the first track

91 Random (shuffle) playback
In the information pane:
- Click 🔀

- Click ⏩

92 Switch to mini player
- Click Window

- Click Switch to MiniPlayer

93 Return to *iTunes* window
- Click Window

- Click Switch from MiniPlayer

94 Play a DVD
In the control panel:
- Click

95 Return to previous view
- Click

Or:

- Press esc (Esc)

96 Show the *System Preferences* overview
- Click ⠿

97 Activate Split View
- Click and hold the mouse button down

- Drag the window to the left or right hand side of your screen

- Release the mouse button

- On the other side of the screen, click one of the small preview icons of the programs to open it next to the other program

98 Deactivate Split View
- Click

The second program is still active in full screen mode. To also minimize that program:

- Click

Appendix B. Opening Bonus Chapters

On the website accompanying this book you will find the bonus chapters *Basic Text Editing Operations* and *Downloading Apps and Music*. These are PDF files. This is how you download and save the files from the website to your Mac:

☞ **Open the www.visualsteps.com/macossierra website** ✇**42, 41**

You will see the website accompanying this book:

Go to the page with the bonus chapters:

🖱 **Click** Bonus Chapters

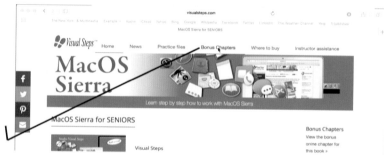

To download the chapter:

⌨ **Press** control

🖱 **Click**
Start downloading »» »»

🖱 **Click**
Download Linked File

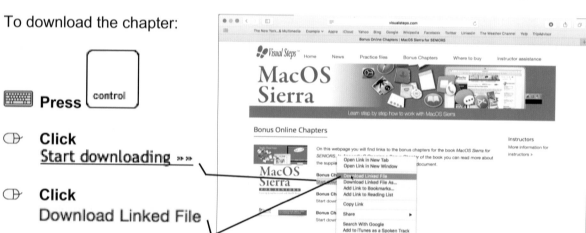

The file has been saved to the *Downloads* folder. You can open it straight away from *Safari*:

🖱 **Click** ⬇

You will see the file:

🖱 **Double-click the file**

The bonus chapters are password protected. To open the PDF files, you need to enter the password.

☞ **Click** | Password |

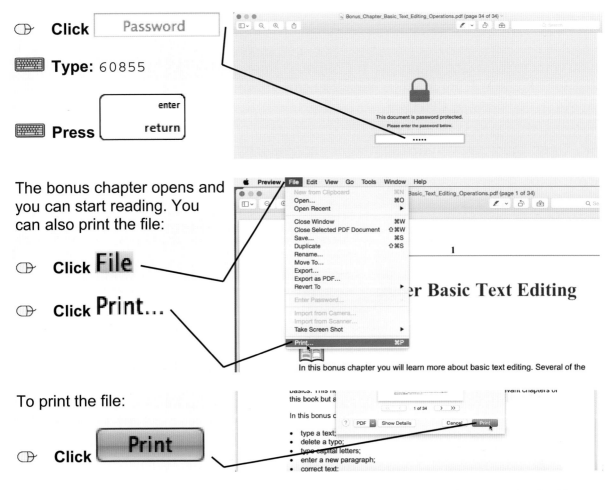

⌨ **Type:** 60855

⌨ **Press** | enter return |

The bonus chapter opens and you can start reading. You can also print the file:

☞ **Click** File

☞ **Click** Print...

To print the file:

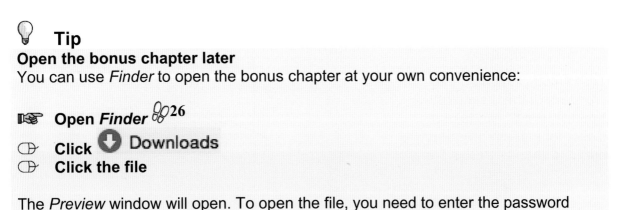

☞ **Click** | Print |

You can work through this bonus chapter in the same way you have worked with other chapters in this book. Once you have read or printed the bonus chapter, you can close all the windows.

💡 **Tip**

Open the bonus chapter later
You can use *Finder* to open the bonus chapter at your own convenience:

☞ **Open** *Finder* 🦶26

☞ **Click** ⬇ Downloads

☞ **Click the file**

The *Preview* window will open. To open the file, you need to enter the password again.

Appendix C. Downloading the Practice Files

If you want to follow the examples in *Chapter 6 Photos, Videos and Music*, you will need to use a few of the practice files. You can download these practice files from the website accompanying this book.

☞ **Open the www.visualsteps.com/macossierra website** ✂️**42, 41**

The web page will be opened:

👆 **Click** Practice files

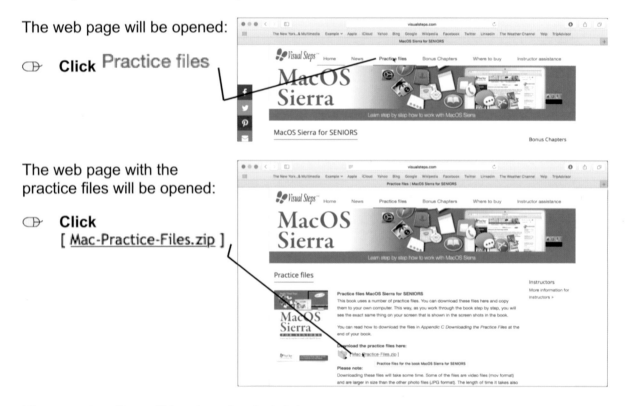

The web page with the practice files will be opened:

👆 **Click**
[Mac-Practice-Files.zip]

The practice files will be downloaded right away.

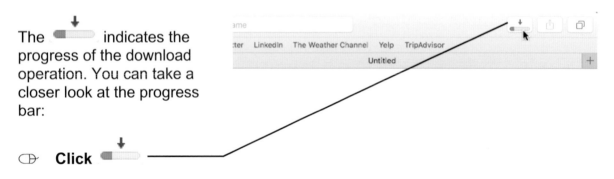

The ▭ indicates the progress of the download operation. You can take a closer look at the progress bar:

👆 **Click** ▭

Here you can see a better
view of the download
operation and how much time
is needed for completion:

The folder with the practice files have been downloaded and are stored in the
Downloads folder. Now you can delete the folder from this list. If you do this, the
folder will only be deleted from the download list; the actual files will still remain in the
Downloads folder.

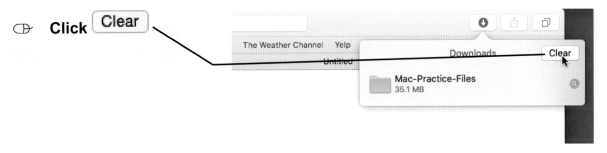

Click `Clear`

Now you can stop *Safari*:

☞ **Stop** *Safari* ⬚⬚**58**

You are going to move the practice files to the *Pictures* folder:

☞ **Open** *Finder* ⬚⬚**26**

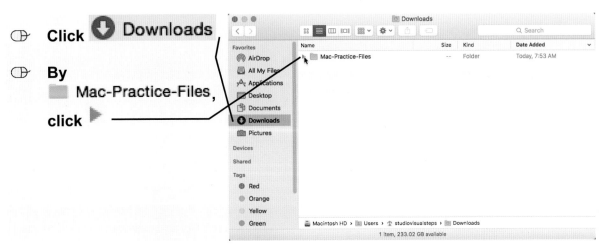

Click  **Downloads**

By ▢ **Mac-Practice-Files**,

click ▶

You can use the Shift key to select a range of files:

☞ **Click the first file**
■ **P1000530.JPG**

⌨ **Hold** [Shift]
down

☞ **Click the last file**
▦ **Video file Mac.mov**

⌨ **Release**
[Shift]

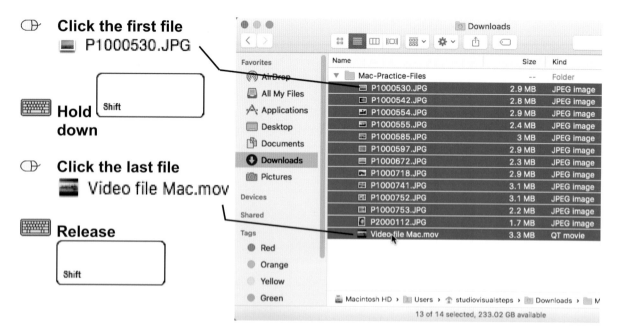

You drag the files to the *Pictures* folder:

☞ **Click a file and hold the mouse button/ trackpad down**

☞ **Drag the files to**
📷 **Pictures**

☞ **Release the mouse button/trackpad**

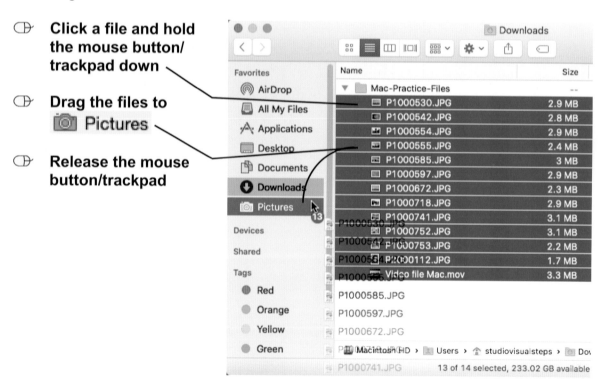

The practice files have been added to the *Pictures* folder:

The *Downloads* folder now contains an empty folder. You can remove that folder like this:

👆 **Click**

   ⬇ Downloads

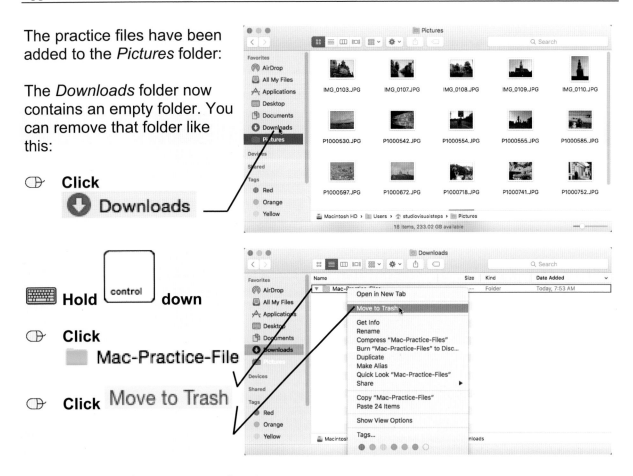

⌨ **Hold** control **down**

👆 **Click**

   📁 Mac-Practice-File

👆 **Click** Move to Trash

The folder has been removed.

👉 **Continue the steps in *section 6.3 Viewing Photos in Preview***

Appendix D. Index